'VOICES FROM A BLUE BOX'

(Tales from a Black Country Copper)

To Paul

Regards

Bry

Bryan Connor

authorHOUSE®

AuthorHouse™ UK Ltd.
500 Avebury Boulevard
Central Milton Keynes, MK9 2BE
www.authorhouse.co.uk
Phone: 08001974150

This book contains adult related humour and just a smattering of
profanity, albeit in consonance with the subject matter!

ISBN: 978-1-4490-9064-7 (e)
ISBN: 978-1-4490-9063-0 (sc)

First published by AuthorHouse 6/23/2010

This book is printed on acid-free paper.

Foreword

My association with the police began way back in June 1962. It was then that Sir Lew Grade, boss of Associated Television bought a six week television series from the United States that, stripped of it's sponsorship material, ran five minutes short of the network slot. In those days the gap would normally have been filled by an announcer in vision drawling on about the exciting programmes you could see next week. A definite 'switch over or 'switch off!' Lew wasn't having any of that!

"Make me a five minute programme that will hold viewers attention" he demanded.   And so 'Police 5' was born. Five minutes of free air time given to the police to invite viewers to help solve crime. I was given the job of writing and presenting it.

With two crimes solved in the first week the show was an immediate success with both the viewers and the police and the idea was copied by Police Forces and television stations all over the world! Lew's six week series ended but the five minute 'filler' went on...eventually clocking up thirty years. Coincidentally a policeman's length of service!

The author of this book, Bryan Connor, served his 'thirty' at the sharp end of policing in the office of what I have always regarded as the backbone of police work...the Police Constable....The 'copper on the beat.'

Whether it be man or woman, they are in direct contact with the public maintaining 'law and order,' no easy job. It requires both authority and understanding to be able to deal with difficult situations on the spur of the moment. Situations that, at times, can be downright dangerous.

Bryan's memories of his career, laced with an irrepressible sense of humour, makes entertaining reading and paints a vivid picture of the work of a dedicated band of men and women so often undervalued by the rest of us.

Shaw Taylor - Star of TV's 'Police 5' and 'Ashes to Ashes'
March 2010

Dedication

This book is dedicated to my mother, Gladys Connor.

She was a born-again Christian lady, who, when she wasn't my 'Mam,' looking after her ever-hungry, problematic and argumentative teenage son, was an active Member of St David's Church of England Parish Church, dumped in the middle of a sprawling post war council housing estate called the Clinkham Wood Estate, St Helens, Merseyside.

She was the hard working caretaker of St David's Church for donkeys years, on her knees each week single handedly cleaning the huge church, its lounge and gymnasium as an errand of love for Jesus, it certainly wasn't for the money. An active member of its Parish Council, Sunday School and Choir, to name but a few segments of the parish life she devoted most of her life to. You name it she was there at all hours of the day and night. She lost her husband and soul mate, Matt, in 1973, being left alone to bring up a turbulent spotty faced, teenager. Then, when her son also abandoned her, to attend a college of further education in the Midlands, God (Whoever he or she is) became her everything until she was recalled & reunited? with my Dad in 2003.

Being a Humanist myself, it is hard to accept that I am not going to see her again, but the memories I hold of that fabulous woman will endure in my memory. The love, the laughter, the tears, the arguments, her tenacity and energy, her honesty, her understanding and her help will forever be a large part of what makes me, me. I see her smiling at me when I look in a mirror. I hear her chuckling when I painfully stub a toe in the bathroom and I strangely feel her reassurance at times when I feel particularly down in the dumps.

Gladys Connor, whose heart was a big as a bucket, loved her family dearly but equally loved watching the local rugby league side St Helens Rugby League Football Club, travelling to both home and via Gavin Murray's coaches, to Saints away games with my Dad and me in tow when I was little. She loved her sport and never missed televised wrestling on ITV with Kent Walton on Saturday afternoon's 'World of Sport', with the likes of Count Bartelli, Billy Two Rivers, Les Kellet, Jackie Pallo and of course the great Mick McManus who she loved to hate! Hysterically contradictory for a God fearing Christian who believed people should always turn the other cheek! Mam was a real 'saint' in more ways than just the spiritual one and to quote the fabulous Daniel Merriweather song *Red*, 'God took something perfect and painted a Red Vee on it!' Any rugby league supporter in the famous glass town would be able to explain that the local team are known worldwide as 'The Saints' and they play in all white with a Red Vee emblazoned across their chest.

There are so many stories I could tell you about this special woman. These are my favourite two. One particularly bad wintry day in 1978, when compacted snow on snow, on snow, had frozen solid due to continually bitter north easterly winds. Mrs.Carlisle, my Mam's best friend at church, rang to tell me that on her way home from a days cleaning at the church, Mam had slipped on some slippery iced up paving slabs and an ambulance had taken her to the local hospital. I ran up to the Providence Hospital, found my Mam, who was sat in A &E, sharing jokes with the medical staff, as she had her fractured left arm plastered up. By the time she was discharged from the hospital it was already freezing cold and getting dark. Rather than go back to a cold house, I persuaded her to come to my nearby flat in a now near deserted snow bound town centre. We walked gingerly, like a couple of apprentice ice skaters, arm in arm along the transparent, frozen float glass, icy pavements of the town, the speech steam trails twisting out of our mouths into the atmosphere as we chatted. I disrespectfully attempted to mildly chastise my Mam for being so clumsy.

She listened, but took not a bit of notice and I started to become a little miffed by the fact that she didn't seem to be concerned about her own well being. It was at this time that my very own left foot decided to disobey the health and safety advice I was giving to my Mam. My left foot (Mmmmm not a bad title for the book that...What do you mean it's been done?) decided to go west when the rest of us wanted to head north! The next thing I know is I felt myself sliding uncontrollably backwards. As my head began to fall backwards I could see my right foot shooting upwards in front of me, in a mad panic I grabbed onto the most solid object I could find to hand, my Mam!

There was a muffled thud as two adult spines hit the ice covered terra firma at a rate of knots. The plincketty plinky ting sounds of loosened objects such as pens, coins and spectacles submitting themselves to gravity at different nanosecond intervals were followed swiftly by an eerie silence. I opened my eyes slowly and admired the beautiful starry night sky. I was stunned but couldn't feel any personal aches or pains. I glanced over towards my

Mam, who had virtually done the same thing as me. I was about to reiterate the chastisement when my Mam started to smile, the smile became a giggle and before we knew it we were both uncontrollably laughing out loud. We just lay there for a minute or so, laughing at the situation. Tears ran down my face as I lifted my shoulders off the shiny cold surface. Luckily, there was no one around to witness our peccadilloes. I gingerly helped Mam to her feet and dusted the snow from her back. We very gently shuffled the rest of the way along the road like a couple of David Suchet Inspector Poirot's (Who always shuffles along, walking as if he's holding a Grapefruit between his knees) back to the warmth of my flat.

The last time I saw my Mam alive, she was 81 years young and sitting up in her hospital bed at Whiston Hospital near St Helens. She was dying and apart from the drugs in her system helping her stay awake in the land of the living, she was happy, because I think she kind of knew she was joining the queue to meet Jesus. I chatted with her about mundane matters and then for whatever reason we started chatting about a shared love for St Helens Rugby League Club and it was then that she started to quietly sing the song, 'When the Saints Go Marching In.' My wife Beverly and I joined in. When the off key singing trio had finished the song, Mam took Beverly's hand and then she took my hand and joined them together, she then patted her hand on top of ours smiling at us both, priest-like, as if blessing and approving of the coupling. With a small group of nurses and other patients acting as witnesses. I felt a tear, several in fact, welling up but didn't dare cry out loud till we'd left her. Then for a very rare occasion in my life the hard rugby playing police officer who had hardened himself to so much human grief and suffering, wept uncontrollably in Beverly's arms.

As I said earlier, when I fell on my backside, I grabbed the most solid object I could find. My Mam was always there for me, a constant rock, whenever I fell or even tottered for that matter. I know she was proud of me and this book dedication is my opportunity to tell the world that the feeling was mutual.

Whether we call you Mam, Aunty Gladys, Gladys or Mrs Connor, we *all* miss you.

I would also like to dedicate this book to the mainly unrecognised & unrewarded, hard working law enforcement officers of Britain for the dangerous, difficult and complex duties they continue to perform well for the law abiding citizens of the United Kingdom despite the interference of naive, greedy and power crazy politicians. To those I had the privilege to serve alongside, you have been as close to me as my family.

The Police service fed and clothed my kids and bought me my house.

Confucius originally said, "Find a job you love and you'll never work a day in your life." Quite frankly, that is so true when it comes to being a police officer, it's the best job I have ever known and I will be forever grateful to have been chosen to serve in it.

Thanks to, go of course to all the friends and colleagues who assisted me with the compilation of the book. You all know who you are....Thanks Folks.

Special thanks must too go to that consummate broadcaster, Mr Shaw Taylor for his welcome assistance and support.

I would also like to mention my daughters Sian, Helen and Lexi who, due partly to years of dutiful shift work, I really didn't see grow up properly, my thanks too go to their significant 'others', Dave, Mike and Chris who I *know* will give them more attention than I did.

I must also thank my fabulous Grand Children Mathew, Teri and Paige for leaving me alone to get on with writing this book!

Finally, very special thanks go to my long suffering wife Beverly.

Bev, thank you for looking after me and replacing my 'Mam' as the constant rock in my life. I love you.

Introduction

How did this book come about? Well, one very warm afternoon in 1984, I was standing at my post, a boring, quiet country lane outside Keresley Colliery near Coventry, during the Miners Strike. I hadn't seen a living soul for hours, let alone a Transit Van full of Flying Pickets from Yorkshire. Tell a lie, I'd been checked at regular intervals by Police Sergeant, Ray Gardner, a very good egg, who visited me every half hour, for a 'meet.' He could see that I was totally bored and paired me up with a work colleague, PC Steve Pulaski. Steve, a Scottish, chain smoking, paratrooper from Dundee, a 'United' supporter, who had toured Northern Ireland with the army on numerous occasions, was the son of a post War Polish German Prisoner of War, who, luckily for Steve, very soon defected to the allies. Steve was a stereotypical long streak of nothing to look at, about six stone wet through and thin as a lath, but of course looks can very much deceive. 'Steve' was that relaxed he was virtually horizontal, as fit as a butchers dog, born again HARD, forever smiling, he was a fabulous bobby, a good communicator, a great team player and a good mate. If you wanted a second opinion, he was ugly too. You couldn't punch clay uglier than Steve. As a boy, his mother used to feed him with a catapult and tied a pork chop around his neck when he was a toddler, so the dog would play with him!

To quell the boredom on that tranquil tour of duty, Steve and I first discussed our families. That's how I learned about Steve's dad. The Nazis had invaded his native Poland and when Hitler's S.S. troops entered his village, all the males where lined up against a wall and given the simple choice of, join the German Army or be shot. Steve's Uncle, his Dad's brother, was dissident and told the invaders that he would never serve them. A single shot in the head from an S.S. service luger pistol was their quick and harrowing reply. It was at that moment that Steve's father reluctantly joined Adolf's Army. Within a few weeks he found himself driving a German army Mercedes truck full of diesel fuel towards the beaches of Northern France.

Upon arrival in Calais, he abandoned the Merc somewhere in a back street, dumped the fuel, set fire to the truck and deserted the German army, leaving Adolf to his fate. Soon, he found himself being carried to Blighty in one of the 'little ship armada' of vessels that took the remainder of the British Expeditionary force back to England. Still dressed in German army fatigues he immediately, surrendered to the allies and after his initial training joined the Free Polish Army, becoming one of the 175,000 allied troops that landed on the beaches of Normandy on the 6th June 1944. I think you know the rest of that story.

On that sunny afternoon in Coventry, Steve and I became firm friends, not realising that our paths would not cross again for another twenty years, when we would both work together at Old Hill nick until Steve retired from the police in 2005.

That afternoon in Coventry, Steve and I exchanged stories connected with the more humorous aspects of the fabulous job we shared. It was on that very afternoon that Steve, still laughing at my stories, urged me to write down my reminiscences and turn them into a book. Unluckily for you dear reader, I started to do just that and twenty-six years on I have decided to go one better and publish them. I think you'd call that a 'slow burner!'

The well thumbed navy blue, hard backed, faintly ruled, A4 note book containing my 'jottings' went with me everywhere. It got fuller and fuller, with ballpoint pen and lead pencil jottings piling up over the years. Known simply for most of my career as 'The Book Project' it grew and grew. Over the years very few others have seen the stories. My daughter Sian read them and has always urged me to publish them ever since. The book never had a working title, however, when it became apparent that I would have to present a working manuscript to the book publishers. The football supporter in me, couldn't bring himself to call it a 'Man U' script, because, like most of the football fans across the country, I hate moneybags Manchester United FC for poaching everybody's best players, purely in a green eyed way of course and being a follower of West Bromwich Albion the working copy of my book project naturally became 'The Albionscript'.

I hope you enjoy the stories, to those people reading this, that are new to police books and the world of policing. I would just ask that you read the stories with an open mind. Lots of people pre-judge stuff these days without looking fully into what they are making a decision on! Even I can still get caught out when it comes to prejudging situations. Just last weekend my own Grandson, Mathew, gave me a lesson in 'fact' finding. During the television advertisements, of course, you know, they come on between the mesmeric programmes on the children's television channels. Mathew, aged ten, dragged himself away from the kids cartoon show

Gormiti, long enough to wistfully say, "Grandad?" With all the inquisitiveness a ten year old boy possesses. "Yeeeessss" I warily replied. "I've got worms" he said, confidently. In his eyes that tinge of truth and sincerity that you rarely see on the face of a ten year old. "You've got what?" I said. "I've got worms" he said earnestly. "Do your Mum and Dad know?" I say to him. "Of course they do." He replied in a matter of fact way. I couldn't believe what I was hearing. I looked at my wife Beverly, to make sure that I hadn't misheard him. He really had said he'd got worms. Beverly had the same puzzled look that soon became one of concern. Now, what I'd understood that if you experience any of the signs or symptoms of tapeworm infection, you should seek medical attention. So I said to Mathew, "Seriously Mat, have you definitely got worms?" He replied in the affirmative. I asked him, "Has your Mum taken you to the Doctors to have you checked out?" He looked at me incredulously with a puzzled grin on his face and said, "No." From what I remembered this sort of problem came from people who believed they'd been exposed to food or water contaminated with tapeworm in animal foodstuffs and their waste products. So I asked him, "Mat, have you visited a farm lately or visited the countryside?" He said, "No, but the woman next door to us keeps horses in the large field at the back of her house and she lets us stroke them." The more this little person with earnest blue eyes was looking directly into mine, the more concerned I became. I looked down at his tummy. It looked ok. I remembered that he'd had a voracious appetite the night before, polishing off a huge plate of sausage and chips, followed by ice cream. I think by now Mathew was beginning to share my concern as I repeated, "You have worms?" "Yes Grandad, why, what's wrong with that?" he replied uncomfortably. "They are in your tummy now?" I said inquisitively. "In my tummy, No, don't be daft Grandad, they're in an empty jam jar in the back garden. Daddy found them when he was digging in the garden and I am keeping them as pets!"

One must always make sure to get ALL or as many of the facts as possible before making a reserved judgement! When I visited school students I would point out that the police service is just like any other large organisation that has both good and bad aspects to it and so when making a considered judgement about the police service, not to base them just on the negative aspects but to make their own enquiries and then judge them as they find them. As I have already said, there are good officers and there are, unfortunately, not so good officers. Luckily, they are in the vast minority, but they are there, I'm afraid. I didn't want the pupils to like me take me home for tea or vote me into electoral office for that matter! All I asked from those students that were a little negative towards the police, was to judge me and the service I represented on the facts and at least give me and a fair hearing.

I also asked them to remember to judge everything they come across in life the very same way, with as many facts gleaned as possible to make a considered and balanced judgement. The rank and file majority of young citizens I have met in my time did exactly that. That's all I ask of you now. Read the book with an open mind and I hope you enjoy it.

I would also like to point out that any of the views or opinions expressed in this publication are the views of the author and not those of the West Midlands Police. Unless otherwise noted the author and the publisher make no explicit guarantees as to the accuracy of information obtained from the writers informants contained in this book. In nearly all cases the names of the people and places have been deliberately altered to protect their privacy.

'AV fone home!'

WHAT's BLACK BY DAY
AND RED BY NIGHT?

Before you venture into the rest of these jottings I think you should at least have some idea about the area I'll keep harping on about throughout.

The Black Country.

I was born in St Helens in Lancashire in the North west of England but I have lived in the Heart of England, the West Midlands, for the last 35 years. The first three spent as a student in Lardy Land, aka Birmingham, but the rest of my life, so far (!) has been spent in what is known nationwide as the Black Country. Made famous by such contemporary celebrities as comedians Lenny Henry & Frank Skinner, BBC TV's former One Show presenter and fellow baggie, Adrian Chiles, Mamma Mia film performer Julie Walters and of course living legend Tommy Mundon. They were all born or have roots in the area. Two famous Hollywood film stars, Sir Cedric Hardwicke (From Lye) and Madeleine Carroll (Born in West Bromwich) hail from the Black Country, they both indeed have stars in the Hollywood Walk of Fame, now there's a bostin' quiz question. Led Zeppelin vocalist Robert Plant was born in West Bromwich. Christine Perfect a founder member of Fleetwood Mac hails from Smethwick. Frank Windsor from BBC TV's.'Z'Cars' was born in Walsall. The infamous Gunpowder Plotters were hunted down to and murdered in the Black Country and of course it is the sporting home of three renowned footballing sides, the world famous West Bromwich Albion, Walsall FC and Stourbridge FC. Sorry, my mistake there's four, I forgot about Halesowen Town. Sorry, Dingles, I mustn't forget Wolverhampton Wanderers, who, as you will see, may or may not be a Black Country football team and just happen to be the biggest rivals of my beloved Baggies (West Bromwich Albion) better known to the Wolves fans as the Tesco bags!

I wonder if that last comment will get me some sponsorship from the international grocery and general merchandising retail chain? After all, they are the largest British retailer by both global sales and domestic market share, with profits exceeding £3 billion & currently the third largest global retailer ho could stock my book. I have both a Tesco mobile phone and have one of their club cards. Every little helps you know!

I like to think that I have been adopted by the place and I am certainly very proud to say I live in the heart of it. I married a girl from the area and my children and grand children were all born and grew up here. The people of the Black Country are a very special breed, bred from good stock. Honest, Reliable, Friendly but most of all Hard Working people.

It's difficult to explain where the Black Country actually is, but here goes. The Black Country is the geographical area west of the City of Birmingham, known affectionately by most of my police colleagues on the western side of the West Midlands Police area as 'Lardy Land' (Birmingham allegedly being full of Lard Heads or Lardy Dah know-alls - Of course being a Northerner and only an adopted Black Country officer I couldn't possibly comment and must remain neutral). Even though its in proximity to Birmingham, the vast majority of the Black Country's population will refuse outright to claim any connection or association with that particular city. Black Country folk do grow sick and tired of mistakenly being identified as 'Brummies' by all Non-Midlanders when on holiday in Britain or abroad and when appearing on TV. For example, whilst on holiday in Florida, some tourist from Berkshire (Berk being the appropriate epithet) heard the melodic tones of a fellow Black Countryman by the pool and instantly mistook his almost poetic discourse for that of a 'Brummie'.

But I digress, the Black Country is an area on the Western side of the hugely populated West Midlands conurbation formerly perched on top of a gigantic coalfield to the west of Birmingham. The South Staffs coalfield supplied coking coal to the massive Iron Foundries & Steel Mills that sprouted up across the area. The Black Country now lies wholly within the West Midlands County, but was formerly divided between the English Midland counties of Staffordshire and Worcestershire. Oddly, a bit like the old capitalist city of West Berlin being frozen inside the old East Germany, the ancient parish of Dudley was once a detached part of Worcestershire County within Staffordshire and some still consider Dudley to be Dudley, Worcestershire. Even more strangely, until 1845, much of the parish of Halesowen, including Oldbury and Warley Salop (but quaintly, not Cradley or Warley Wigorn) was a detached part of Shropshire. There is, to this day, a main carriageway named Threeshires Oak Road in Smethwick where funnily enough the three shire boundaries originally met. I don't suppose local scholars know that though. You know it's an odd (and quite sad) sign of the times that the average ten year old can tell you who Luke Skywalkers Dad really was, but can't tell you who Winston Churchill was or what he did, let alone anything about the history of his own locality.

Most local historians (Mainly Brummies, like Professor Carl Chinn from BBC's Midlands Today, regional news programme, who by the way has an exceptional passion for History that is truly admirable) like to mute, somewhat romantically, that Her Majesty the Queen (We are not amused) Victoria went through the middle of the Black Country on the Royal train on the way to somewhere beautifully nice and clean like the Balmoral Estate, when she purportedly looked through the net curtains of the Royal Carriage and supposedly exclaimed, "Oh what a Black Country, this place is". Hence, introducing the name which, was then supposedly adopted by the media of the time? I can't see that happening. If you examine the railway system across the United Kingdom at the time of Queen Victoria there were many routes that would have taken Her Majesty around the dirtier and filthier parts of a realm on which the Sun never set. Whereas, kids in Dudley in those days would have asked, "Mom, whats that bright ball of light in the sky?" Protectedly covering their little eyes on the very rare occasions that they caught a glimpse of that particular star through the mucky, smokey, crap they normally squinted through & breathed into their young damaged lungs, preparing them for their careers in the pits and foundries to come. There is no way Queen Vicky would have been taken through an area that could only be described as an open festering carbuncle on the Industrial face of Britain. No one of breeding in Victorian Society would have ventured anywhere near the place, for fear of catching some fatal disease, let alone royalty. It was too near the real world for the likes of them, mind you, speaking of carbuncles, her

Great Great Great Grandson, whose name escapes me, the one who chats to plants and vegetables (no not his relatives) visited my old patch in Smethwick once, inspecting work on shabby old run down Victorian terraced houses modernised by young offenders working with the Princes Trust (I like his tinned Salmon)! Industrialisation in the Black Country goes further back than the Industrial Revolution. It was already an area where metal working was important as far back as the sixteenth century, due to the presence of iron ore and of coal in a seam recorded to be thirty feet (Nine metres for you thick) thick, the thickest seam in Great Britain, which outcropped in various places. This severe industrial landscape made the place one of the most begrimed and miasmic places on the whole planet, not just Britain. Everything was covered in virulent black smoky dust that branched out twenty four seven from a forest of chimney stacks, so much so, that it automatically got the title, 'The Black Country.' You have to understand that by the late nineteenth century, the area had become one of the most intensely industrialised regions in the world, let alone Britain. With numerous coal mines, iron foundries and steel mills producing what nowadays would be illegal & unacceptable, enormous levels of air pollution with few equals anywhere else in the industrial world and would now be compared with the huge unchecked Industrial plants of Beijing.

In 1841 Charles Dickens described how the Black Country's factory chimneys "Poured out their plague of smoke, obscured the light, and made foul the melancholy air" in his novel The Old Curiosity Shop, the said melancholy air, being breathed in by the dying populace that worked in it. The great landscape artist JMW Turner visited Dudley in 1832 (Just after half past six in new money) to 'paint his representation of his personal hatred of industrialisation and what it meant to the towns and villages of Britain'.

In the early 1860s, his excellency the American Consul to Birmingham, Mr Eli Burritt (Inventor of the Flying Burrito) described the region as "black by day and red by night", because of the smoke and grime generated by the intense industry of its inhabitants and the red glow in the sky from constantly blazing furnaces at night. Harping back to the romantic historians, some of whom link J.R.R.Tolkien, he of Lord of the Rings fame, with the area stating that he based the grim region of Mordor on the heavy industry of the Black Country. Claiming that in the Elvish Sindarin language, Mor-Dor means Dark (or Black) Land, and is sometimes even referred to within the novel as "The Black Country." Mmmm, well maybe so JRR, maybe so.

I personally believe that the place got its name because of the horrible crap that was pumped into its atmosphere from its heavy industries, covering the area in a thick black soot that rested uneasily on all those young lungs. However, there are some local historians that also mute that the name might have already existed long before Britains Industrial Revolution. Stating that the outcroppings of black coal that covered the surface of the local heaths and the presence of coal so near the surface supposedly rendered soil in the area a deep black hue, hence, The Black Country.

However it got its name, the Black Country is known the world over for its engineering feats. The anchors and chains for the ill-fated liner RMS Titanic and her sister ship RMS Britannic were manufactured in the Black Country in the tiny hamlet of Netherton. The Titanic's three anchors and their accompanying chains were manufactured there; the set weighing in at one hundred tons. The centre anchor alone weighed 12 tons and was cheered by crowds of local schoolchildren (No doubt cheering because they'd got a day off school)lining the route as it was pulled through the streets of Netherton behind a brass band on its sedate journey to

Belfast by way of Liverpool by no less than twenty powerful shire horses.

Whatever the reason, The Black Country is also known for its distinctive dialect, which differs slightly across parts of the region. But has become popular again over recent years with the growth of periodicals such as the Black Country Bugle and the popularity with youngsters of the Black Country Alphabet song on youtube.com.

The modern day Black Country has now merged into a single geographical area, but is unusual in that it has no single centre, having grown up from a number of historic market towns and industrial villages that have joined their boundaries as they expanded during the 20th century. The boundaries of the Black Country, are to this day, still hotly contested and controversial, with the whole of Wolverhampton included by some and not at all by others. The usual twenty-first century definition of the Black Country encompasses the three Metropolitan Boroughs of Dudley, Sandwell & Walsall joined by the City of Wolverhampton (By some). The town of Dudley being generally adopted as the Black Country's (unofficial) capital.

Linguistic Scholars agree that the traditional Black Country dialect preserves many archaic traits of Early Modern English and even Middle English and can be more than a little confusing for outsiders. I remember my early days in the police were challenged constantly by members of the public asking me, "Ow B'ist?" (How are you, Officer) Only to be answered initially by a silent, slightly puzzled, grinning young member of the constabulary, blankly staring at them wide eyed, thinking to himself, "What the bleeding hell is this person saying to me?" When saying goodbye Black Country folk blurt out,"Tarra for a bit" a phrase you probably last heard used by the Tim Spall character 'Barry' in ITV's *Auf.Weidershen Pet,* unless you live in the

Black Country of course. When encouraging someone to try harder at a task, they will shout, "Gi it sum 'ommer" (Give it some Hammer or Hit it Harder!). Or, when asking if someone had seen a local girl who was missing from home, I was met with,"I ay sid 'er ma mon" (I haven't seen her, officer). I very soon got used to hearing "Ar" instead of "Yes" and "Yow" instead of "You" and soon picked up phrases like " Cuffin an Hayvin" (I have been Coughing and Heaving or I Have a Bad Cold) or "I got some fluff in mi clack" (I have a blocked throat). "Go" pronounced "Goo", thus "Goo-in" becomes "Going." "Ah cud eet' hos b'tween two bread vans" (I am that hungry, I could indeed eat a horse). I remember attending a domestic dispute in my early days of policing, where the male partner of an arguing newly married couple in Rowley Regis stated, "Mate, it's mi wench, er's in pig loike an er's drappin' it Chrismuss. Cuss o' that er's bin a bloody pane aw dae, so I gid er a bit of a paylin" Which I eventually, after several years in fact, understood to be, "Officer my wife is expecting a child and the happy day will be around Christmastime, however, she has been getting on my nerves all day and so I hit her". Yes unfortunately, there are still worryingly large parts of the Black Country were some of its Troglodytes still think it is the dark ages and therefore OK to hit women. In fact, there are some Black Country women that feel that they haven't had a decent night out, unless they've had a domestic dispute with their chosen cave dweller! Yes reader, it is the twenty first century, even in Blackheath. Thankfully the vast majority of Black Country Men treat their other halves with the utmost respect. Luckily the RESPECT message is getting through to the moronic minority too!

As I have already stated, residents of Birmingham often refer to their Black Country neighbours as "Yam Yams" and both Aston Villa and Birmingham City fans on their travels into the Black Country to either The Hawthorns, The Bescot Stadium or even the Custard bowl er, I mean Molineux at Wolverhampton are often welcomed by the locals singing, to the tune of 'She'll be coming round the Mountain when she comes', they substitute the words, "Well I'd rather be a Yam Yam than a Brum. Well, dear reader, I would rather be a Yam Yam too and proud of it, 'ar kid. Black Country folk are often the butt of a Brummie jokes and vice versa. Like the one that states, How can you tell film star 'legend' ET is a Villa Supporter? Because he looks like one! Its just a joke....no offence was intended, I hope none was taken. The truth is that these days the Brummies have been magnanimous enough to recognise that the Black Country exists and thats at least a start.

Mentioning the Villa and the Blues. I am reminded of something Richard Starling a Villa loving colleague of mine once told me. It is true that the 'Blues' (aka Birmingham City) have never won the English FA Cup, a trophy that their bitterest rivals Aston Villa have won on numerous occasions. It is also true that the FA Cup has only been stolen once in it's history, when it was on display in a shop window in Aston, Birmingham, whilst in the safe keeping of the holders Aston Villa FC! The cup was never recovered, it was probably melted down somewhere in the Black Country! As a result, the 'Villa' fans still goad the Bluenose fans by stating that the 'Villa' have even had the FA Cup stolen more times than the Blues have won it! Ironically, it was recently reported that when they'd just won the European Cup in the early Eighties the Villa had that stolen too! Perhaps they should invest in a better safe deposit box at Villa Park? Mind you, they've nothing to put in it nowadays have they? Heh heh heh.....

The Black Country, credit crunch permitting, even has its own evening newspaper. The Express and Star (Black and White by day and Read at night, with apologies to his excellency the American Consul to Birmingham, Mr Eli Burritt) a quality Black Country newspaper that is still going strong, in spite of the current financial crisis, a great Black Country stalwart.

THE BLACK COUNTRY, WHAT A BOSTIN' PLACE, INNIT 'AR KID!

'Come Aboard!

HANDCUFF 'EM ALL TOGETHER

Remember the old joke, How do you join the Police? Handcuff 'em all together! Well, as I embark on this book, I am currently employed by West Midlands Police as a Co Ordination and Tasking Officer on the Sandwell Local Policing Unit, West Bromwich. Having served over thirty years as a Constable, I stayed on in the job as a Thirty Plus officer with the West Mids. As a CATO Officer I help arrange police resources for various operations that require the attendance of varying levels of Public Order trained officers from my LPU. Mainly for Football matches at our varied West Midland footballing venues, but mostly for games at the Hawthorns, home of the great West Bromwich Albion Football Club, located on our LPU.

After being on operational front line duties for nearly twenty of my thirty years of service, I had an operation on my lower back in December 1999 following a serious road traffic accident, which resulted in me having one and a half discs in my lower spine, removed. A full and partial laminectomy to give the procedure its exact title, where a leading orthopaedic surgeon, removed bone by shaving it from my right hip. He then removed my worn and prolapsed discs wedging the newly removed bone tightly into the space left, fixing them firmly in place with four titanium screws. Since that day, I became what rank and file police officers very unpolitically correctly refer to as a 'Raspberry Ripple' (Police euphemism for physically 'permanently' restricted or disabled officers).

When I listen to the speeches made by retiring colleagues who state that when they joined the police, it was the fulfilment of their childhood ambitions, hopes and dreams, I have to admit that I cannot really say that about my own career in the police service. When I was a kid I remember wanting to be a school crossing patrol officer (Can't say Lollypop 'Man' - It's sexist), because you only start work when you are sixty-five! Neither, did I dream of a career in anything really. To dream you have to be asleep! I was always half asleep in the classroom, I had to be, staying on the look out for the bully boys. I was never fully asleep enough to have dreams!

I honestly cannot remember having any ambitions when it came to a working career. I started my police service way back in 1980, The 2nd of January 1980 to be exact. That, twenty two year old Bryan Connor, had been married for three years, but having no children yet had little or no experience of life or the responsibilities that go with it and was mystified at how anyone could be employed in the police or any occupation for that matter for thirty years! People retiring from the police service in my formative years of policing had done their police training when I was still a twinkle in my Dad's eye, literally! Likewise now, literally at the end of my own thirty year career with the police service, the brave young folk who stand on the front line on my LPU, that face the same social diseases that I faced decades before them, didn't exist when I started my stint at the sharp end.

It honestly doesn't feel like thirty years ago that I came nervously through the hallowed portals of Lloyd House, the West Midlands Police Headquarters, in my bid to become a Police Officer. The police service are always looking for men and women who thrive on challenges and are willing to work hard to learn the skills necessary for this difficult but critical role. Police work can be a tough and unpredictable, but it is the most rewarding position I have ever experienced. Every day that I donned that uniform and went to work, I knew that I was helping make life that bit safer and more secure for my loved ones, my friends, my neighbours and the general populace of one of the greatest places in the United Kingdom. In fairness I wasn't sure whether I fitted the bill (No pun intended) when I was that young wannabe but having received my, black ink only, handwritten application form, the West Midlands Police had checked my eligibility and marked the answers to questions about my aptitude. I had applied to both Merseyside Police who covered my home town of St Helens and West Midlands Police where I had been a student and where I had lived for the last five years before returning to work for a short time to Merseyside. Thankfully, it was the West Midlands Police who wrote to me first, inviting me to attend Lloyd House, the force headquarters, in the centre of Birmingham, for an assessment test. Had I known then what a roller coaster ride I was in for, I might have trembled a little bit more or even turned right round and got the train back to my hometown St Helens, but ignorance was bliss in those days, wasn't it? The selection process for the job was so scrupulous, not like nowadays. Checks were then made not only into your personal background, but into your families backgrounds! Information I gave on my application form and from police systems such as the Police National Computer (PNC) are used to verify the applicants identity and his/her background. On my application form I had to provide the names of references who could provide supporting information about my character and employment history. When you finally pass all the initial phases of the application process, all the people you named as referees are visited by police recruitment officers. Police officers visit them at home to confirm that the details you have said about yourself is genuine! As I still lived at my Mum's address in Clinkham Wood, St. Helens in Merseyside I was visited by an Inspector and a Sergeant from the Recruiting Department of the Merseyside Police Force. I saw them pull up in a marked police vehicle outside my mothers council house on the Clinkham Wood estate, the sort of estate that had grown accustomed to seeing that mode of transportation quite often. As the curtains of my mothers neighbours windows twitched, I answered the door. They took one look at the stocky, long haired, bum fluff bearded, denim clad, youth and community worker that opened the door and the broad scouse accented Sergeant asked, "Excuse me son, does a Bryan Connor live at this address?" "Yes," I replied, in friendly way, "Thats me!" I may well be mistaken, but I'm pretty sure I saw the Inspector glance over at the Sergeant and then roll his eyes toward the sky! They came in and asked that dubious looking, would be pillar of the judicial system many relevant questions as they eat my mothers cake and washed it down with copious amounts of Co-op '99' Tea. That was really only the start of a very lengthy and thorough recruitment procedure. Once an expectant recruits' references had been verified, their application would continue to greater security clearance levels – and then to a final stage of recruitment at Lloyd House itself, which was and still is the Headquarters of the West Midlands Police, in Birmingham. The final interviews began with a thorough medical, then finally a formal interview. I remember in summer 1979, sitting next to a bloke who looked a bit like entertainer, Rolf Harris, in the lecture theatre at Lloyd House with about seventy-five other hopefuls. 'Rolf' told me that he was currently based in the mobile frozen confectionary retail trade (He was an Ice Cream Man) and had come all the way from the City of Coventry to be there. I told him that I came from St Helens in Lancashire. "That's by Blackpool ain't it?" said Rolf. "Close enough" I replied, too nervous to explain the mistake fully. A lot of people in the Midlands get confused and think I mean (Lytham) St Annes, when I tell them my home town is St Helens, the large Industrial town stuck between Liverpool and Manchester in the North West of England and I just get fed up of having to explain that I don't come from the clean, well to do, affluent suburb south of Blackpool, but the grubby industrial glass town known for its glorious Rugby League team.

Now, because I hadn't passed my GCE Maths qualification (I was thick at 'sums' I'll be honest with you) I had to take the police entrance examination. Which I found quite easy, no disrespect to those people who have failed it. The first question was, What is your name? I got seventy five percent for that question (Thanks Peter Cook)! They were the sort of questions that you dread, you know, If Mr Blue has twelve gallons of water in his bath and Mr Red adds two pints, then how big should the sponge be, that Mr Purple buys to suck up all the water? When we'd completed the 'exam', which as I say, didn't seem that hard, really, just a collection of simple mathematical equations, spelling and comprehension tests. The sergeant from the West Midlands Police Recruiting Office announced that he would read out a list of names. The people whose names were read out where to file out of the right hand door as it was called. When he got to the end there were only about six of us left left in the large lecture theatre. I thought to myself, 'Rolf's gone out of the door, he seemed a level headed chap, he dribbled from both sides of his mouth at the same time, so, I must have failed!' I looked around at the remaining group. They looked like me, in a gormless fashion! I couldn't have failed, I thought, I can't be that stupid? The sergeant smiled at the few of us that remained and I thought, 'Here it comes, the thanks for coming lecture.' He said, Ladies and Gentlemen, Congratulations, you have all passed the entrance examination, you'll get a letter shortly inviting you to a selection board interview, where an Assistant Chief Constable, a member of the Police Authority and a Chief Superintendent will ask you various questions regarding your application to the West Midlands Police." As we few, we happy few, prepared to leave. The same sergeant said. Mr Connor, would you mind waiting behind in the adjoining office before you go please?" Well, at the time, I was very busy, being an unemployed ex-student, with zits to squeeze and long playing record albums to listen to, but what the, "OK" I said (Anything to help the police, I thought). When the others had left Lloyd House, the recruiting sergeant said, "Because you have had to come so far for the procedure we thought it best to set up a special interview board for you this afternoon, if that's ok?" 'Ok? Not really,' I thought, but I have learned in life that some doors open as others close. I remembered as a child, having the opportunity to stand on the footplate of a real steam engine at the invitation of my Brother in Laws Bill's Dad, who worked for British Rail on the Rail System in and around my hometown of St Helens, Lancashire, when I was nine years old and waiting on a platform for a train to take us on our holidays. I diffidently declined this once in a lifetime, never to be repeated proposition. A regret I still bemoan to this very day. The lesson I did learn from that overlooked prospect was to never ever turn down a life-changing opportunity when it is presented to you. This was the hand of fate knocking on my door of Opportunity as Hughie Green might have put it. Some of those doors that do open for us only open temporarily and you must take those opportunities when they happen. This was one of those junctures. Apparently the Assistant Chief Constable had a cancelled appointment that morning with members of the West Midlands Police Authority. The recruiting sergeant had suggested to these significant protagonists that it would only take half an hour of their demanding schedules. So they agreed to alter their diaries to accommodate my formal interview. Straight away I had a fitness test in the forces Occupational Health Department, this incorporated an eye test and a medical examination. Police officers must of course, be physically healthy to carry out their duties, all applicants need to be examined to ensure that they have no serious health problems, after all, the Home Office are investing a lot of tax payers money into a police officers career development. Accordingly, it is a thorough test, but at the time I had mine, I was Twenty-two years of age and playing Rugby every weekend, I wasn't super fit, but I was more than fit enough to carry out the demanding duties of the office of constable. While I was taking the tests, the sergeant had collected the panel together and delivered them to a small office opposite the recruiting office. I'm certainly glad they made the decision to stay for half an hour. For them it was half an hour out of a hectic timetable. For me it was a life changing decision. In that small window of opportunity I was seen and positively scrutinised by a set of professional principal elders. I had just finished reading a library book entitled, 'A Man Apart: The British Policeman and his Job' by Tony Judge. It's a warts an all profile documenting the pros and cons of being an operational contemporary police officer. It was this book that first aroused my interest in the police force as a career. I had just read it for the second time on the train coming down to Birmingham for the examination! The details covering every question that the panellists posed had been highlighted by Tony Judge in the book! They could see that I had an obvious enthusiasm to join the police and gave me the chance show it. After asking me to leave the room momentarily I was asked to return and again, breaking all the usual rules of recruitment protocol the Assistant Chief Constable, who chaired the panel told me, there and then, that my application to join the West Midlands Police had been successful. I felt like Charlie Bucket unwrapping Wonka's Golden Ticket! That moment was one of the most memorable points of my entire life. It was your first trip to Wembley, your first date, the unwrapping of Christmas presents, your first flight in an aeroplane and scoring your first try all wrapped into one! I told the world and his dog, everyone. It was in the days before mobile phones and texting. If I'd known the number of the editor of the Express and Star, I'd have rung 'em with the scoop. Lets face it. Not just anyone can become a police officer. There are literally thousands of applications made per year and thousands are turned down. To be selected for this task literally in the words of Tony Judge makes you a Man Apart a special individual. The reassuring feeling that I had what it takes, was for me a proud feeling. They were looking for individuals who had the qualities, the initiative and the willingness to learn new skills and methods for combating crime and violence. As I stated earlier the Home Office invest thousands of pounds in an officers comprehensive training. I learned how to protect myself, how to reassure Joe public, how to assist crime victims and offer aid to those people who have witnessed crimes. I learned how to investigate complex criminal matters utilising both new technology as well as time-proven traditional methods of locking up criminals.

The last thirty years have literally whizzed by. As I said earlier, it's been a roller coaster of a job to be in. Was it worth it I hear you say? Oh Yes, every minute of it. What other career can boast that no two days will ever be the same, is a constant challenge and brings the opportunity to contribute to your local community with continual opportunities to advance? How many people can say that they have spent three decades in a job they love and get well paid for doing it? I rest my case your worships.

I will take this opportunity to say a few words to those colleagues I have had the privilege to share that ride with. Folks, I want to tell you how much I have appreciated knowing each and every one of you. You will see that all the names of officers accompanying me in the stories in the book have had their names changed, purely to protect them from any future Google searchers! Folks, You all know who you are....and I repeat, It was a pleasure and honour to have served with you all. Even the officers I had a bad time with. I can literally count on one hand the bobbies I couldn't get along with in the job. Even then, although I don't get on with them (and the feeling was probably mutual) they shared the same ethos as myself. That was a desire to serve the community to the best of their ability. After thirty years, that isn't a bad epitaph for any profession is it? That even the few people you disliked in your chosen calling shared your principal views?

Everyone of my working colleagues the good, the bad and the indifferent, have all made this job so very special for me not just the 'serious' fundamentally sombre features, but very much the amusing and entertaining aspects that I have experienced working alongside you all. Some of the more memorable experiences have been retold in these scribbles of mine. Fellow West Mids members both past and present, all laboured for long protracted hours either standing frozen at fixed points or trudged freezing; along pavements, passageways, alleyways, trails, ditches, rivulets, canal tow paths and corridors, outside, in all extremes of weather conditions, preserving and protecting crime scenes, we have escorted more prisoners than lived in that village in Wales with Patrick McGoohan, we have ejected hooligans out of the Smethwick End at the Albion home games, directed irate motorists down streets they didn't want to navigate, towards places they didn't want to go! Learned how to use a typewriter (They didn't mention that at the interview!) the hard way, been bombarded with missiles from proper rioters and our own training police officer 'pretend' rioters, been erroneously sprayed in the face with Cs spray by our workmates, done plain clothes 'obs' in very cramped locations with bobbies who had chronic body odour, halitosis and very irritable bowels, drank enough cups of tea, coffee and soup to float the QE2 and attended more court cases than Perry Mason. Been bitten by police dogs and other hirsute life forms, grabbed grannies at pay day disco's (Of course I can assure my lady wife that I was never present at one of these gatherings, someone told me about it – Is my nose growing?), I have run around aimlessly wearing adapted motorcycle helmets whilst carrying huge clear (?) perspex shields and dodging Molotov cocktails, witnessed enough political incorrectness to challenge and raise a dead looney left euro politician from the dead, received countless bollockings from countless supervisors, interviewed more 'guests' than Michael Parkinson, attended more Hospitals A & E's than Charlie Fairhead and had more domestic disputes than Liz Taylor. Explained the caution to more illiterate Britons than we can remember, moved offices enough times to be added on to Pickfords Removals Christmas Card list, dealt with innumerable obnoxious acne ridden persistent young offenders (not to mention custody officers)! People, I could go on and on!

I am enormously proud when I say that I have been a Police Officer in the second largest force in England and Wales, the West Midlands Police. I have worked at some great nicks over the years. I started at K3, Piddock Road Police Station,Smethwick. The irony there being that I got a bus to Smethwick on my first ever tour of duty, a late shift (1400x2200hrs) and had to ask the bus driver where to get off the bus for the police station! Then to K1 West Bromwich, then Old Hill, back to Smethwick, then Oldbury, Warley, then onto Hawthorns House an office block where a floor is rented by the job, where I was based as the OCU Planning officer. I could even see 'Mecca'......No not the City in Saudi Arabia or the Bingo Hall! I meant the Hawthorns Stadium of course (The home of West Bromwich Albion FC)Albion FC, Association Football Stadium) from my office window! Recently I moved to West Bromwich Police Station as a CATO Officer where I think I will finally end my time as a police officer. I won't be sorry to leave though. I will be leaving a job that has been my life (So Far anyway!), but the job has changed totally from the job I joined thanks mainly to modern influences like Political Correctness!

Over the years it seems that the thin blue line has got increasingly thinner. Certain factions of society have always hated the police and what they stand for. Many members of the public tell us that they are losing confidence in us. But all I can tell them is that the vast majority of front line officers out there now, still have the right credentials, in spite of the regimes they have to endure to get the job done. If they try to enforce the law as most of society would expect them to (catching burglars and muggers) then they may well incur the wrath of the politically correct contingent and if they don't enforce the law then they incur the wrath of the the rest of society! Its a thankless task and a no-win situation most of the time.

As I finalised this book the despicable Ali Dizaei, a thoroughly bad apple, seems an apt example of how low the modern police service has sunk. This disgraced former Police Superintendent and the most senior police officer to be convicted of a serious criminal offence in the United Kingdom since 1977, when two Metropolitan Police Commanders were found guilty of accepting bribes from Soho pornographers, was jailed in February 2010 for four years. Dizaei was branded by the media as a 'criminal in uniform' and was found guilty of trying to pervert the course of justice among other things. He had been out with his wife at a Persian restaurant when he was spotted by a web designer, to whom he owed money, a Mr. Waad Al-Baghdadi. Mr Al-Baghdadi was chasing just six hundred pounds for updating Dizaei's own website. Mr Al-Baghdadi had originally been commissioned for a fortnight's work by Dizaei, the former president of the Black Police Association but it turned into several months of demands to continually alter the egotistical site with speeches, pictures and articles concerning Dizaei's police career. The prosecution and defence teams at Southwark Crown Court understandably disagreed on how events unfolded at the lush Kensington restaurant that Friday night in July 2008. The prosecution claimed that a row broke out between the pair over the work and Dizaei, who was in police 'half blues' after a ceremony for recruits at Scotland Yard, challenged Mr Al-Baghdadi to a fight in the street. Most becoming of a very senior police officer eh? The injured party stating that he was left "scared" and "shocked" by the suggestion also claimed that Dizaei was drunk. Dizaei dialled the nines and asked for assistance from his Metropolitan Police and handcuffed Al-Baghdadi telling him he was being arrested, although he failed to say what for. Mr Al-Baghdadi consequently complained that he was being restrained so tightly that he feared his hand or arm might break, comparing Dizaei to an aggressive gangster, saying he was like, Al Pacino's character in the film Scarface, 'Tony Montana.' It of course transpired that Dizaei was lying and had even self inflicted the wounds that he said had been made by Al-Baghdadi during his arrest! Good Riddance to bad rubbish! There is only one thing worse than a bombastic egotistical bully as a gaffer in the police force and thats when they are *bent* bombastic egotistical bullies!

I used to be proud to tell people I was a police officer. Now, I don't divulge my occupation to any strangers I meet, when asked what I do for a living. Thanks to all the bad publicity brought on the job by criminal coppers just like Dizaei. I tell people that twig that I know something about the judicial system that I'm an admin assistant in the Crown Prosecution Service, a local government event planner or even a portrait painter in oils (See www.bryanconnor.co.uk - Very Reasonable rates folks!) *anything* but a police officer!

Nowadays: When Judges impose contemptible sentences for serious offenders and offences. When someone is being burgled or robbed at knifepoint or God forbid worse, members of the public who are still supportive enough to ring the police with good intelligence on criminals are put off totally by the unprofessional way they are treated by the judicial system. Who can they turn to?

They turn to Police Officers and lets face it: Would any reasonably sane person willingly rush to a report of a violent youth robbing a shop with a firearm or to a call where a someone is wielding a knife in a busy shopping centre?

It's not easy being a copper these days. In a modern world where there are Closed Circuit Television cameras literally everywhere you go, watching every move police officers make out on the streets, both on and off duty. Where the media, left and right wing agitators, both parliamentary and local politicians, even some senior police officers and of course the law breaking three percent of the population that have opted out of the general law abiding civilisation, all constantly try to find examples of a police officers wrong doing and rarely, if ever, does anyone look for examples of the fantastic work, the latest generation of officers who are, overworked, underpaid and under appreciated for the hard front line operational street work are performing.

To paraphrase our famous founder, The police are as much part of the community now as they were in Sir Robert Peels day, they are the public and the public are the police; the only difference being that police officers are paid to give full time and attention to such duties which are incumbent on every citizen of the UK in the interests of community welfare and existence. I say to all those police officers working hard to make a better Britain. My good friends, be careful out there, keep your integrity, keep the faith, know all your powers (They'll help keep you safe) & never stop believing that you can make a difference, retirementshire will come a lot sooner than you think and in the meantime...

Don't let any of the *******s grind you down!

'A Greycockapoo'

A CLOSE ENCOUNTER
WITH A GREYCOCKAPOO

You always have to be careful with the origin of some police yarns. Whether you're hearing them from a bobby, or amongst people who know the world of bobbies and policing, you know that there are stories that circulate across time, permeating all police force and even international boundaries, funny stories, that a law enforcer, wherever he or she works will identify with and adopt as his or her own or say 'Oh, I knew this bloke once who did this'. Educated folk call this plagiarism, a copper would call it,'Gilding the Lily' and you all know it as that waste stuff that a bull leaves, at the rear end, not the horny end! This is one of those stories, and I'm going to tell you how I found out that it was bull-shine later. It's a great story and I love it to bits, here goes:

A couple of detectives that I knew told me that they visited a location to get a witness statement, a house in a place called Tipton, which is a infamous little town located between West Bromwich and Wolverhampton in the West Midlands. Tipton has a notorious reputation, as a place where the people are rough and ready but really they are the salt of the earth. An anachronism, it's a little like the land that time forgot, a place where, you would not be surprised to find people still storing coal in the bath, or stabling a pony in the back kitchen. I jest not. Tipton has a reputation for being a tough Black Country town full of eccentrics and it is!

So the police story; Two D's (Police term for Detectives who work in the CID that's an abbreviation for Coppers In Disguise) go to a council drum (Police Term for House) in Tipton to cop a statement from a witness. They knock his door and while they're waiting, standing in the front garden of the premises is a dirty, salt and pepper, woolly, scabby mongrel dog, which in the Black Country we would call a 'Tipton Flock hound', you may know it better as a 'Heinz 57' or a Greycockapoo Hound. Why Greycockapoo? Well, it looked like a cross between a Greyhound, a Cocker Spaniel and a Poodle! Anyway, you get the point; it's a mongrel dog, a 'Heinz 57' or Tippon' Flock Hound. I like Tipton Flock hound, it's a good phrase isn't it, and this dog of dubious parentage and grand damme-age (Is that a word? Certainly caused some damage somewhere) or whatever they're called? The geezer at the house answers the door, one officer says, "All right mate, are you Mr Blinge?" He replies, "Yeah mate." "We've come to get a statement from you", says the officer, "Yeah, av bin expectin yer, come in lads", says the householder, and they walk into a dimly lit, sparsely decorated and besmirched hallway. The gumshoes immediately upon entering the establishment sense that distinctive bouquet. A fusion of the householder's lunch, animal waste, rancid cooking fat, soiled sweaty clothing and a long standing total disregard for personal hygiene. Those brave souls that who have entered a busy police cell block, worked in the housing department of a municipal council, worked for the Department of Social Security or worked in the prison service will have experienced this stench. I've personally perfected the art of blocking up my nasal passages and pretending to have a cold when visiting such places, why? Because, I once took a deep breath upon entering a flat in the Hill Top area of Smethwick where there was a similar fragrance, with the intention of keeping it held, like a deep sea diving pearl fisher. As my Doc Martin boots bonded with the grubby excuse for floor covering beneath them it suddenly dawned on me. How am I going to converse? I regretted not taking the sign writing course as I can only hold my breath for about sixty-seconds. I would have to breathe again otherwise I could die! I breathed in; receiving the full bodied strength of the pong through both nostrils. I uncontrollably vomited all along the hallway; it plastered most of the front door as I struggled with one hand to open it whilst trying to quell the projectile flow of the vomit by holding the other across my mouth. My amused partner, Mick Benyon, made some scant excuse to the householder who, unsurprisingly, did not own a mop and bucket. I used the brush from the boot of the panda, normally used for broken windscreen fragments and blood on tarmacadamed roads from car accidents. This, dear reader, is literally the smell of years of neglect. Houses and flats full of grubby people, who, never had or lost any of the self respect they once had, a very long time ago, living in hovels, that haven't been spring cleaned in donkey's years.

Back to the tale, the witnesses dwelling was that sort of venue! It was really, middle of a hot summers day stinky, and unsurprisingly, to the officers, the mutt follows 'em in, they think nothing of it, Mr Blinge thinks nothing of it, even the dog thinks nothing of it, so all parties carry on their business as normal. Nevertheless, they get talking about the incident that he's witnessed, an assault or whatever, taking a swift statement from him. Going along the lines of, 'At such and such a time and date, I was outside the local Sauna Baths (He wouldn't be visiting them of course) in such and such a street with me mates, when I see Mr Bully come out of the slipper baths and swiftly kick the local vicar Reverend Victor Timm in the arboretum (That's makes your eyes water) etcetera, etcetera, that's it, and I'm prepared to give evidence at court and Blah, blah blah, whatever'. These were places existed for people who hadn't a bath or shower at their home, usually old terraced houses, who could visit and have a hot bath for a small fee. Usually run by the local council, it's like something out of a Dickens novel isn't it? They were still around in the eighties in Britain. The detectives finished taking the statement and the witness is happy to put his identifying moniker on the bottom of it, but, as he's having the statement read out to him, the flock hound, which has been in the front room all the time, lying on the floor in front of this guy's two bar electric fire licking his guild halls, gets up and squats, and that's the only word for it, squats, I think you know what I mean, sits on its heels, hunkers down, cowers, it's front legs splayed straight and its back legs doubled up in a squat! It then starts to perform a natural bodily function, a movement from its inner body, evacuating, if you get my drift. Leaving an oversized deposit on the living room floor that was hotter and steamier than the sauna bath mentioned in statement they'd just taken. The two detectives glance at each other and instinctively think 'Mmm, that's strange', then, with Chaplinesque timing, turn their heads toward the witness Mr Blinge, who shows no emotion whatsoever, ostensibly thinking nothing of it, therefore the bobbies professionally carry on regardless, reading over the statement to the witness, making no comment about the canine kack, they just think, 'Well we are in Tipton, its not unusual (Ask Tom Jones) we'll get this done and dusted as soon as we can, get it signed and then we'll Foxtrot Oscar'. (Foxtrot Oscar being Police code for going on a corporeal mystery trip.) The two law men got up to leave and as they Foxtrot Oscared, they stated the necessary judicial comments, thanked Mr Blinge very much for his aid and told him that he'd be hearing from the them in due course. The detectives hurriedly 'do one' down the drive of this blokes house and he is standing at his front door like, 'cause it's Tipton y'know, he's probably gonna wave to them as they drive off! They're friendly like that in Tipton. As they get to the car Mr Blinge starts running towards them shouting, 'Scuse me, officers! ' The detective sitting in the front passenger seat rolls the passenger side window down and says, "What's the problem squire?' Chummy says,' you've forgotten to take your dog with you mate!'

What a belting story. Mr Blinge thought it was the officers flock hound! This is Tipton remember? Where Of course, for security purposes you understand, police officers, especially those from the Criminal Investigation Department of the West Midlands Police, usually go to enquiries accompanied by dirty smelly mongrel dogs that relieve themselves wherever they like, for protection! Now, I used to genuinely believe, naively, that the officer that first told me that story was the detective that made the actual visit for the statement. I believed and trusted him implicitly, as far as I was concerned, it happened to him and his work partner, in Tipton, West Midlands. I have told people that very tale when I've gone on holiday, when I've been having a quiet drink with mates in my local or at family get-togethers. I've told that story for years and got laughs and much mileage out of it socially. I thought nothing of its authenticity until I reread an old book of police yarns by a retired bobby called Harry Cole. Harry, a former Met bobby, wrote many books, containing amusing and strange anecdotes that had happened to him, that he had heard or had forwarded to him by likeminded bobbies, that he had collected over his own thirty year stint in the greatest job on earth. That's what gave me the inspiration to write down this collection of stories now. The story about the dog was one of Harry's and the Detectives had nicked it or should I say appropriated it! It's not like Police Detectives to guild the lily like that is it?

Folks, the stories that I've retold in my collection of jottings, really are genuine, unique stories that I, or some of the wonderful colleagues I have had the privilege to have known and worked with, have witnessed, they're not made up and they haven't been plagiarised from other works (well except for this one), the story I've just told you about the Dog leaving a surprise parcel is Harry Cole's. Harry was born and brought up in Bermondsey, South London. He left school when he was fourteen, during World War 2 and became an apprentice cricket-bat maker, until he was old enough to join the army. Upon leaving the army he first tried his hand as a stone mason, but in 1952 he joined the Metropolitan Police (Only two years after George Dixon had been shot dead in 1950 by Tom Riley but then, Jesus-like, had ascended from the dead to live again for twenty-six more years service. George Dixon finally retiring from the Met when the actor who played him, Jack Warner was eighty years old!). The other connection between where I worked all my police career and BBC televisions Dixon of Dock Green is in the name of its protagonist, George Dixon. Who, I have read, got his name from a local comprehensive school in City Road, Edgbaston, Birmingham. The school the director of the Blue Lamp, Michael Balcon attended as a boy. George Dixon's High School is only half a mile away from my old patch at Cape Hill.

After thirty years in the job, Harry retired in 1983, he'd worked at the same police station in London throughout. He became a qualified Football Association coach running numerous junior football teams in the local community, a referee and a keen cricketer. Harry had a regular column in *The Warren*, the metropolitan police magazine. His books include 'Policeman's Progress', 'Policeman's Lot', and 'Policeman's Patch.' In 1978 Harry was awarded the British Empire Medal for his voluntary work. After leaving the force, along with writing he took up after-dinner speaking. I tried to contact him a few months after he'd sadly passed away. That is typical of my timing!

Harry, thank you mate, if there's anybody reading this that knew him or was related to him, I cannot fully relate just how much of an inspiration Harry has been to me. His books inspired me to write my stories down. Harry died in 2008, which means he also had a Home Office police pension for twenty-six years. Good on you, Harry!

Another such story with such dubious origins which I love, is the sprog (Police Constable in his or her first 'probationary' two years) attending their first PM, Post Mortem that is and not 'autopsy' as the Yanks call them. Pathetically, even British cop drama's refer to PM's as autopsies! Sacrilege! A Post Mortem in the United Kingdom is always carried out in a Mortuary, Not a Morgue! Another modern television drama inaccuracy that bugs me. When I first heard this next story it was set at the central mortuary in Birmingham. Two young probationers (Sprogs as they are colloquially known) where sent there early on in their police training to observe their first Post Mortem. Not pleasant, but a necessary 'must do' part of any new police officers training. The Birmingham Mortuary was a very old Victorian building with hundreds of cadaver sized metal drawers distributed about five deep across one huge wall. These drawers temporarily held the poor unfortunate ex-sentient humans that were to waiting to be dispatched.

Having already eaten a very greasy, unhealthy, fried in lard, full English, greasy breakfast, the first sprog was summoned into the PM room to see his first examination of a cadaver. The mortician's assistant led him along long, narrow, cold, draughty, Victorian tiled corridors, through a pair of huge clear plastic swing doors into the white tiled examination room, handing him over to the Mortician. The assistant left the room to fetch the next victim, er sorry, willing police probationer spectator. The smirking mortician asked in a deep Vincent Price type inquisitive voice, "Young Man, have you ever seen a dead body, in the flesh as it were?" After the negative reply of the young apprehensive probationer, the mortician re-assuredly smiled and said, "You'll get used to it. The first thirty years are the worst. "Walking over and gripping the handle to one of the stone grey metal drawers lining the wall he gave it a slight tug and as it easily slid open said, "Shall we get on with it then?" He pulled open the sliding drawer with ease and there on the open drawer covered by a white linen shroud lay a body, with its head towards the drawer, lying on its back facing the strip lighted, tiled ceiling. The mortician said to the probationer, "Go on then, you pull the cover off." He tentatively took the corner of the sheet in between his right thumb and forefinger and as he pulled back the cloth, the male, naked cadaver shot up, bolt upright, looked the sprog directly in the eyes and shouted, "Fucking Hell its cold in there!" The astonished sprog shot twelve foot in the air and was having palpitations! The 'dead' body was the mortician's assistant, who had initially brought him down to the examination room earlier. With very lively cheeky grins the Mortician and his assistant managed to calm the young probationer down. They then proposed the question, "Do you want to play that trick on your mate when he comes down here?" "Oh Yeah!" says the probationer readily. "OK go into the changing room next door and undress down to your undies and come back in here. "OK says the willing sprog removing clothes as he started off towards the changing room!

He gets back into the examination room in just his Y fronted grundies. With the mischievous grin of a naughty schoolboy about to put one over on his classmate, he climbs onto and lies down upon the open vacant drawer and is then covered with a shroud by the winking Mortician who closing the drawer says to the would be 'dear departed' sprog, "You OK?" "Yeah," he unconvincingly says, with a nervous quiver in his voice as the drawer closes and the light vanishes. You have to imagine what it must have been like whilst his eyes were not yet accustomed to the light it must have been more than a tad cold. As he started to get his eyesight back he could see the drawers above him and more to the point, parts of their wan coloured, lifeless customers. There are no sides to the drawers in these places, why would there be? All the insides of the oversized filing cabinets are open. In the still, dimly lit cabinet world of the newly deceased he started to feel he'd been there for an inordinate amount of time. His eyes gradually getting used to the darkness, he lifted up his left hand to looking at the wristwatch shaped pattern on his left wrist to check how long he'd been there. No watch! He had taken it off. He tried not to look up at the gory sight before him, that of rows and rows of dead bodies. Instead, to get his mind off his predicament he thought to himself, 'Come on, pull yourself together, they must have brought the other officer down stairs by now, I won't have to wait much longer he'll be here anytime now, they'll open the drawer and I'll be ready to shock the living daylights out of him'. He started to cautiously sing under his breath, 'Happy Days are here again' as he glanced towards the drawer to his right. There, on the next drawer lay a gruesome sight. 'The skies above are clear again' he jerkily continued as he surveyed the green tinted, slime covered monster man, bloated through lying at the bottom of the Birmingham and Fazeley canal for several weeks. He abruptly stopped singing under his breath and with an extremely large intake of breath the sprog quickly looked away from the horrid sight, then instinctively glanced over to the left of him, and there, staring directly back at him was a bright white, familiar face with large spoon shaped hazel eyes. One of the eyes winked and then the face frowned and said, "Fuckin' cold ain it?" The sprog in total fear and panic shot bolt upright hitting his forehead firmly against the bottom of the upper drawer with considerable force. Splitting his head open and knocking himself out cold! He later received several stitches to a nasty head wound. The giggling mortician's assistant in the left hand drawer suddenly didn't see the joke and the mortician and him must have had very troubled thoughts as they went to assist the stricken sprog and wondered if they would still have a job by the close of the day following their workplace prank.

Now, whether that is a true story or not, it's a great yarn over a couple o three pints with a few mates! I certainly don't know whether it happened or not. Mind you, you could say the same about the Bible! It makes you wonder just how many different forces up and down the country or around the world for that matter have heard a similar tale told to their intake of probationary officers. I remember my first Post Mortem. It was one spring morning in 1980 and traditionally followed a hearty, full English fried breakfast in the police canteen! PC Pete Connolly, the Sandwell Coroners Officer at the time and a great friend of mine since then (He even had a hand in bringing my wife Beverly and I together). Pete took me around to the Little Red Brick Mortuary built onto the end of Smethwick Police Station. For those who know Smethwick, it's gone now but on the site where it stood is now a tastefully designed Garden to the memory of fallen police officers. By the small, overshadowed, discreetly concealed doorway entrance of the mortuary, in a tiny courtyard, is where Pete introduced me to the Mortician, Mr Sly (You can't make it up can you?). He was a short, thin, wiry man in his early sixties with greasy short, wavy, mousey coloured hair, greying at the temples and receding at the forehead, he looked a bit like the old Sunderland football manager Bob Stokoe. He had a grin to match his name with a half smoked unlit Woodbine hanging off the edge of his mouth he shook my hand and coughed as he said," Charmed, I'm sure", he thrust his bony right hand through the morning mist into my dry nervous palm. It was then, in the dim light of the weatherproofed illuminated lamp over the door that I saw the largest cyst I had ever seen, before or since. It had grown & was stuck like a large rose red oval limpet on Mr Sly's neck. It must have been at least four inches long by three inches wide and it shone like a new ball at the Oval. Talk about looking the part, Mr Sly wouldn't have looked out of place on the set of a Hammer horror film! When we went into the spooky darkness of the Mortuary the first thing that hit me was the pungent smell of formaldehyde, the preserving fluid used in such places. It is a smell one never forgets, believe me. I can smell it now as I type these words its awful smell clinging in the nostrils. Then, as the strip lights along the corridor flickered and tinkled into life, I could sense the smell disinfectant, a strong Jeyes fluid type smell. It was mixed with a strange odour that I couldn't recognise from the built in library of odours I had hidden somewhere in my memory. It was the smell of death. A smell I would unfortunately get used to over the next thirty years. It was nippy in there too, the sort of cold draught that you get on a hot day when you walk past the freezer compartments in supermarkets. The sort of cold that makes you shiver uncontrollably as if someone just walked on your grave, very apt. The walls were covered completely in small, plain white, shiny tiles, like an operating theatre in a hospital. The floor was tiled with worn terracotta coloured tiles, the sort you get in the changing rooms at the public baths. In the centre of a round medical room with no windows, was a large aluminium trolley or gurney on large ten inch diameter wheels with an ominous body shaped white heavy cotton sheet draped across it. Mr Sly threw off the sheet as if he was clearing a table top after a meal, a little like a magician doing the tablecloth trick, so matter of fact and there he was, the deceased, the poor sod, just as he entered the world, as naked as a jaybird. I stood there mortified, no pun intended, just staring at what used to be a fellow Briton. Now, he was the deceased, an inanimate object just waiting to be examined, a lump of meat waiting to be scrutinised, the learned physician waiting to ply his trade to find out why this former life had now ceased to be. It was then that I noticed another smell, the unmistakable, very strong whiff of domestic gas, looking at the old gas fire in the room, we all could hear the unmistakable Sssssssssssssss of escaping gas searching an enclosed space for a naked flame. "Well, if ee wor dead last night at eleven o'clock when we brought him in, he is now" chuckled a dry, grinning, Mr Sly as he washed down and prepared the body for its final medical examination.

Pete opened the outside door widely, fanning it to and fro, producing a welcome gust of outside world that rushed in to this bizarre location inquisitively. It wasn't the first dead body I'd seen. I'm from an Irish family background. So, I'd seen my Dad at his wake when I was sixteen years old and this poor bloke bore the very same pallid, grey skinned, but peaceful, calm, deep sleep appearance, that my Dad had. Just like then, you think that the eyes are about to pop open and the dead man start to speak, its a surreal situation. Memories of my Dad soon dispersed as reality kicked back in all too quickly. You never ever forget the sight of a Pathologist opening the chest cavity of a dead person with a bog standard Bosch commercial mechanical saw. I watched in strained silence, my dry mouth crammed with minty round sweets, the ones with the hole, to blank the smell (Doesn't work mind) as the doctor took out all the dead man's vital organs ready for inspection. Mr Sly placed each one on the weighing scales, then neatly on a white enamel tray beside the Doctor. Just when the young twenty-two year old Probationary Officer thought it couldn't get any worse, the Doctor sawed off the top of the dead man's head and took out his brain. A soft spongy ball that up until a few days ago had controlled all the other organs lying sprawled out on the tray. It also ran the living systems of the body that now lay motionless, by either activating his muscles or causing the secretion of chemicals such as hormones. Yes, I felt light headed and swooned, yes, I really thought I was going to faint. I even started to survey my surroundings, choosing the best place to flop! So, four more 'holy mints' were hurriedly crammed into my mouth (Which reminds me of a police joke. What's the difference between a Polo Mint and a Police Officer? Answer: People like Polo!).

"Pull yourself together Bry", I told myself, not wanting to lose face in front of my new work colleagues. A phrase I have repeated to myself on many similar occasions since believe me. The organs, left on the side of the trolley, ready for the examination, were scrutinised closely by the Doctor, who; unlike every Jack the Ripper film I have ever watched looked extremely normal and did very little slashing movements with the blades he utilised. The Doc made numerous cross cut slices in the heart, it looked like a small sliced hovis loaf and the Doctor held it under my nose tenderly like a tiny, dark crimson bouquet of flowers, as he said, "Look at the fatty deposits in this pulmonary artery", holding the said organ directly under my proboscis as if showing me a good card hand. It surprised me that the Doctor then lobbed each organ he'd inspected quite unceremoniously into a white melamine bucket, but the most surprising thing was to see Mr Sly at the end of the examination replace the contents of the bucket back into the body before sewing up the chest cavity. As Pete, who's claim to fame in the job was that he had been first police officer on the scene of one of the notorious Black Panther murders at the post office in the small village of Langley near Oldbury, in the early seventies, asked me if I was OK and kind of debriefed me on the why's and wherefores of dealing with sudden deaths. With great relief, I saw Mr Sly rolling the body back into the walk-in mortuary chiller cabinet, only to return seconds later clutching at and munching on, a huge cheese and beetroot sandwich, with the red vinegar soaked into the bread. He was holding a tall, narrow almost empty bottle of milk from said refrigerator. As I looked ominously at the milk bottle in his hand, he grinned at me and said, "It's ok lad, it's been sterilised, now put the kettle on we'll have a brew."

The next time I had any dealings with Pete, he was investigating a suicide where we had a 'jumper', who had previously been reported to us as a depressed misper (Misper is police speak for someone missing from home). The jumper had aimed to catch the Liverpool to London train as it rattled through Smethwick at approximately 125 miles per hour from the top of the wall in middle of Galton Bridge, Smethwick which, when built, was the highest and longest spanning iron bridge in the world and was some fifty feet above the rails. I can tell you're impressed! He didn't miss his train. It all started for me on the following morning of earlies when, as front office constable got a telephone call from a British Transport Police officer at Euston Railway Station in London. The officer enquired if we had had a suicide overnight and if we had, was the body missing anything. Namely, it's bonce, *head* that is. A routine call for a police station you know. He'd called every police area on the route the train had travelled through and had finally got as far as the West Midlands region. I told the officer that I was not aware of anything but I'd make some enquiries. I spoke to Pete who confirmed that we had indeed had a headless corpse reported to us that morning and that our search officers had found several discarded hats but couldn't find the head anywhere. I informed him that the deceased mans head had been found jammed tightly in the front axle of the 22:57 Liverpool to London express train that had arrived in the capital in the early hours and that BTP (British Transport Police) would put the said cranium back onto the 10:24 to Crewe which would make a special stop at Smethwick's Rolfe Street Station to drop it off and reunite it with the rest of the body as it were. The controller, Sergeant Stan Roby called upon a new probationer to the shift, WPC Julie Tanner, who the shift had christened, 'Elsie', after the ITV *Coronation Street* television soap character (Yes, I know, she'd now be PC Tanner, but that is now and this was then). So, WPC Tanner was called on the radio by Sergeant Roby, who told her that she was to visit Rolfe Street Station to collect a special parcel for the coroners officer, PC Connolly and bring it straight to him without fail. He then added an important caveat that under no circumstances, whatsoever, must she open the parcel and view the contents. "Understood Sarge," Came the speedy reply from the eager young officer, "I'm only about ten minutes away from the station." She said keenly. About fifteen minutes later, I was still in the front office when I received a landline call from a very concerned member of the public to the effect that one of our policewomen had apparently fainted on the High Street, Smethwick. The traffic in the area was completely gridlocked for half an hour. Just couldn't resist could she?

Years ago Michael Miles hosted a quiz programme on the telly called Take Your Pick, where contestants were invited by the host to answer general knowledge questions and then rewarded by either being allowed to take a reasonable amount of the money on offer or taking a gamble and opening the box. If they opened the box they could win a fabulously expensive prize, worth a hell of a lot more than the money that they had rejected or on the other hand they could take home a booby prize, for example, an old boot. I bet Elsie wished she'd taken the money instead of opening the box! She was ok though. Only her pride along with her elbows were bruised! Another observation from that particular case was that the original misper had been described as being five foot eight, but I could have sworn he was only four foot six when I saw him.

HARD SUMS FOR SKIDS
IN THE UNDERPASS

Mathematics aka 'Sums', is a subject that many us left behind at our place of learning. I for one thought I would need only the usual day to day calculus to get through life once I'd left school. You know, calculating 15% of a restaurant bill, working out how many carpet tiles I needed for the kitchen floor or checking my monthly pay check and Taxation! Oh yes, Tax, there's another story, you go through approximately 12 years of schooling and no one, but no one, during those formative years mentions the subject of Income Tax and the fact that someone known as the Chancellor of the Exchequer takes a massive lump of your hard earned wages at source, before you even get hold of your pay packet. I found this out in my first job as a storekeeper at a Chrysler Motors main dealership in St Helens when I was 16 years old. I left school early following my Dads passing away, to get some cash into the house. I was told at the interview that I'd be on £14 per week and when I got my pay I excitedly opened the little brown envelope expecting to find fourteen quid. What was there was £9:76p! After questioning where the rest of my money was and crowing that there must have been some sort of mistake, Barrie Swain, my new Manager, took me to his office and explained briefly the British taxation system. The teenage 'Connor' equated it to Legal theft on behalf of the Government of the day. What a Gyp! It's only much later, when you start to obtain responsibilities in life, that you realise that this cash is utilised for all the services the Government supply and that most people take for granted, like the Prison Service for example!

Getting back to the subject of arithmetic, the very word 'arithmetic' derives from the ancient Greek word for learning. Now some people would argue that Mathematics holds the secret to life, the universe and everything. It certainly aids police officers in their day to day tasks. Apart from calculating wages, it can be of great personal advantage for Police Officers to revive an interest in 'learning' mathematics, one of life's essential core disciplines, for more reasons than just salary inspection. Mathematics play a big part in day to day policing. For example, working out speeds of vehicles from the skid pattern they have burned onto tarmacadam surfaces following a Road Traffic Accident or for the more ignoble readers among you, skid marks......a phrase that never fails to extract schoolboy titters from most police officers who immediately think of soiled grubby 'Y' Fronts!

There are many mathematical equations used for police scenarios and maths makes our life easier. Bobbies, Traffic Bobbies in particular, are remarkably good at judging distances. Especially over short distances, the human sense of perspective allows us to make informed guesstimations for example the width of a carriageway. But if I want to know the distance of an object, usually a vehicle in police cases, from a fixed point without leaving that location I use the rule of thumb.

Your thumbs are very valuable instruments. Every Time we estimate distances our eyes fine-tune the gap in between while the grey matter cleverly calculates the optical angles. So to calculate distance, using the rule of thumb we need to know roughly how big the object, the car, is. An average motor vehicle is around one point five metres tall and as a rule if you stretch out your arm (Either arm… we're very diverse in the police you know) fully with your thumb stuck out at the end. The distance between your thumb and your eyes will always be thirty times the width of your thumb (Strange but true). So anything that appears to be the same size as your thumb is, thirty times its true height away from you. Get it? So, if a vehicle is one point five metres tall and two motors can 'fit' your thumb at a particular distance, then two times one point five is three and we multiply this by thirty (The strange but true distance between your thumb and your eyes) and voilà a result of ninety. So the vehicle is approximately ninety metres give or take. I don't know why it works but it does. Try it.

The 'rule of thumb' has been said to originate from the belief in the eighteenth century English law that allowed a man to beat his good lady wife with a stick so long as it is was no thicker than his thumb! Judge Sir Francis Buller (Worryingly close to being a bully) is reported to have made the legal ruling in 1782. In 1783 James Gillray attacked Buller and caricaturing him in a satirical cartoon as 'Judge Thumb' making him a laughing stock across the country, no change there then, crown court judges of today, still manage to make the tabloids. British common law did once hold that it was legal for a man to chastise a wife and added the words 'in moderation,' therefore; paradoxically, both condoning and tempering the punishment, thankfully, today we live in more enlightened times.   Mind you.   In some parts of Britain there are still a few troglodytes, mainly short, stupid men, that unfortunately still think it 'normal' to use their spouse as a punch bag.

The origin of the phrase The Rule of Thumb remains unknown but it's likely that it refers to the one way I have explained, where it was used by our predecessors to estimate the distances of objects by holding the thumb the eye-line at arms length.   I sometimes used it used it to approximate the distance cars were away from traffic lights.

I was parked early one Sunday morning on the car park of the Hen and Chickens Public House which was situated on the main A4123 Road into Birmingham.   My partner for the day was PC Doug 'The Thug' Froggitt, also affectionately known as 'Thrombo' (The slow moving clot).   He was a big Brummie lad, from Longbridge, home of the famous Morris Car Plant in the South of Birmingham,the kind of lad who would take a motor bike to bits in his mom's Kitching and put it all back together minus the one important component which had rolled underneath the fridge.   Six feet two inches tall and built like an 18 stone brick shithouse.   Doug was much too friendly to be a Thug; he was probably too friendly to be a copper in fact.   He was a bit slow up top, hence the 'Thrombo' soubriquet, but he was as honest as the day is long and had a heart as big as a bucket.   He was certainly a good lad to have with you at a pub scrap.   There are quite a few 'Thrombo' stories.   I first knew him on the shift where when on nights where he exhibited strange and annoying habits, above and beyond the ordinary annoying habits that coppers have, like evacuating gas from their bowels in the close confinement of a police carrier.   One of which was that he'd clean the wax out of his ears with the car keys to the panda and I would see this and make car engine starter noises to coincide with each twist of the key as it vanished into Doug's ear cavities. Another one was that he would always wear the same police uniform shirt for the whole set of seven nights. With the obvious aroma this habit inevitably brings! How did we know it was the same shirt? Well, because we had our suspicions, with the odour. One night during our snap break. I put a small dot on the back of his collar with a ball point pen while he was watching TV. That little black dot remained on his collar for the rest of that set of nights!

When he was working with a colleague, PC Mick Fieldhouse in the Permanent Beat office, a Neighbourhood Watch Co-ordinator had mentioned to Mick at a community meeting that he had suspicions about him becoming a drug dealer because he'd been seen walking along the Oldbury Road with 250 lbs of dope. Poor old Dougie, even the public took the pee out of him!

On this particular morning, about 0630hrs, Doug and I were parked up making up our pocket books (Of course, they're never made up...everything's true......Ah, the old ones are the best!). I was in the gopher (Front Passenger) seat and Doug was driving. Both of us writing up our reports and occasionally, glancing up to watch a solitary vehicle coming ourway, conspicuous because of the time of day, a normally very busy main artery into the second city was almost deserted in those early hours of the morning.

Now, by the Hen and Chickens was a busy, major, traffic light administered junction and it was not at all a rare occurrence, given the time of day, to see the odd approaching vehicle, it's driver in a hurry for work, attempt to 'jump' the lights and drive across the crossing against the red (Stop) traffic signal.

On this particular morning, we both saw a saloon car drive up, at speed, towards the lights as the light sequence was still at amber. I tapped Doug's arm and as I did so the lights for the oncoming saloon car turned from amber to red but the car continued over the thick, white painted, stop line in the road and continued to drive across the junction without even attempting to slow down, let alone, stop. Doug started up the car as I said,"We'll tug this one." We pursued, caught up with and overtook the nervous looking driver. We 'pulled' (stopped) the offending vehicle, which came to a halt at the next lay-by.

I spoke to the driver and after ascertaining that it was his car and obtained his driver details I told him that the facts would be reported and that he may be summonsed for failing to stop at a red signal. The driver, a smartly dressed executive, late for his appointment in this world, was very irate and stated that the light was at amber when he crossed. I informed him that it was well on red when both my colleague and I saw him cross the stop line and indeed reminded him that the amber signal also means STOP. I cautioned him and he replied, "Your Superintendent is a personal friend of mine" to which I replied, "I'm glad to hear the Superintendents a personal friend of yours at least you have someone who can act as a character witness for you at court won't you." The gentleman not only pleaded not guilty, he decided that he would do a 'Perry Mason' and dispense with a professional solicitor in favour of defending himself at court! What is it about the Brits when it comes to by passing up on the use of professional people? The do-it-yourself culture that means half the fixtures and fittings of homes the length and breadth of the nation have been fitted by semi literate morons, who not only haven't and sometimes can't read the instructions but have the nerve to tell their grannies how to suck eggs. For example, the type of people that tell a fully trained Barber how to cut hair, tell window cleaners how to clean windows, tell decorators how to hang wallpaper, plumbers how to plumb, chefs how to cook, I could go on, you get the drift. Well, when it comes to the legal system a few members of the public have the opinion that that they can defend themselves just as well as any learned Solicitor or Barrister, thus saving the fees!

The barrack room lawyer questioned me in the box and failed to ask me one pertinent question. Luckily for him, the British justice system assists such morons in this very instance when a court official in Magistrates Court known as the Magistrates Clerk, who is normally there to assist the Magistrates, who, by the way, are unpaid lay Justices of the Peace, sitting voluntarily. The majority of which are seen as middle class, middle aged and middle minded, with over a third of them retired from full time employment. No formal qualifications are required but magistrates allegedly require intelligence, common sense, integrity and the capacity to act fairly. Membership in the Sandwell area is widely spread throughout the borough and drawn from all backgrounds.

The Magistrates Clerk asked, on Perry Mason's behalf, if I had a clear unobstructed view of the stop line and how far from the stop line the defendants car was when the traffic light turned to red against the defendant. I answered confidently that yes, I had a clear and unobstructed view of the stop line in question and yes, I could confirm that when I first saw the vehicle it was approximately ninety metres from the stop line (Rule of Thumb) and that when the light turned to red it was approximately seventeen metres from the stop line and had ample time to stop safely and that no vehicles were in close proximity to the defendants vehicle.

One of the magistrates then asked me how I estimated the ninety metres. So it was time to wow 'em with science. They loved my explanation of the Rule of Thumb.... I nearly got a nine point nine from the Czechoslovakian judge! Sorry, getting cocky now! The magistrates then asked how I could state that the vehicle was approximately seventeen metres from the stop line and that it seemed a strange figure to approximate it to. "It might have been APPROXIMATELY ten, fifteen or even twenty metres away. How could I possibly approximate it to seventeen?" said the magistrate. I told her that I agreed, it did sound a strange figure to approximate to but explained that I had counted seventeen slim curb stones, the narrow concrete edges of paving stones that divide a pavement from the roads edge and that as these curb stones are about a metre long, I guesstimated the distance from where the defendants vehicle was when the lights turned red to the stop line as approximately seventeen curb stones in length. She grinned at me over her horn-rimmed spectacles and nodded in agreement.

Perry Mason had no further questions for me. So I went and sat at the back of the court as Doug entered the witness box. Straight from the 'swearing in' Doug asked if he could refer to his pocket note book, which officers are allowed to do to help them recollect events pertinent to the case. The Magistrates Clerk asked, "Officer, when was your Pocket Book made up?" This is where I would have been tempted to reply, "It's not made up, it's all true!" The actual reply that should be made is "They were written straight after the incident your worships" or something to that effect. Doug wasn't sharp enough for such a retort. He replied, "Well, I usually make my notes in my pocketbook straight after the incident." The Clerk said, "What do you mean usually?" This ended after several strained minutes' of conversation just to establish that Doug, a very experienced officer, had written the notes at the time. So an exasperated Clerk then invited the defendant to cross examine Thrombo, which he began as ineptly as he had with mine. Then, adopting a phrase that the Magistrate's Clerk had used during my cross examination he looked up at Thrombo in the witness box and enquired, "Officer, did you have a clear unobstructed view of the stop line?" Doug thought for a minute, both eyebrows sank deep into the bridge of his nose as he looked around the court, he looked slowly at me, he looked slowly at the Magistrates and after a pregnant pause the defendant said "Well?" urging an answer from the uniformed hulk that now looked like a tiny rabbit caught in the headlights of a truck as he blurted out, "Yes, I had a clear unobstructed view of the stop line, apart from the tree and the telephone box!" he said hesitantly and with some uncertainty in his voice. A stony silence in the Magistrates Court was ended by one of the Magistrates saying to the Clerk, "I think we've heard enough, we'll adjourn to the next room to make a decision.

Now, in English law a case prosecuted at a court of law must be proved beyond a reasonable doubt. In this instance the police had to prove (beyond doubt) that this man intentionally, purposely or recklessly failed to stop at the red traffic sign thus being a danger, not only to him but to other road users. In my opinion he was and I saw him commit the offence. If the police have enough evidence to prove the accused persons guilt then that guilt MUST be established beyond all reasonable doubt. This is the central pillar that our justice system is built upon. The Magistrates decision that day was surprisingly swift and clear. In spite of Thrombo, they found that there did not appear to be an element of doubt upon the clarity of the view we police officers had from the police vehicle and that we did see the car go over stop line. Perry Mason was gutted, the man defending himself looked unbelievably forlorn and scowled at the Magistrates as the verdict was read out. It's the only case I have ever thought I may have lost at court thanks to Doug. Before you ask. Yes, there was a tree and a telephone box nearby but, they were nowhere near the stop line I was looking at and they certainly didn't obscure the view I had! I used to wonder why they called him Thrombo until that point. He was the kind of gentle giant that would give you the shirt off his back (Even if it did stink and have an ink spot on the collar) if you asked him for it, but oh my God, he really was a slow moving clot!

'Yoom Shaw Taylor aye yer?'

HOW DID SHAW TAYLOR
GET KILLED?

Do you recall Shaw Taylor? Shaw Taylor was the man who first introduced the Great British public to a television show that reconstructed unsolved crimes with a view to gaining information from members of the public. Shaw presented a long running programme called *Police Five*, which I know, from Shaw's own internet website; (www. shawtaylor.com) was first broadcast in 1962. It was a five minute (Hence *Police 5*) slot that followed the local regional Independent Television news, Introduced by another Midland, TV legend, Bob Warman. Firstly, on the Midlands regional Associated Television (ATV) then Central Television, based in the Second City, Birmingham.

Shaw, affectionately called the 'Odd Job Man,' in the business, because he'd been involved in so many different types of TV show ranging from quiz programmes to sports commentary, was the brainchild of what became the precursor to the British Broadcasting Corporations (BBC) *Crimewatch* programme. The consummate professional, the 60's version of Nick Ross, went two steps further than

Ross, by both scripting and presenting the programme,as well as inviting viewers to help solve actual crimes that had been committed in the Midlands region of the England. He would travel to police stations length and breadth of the Midlands region of the England, liaising with Centrally based Detectives, to bring topical incidents that were the talk of the town to the their screens. On just a few scraps of information Shaw would wonderfully re-create enough of the proceedings at the actual crime scene to have the public ringing police forces with information; literally within seconds of the show going off-air. Police Five genuinely reaped rewards, with thousands of crimes being solved through the medium of the cathode ray tube. Viewers volunteered constructive information that aided the boys in blue in locking up dangerous individuals and bringing them to justice. Simply by watching Shaw on that warm little box in the corner, doing his stuff and dialling the telephone number displayed on their screen!

Shaw Taylor was one of those 'Peter Pan,' never grow old, TV Presenters. He looked like a cross between a trusty sales rep and medical consultant. He was a clean shaven, sophisticated broadcaster. Always well dressed in stylish seventies and eighties garb, you know wide lapels and flared trousers. He spoke plainly and simply. His obvious trade mark being, his thick jam jar lensed, square rimmed, black plastic spectacles. Were you a little bit of an introvert Shaw? The design of your specs, emulating two enormous TV screens, may have been a purposely used prop to hide behind, in the glitzy world of showbiz, as they covered most of your face!

On a bleak autumn morning in Derbyshire our leading man would be on location at the scene of some dastardly misdemeanour. Looking directly into the viewer's front room. Shaw would narrow his eyes in menacing disdain, slowly delivering his opening line, "Were you anywhere near this eating establishment last Thursday afternoon?" Camera pans out a little to show presenter is standing (Almost hiding behind one of those huge microphones you used to see David Coleman use when doing an outside broadcast, it looked like a big wooden spoon with a huge dark brown boiled egg bobbling on the end of it) outside a squalid transport cafe on the main A514 trunk road, with apprehension in his voice, he continues, " The Nell Gwynn Tea Rooms, Swadlingcote, last Thursday afternoon at three thirty five, when two men, wearing pink, Pretty Polly type stockings on their heads & armed simply with blue plastic peashooters; threatened staff before stealing the cafe's two foot high hollowed out statue of a young polio victim wearing leg braces, He contained an unknown quantity of charity donations?" The screen would then show a photograph of a pristine dark grey (Black and White tellies remember) Morris Minor Van (A graphic, possibly 'borrowed' from the ladybird book of getaway cars) with the number plate crudely covered with black sticky tape. Shaw would voice over in that distinctive voice of his, "They were seen to drive off in a vehicle similar to this one in the direction of Ashby de la Zouch." Shaw now back on screen looks deadly serious over everyone's supper as he tells them, "We are not sure if these assailants had peas in their mouths during the raid, but if they had, heaven knows what damage they could have done. Has anyone offered you a suspicious little crippled boy charity collection statue? Do you know anyone who drives a van like the one depicted? Perhaps you work in the retail trade and sold them their peashooters? One of the men had a strong Potteries accent. If you think you can help catch these men then contact Swadlingcote CID on Swadlingcote 47892 or contact your nearest police station." He would then smile reassuringly, for all the elderly viewers out there in TV land, telling them that a wealthy local scrap metal dealer from Barton under Need-wood, who wished to remain anonymous, had heard all about the robbery on local Radio, east mid FM, donating a hundred pounds to the charity victims. He would always close the show by wishing his viewers a safe and happy week and then, as if it had slipped his mind, he would, with a heedful expression on his face, wave his right index finger across both eyes and deliver his memorable catchphrase, "Keep 'em peeled!" (A pun on peelers, the nickname given to early police officers, after their founder Sir Robert [Bobby] Peel. Then pointing nonchalantly at the camera prompting viewers to be vigilant. Winking to them with a glint in his eye & flashing them a cheering smile as the closing credits hit their screens. Alas, we don't see much of Shaw any more. I know he's still about though, I saw him on a TV cop show, playing himself, hosting a Police Five, as part of the recent BBC drama, Ashes to Ashes, at the ripe old age of 83. Well done mate, you were great!

It really wouldn't come as a surprise to anyone who knows the area, that Shaw Taylor was a regular visitor to Smethwick Police Station. Where I spent the vast majority of my police service. He was held in great veneration, almost like sainthood, by bobbies of all ranks. He was an honorary detective! I know, one good Shaw Taylor story at Smethwick was told to me by my wife Beverly, who at the time, about 1981, was one of the station typists. Shaw had been filming in the Smethwick area. He always visited the local station when he made TV reports for Police Five. Usually before, liaising with the CID and then afterwards to thank the Superintendent of the division for their co-operation. On one such visit to Smethwick, whilst Shaw was chatting to Superintendent Tony Eastmond in his office, the Chief Inspector at the time, Ken Goulding, Swanned into the typists office with a piece of letter headed station notepaper in his hand containing the communication, 'To Debbie and Family, Kindest Regards, Shaw Taylor,' to Debbie Hayes, one of the typists, who had asked him to obtain a copy, for her twin boys (She said). He handed it to a blushing Debbie, saying, "Shaw has just signed this for you, Debbie." Wendy Ward, another typist asked if she could have his autograph, the CI says, "Sure!" and off he trots, along the corridor towards the Superintendent's office, coming back, only moments later with another piece of letter headed paper, which this time containing the remarks, 'To Wendy, Kindest Regards, Shaw Taylor.' He then said to Beverly, "Would you like his autograph Bev?" Beverly replied, "Ooh yes, my mum likes him. "After confirming the name of the individual, Pauline, who of course, is now my Mother in Law, he shortly returned to the typist's office, again handing over a pink police calling card containing the dedication, 'To Pauline, my number one admirer, much love and undying appreciation, Shaw Taylor. Shaw adding a scrambled and quite unreadable phone number, scrawled underneath the signature! The typists all had a giggle about him writing his phone number on it. Beverly embarrassingly, quickly folding it and putting it in her bag. A short time later they saw and heard (It was a small corridor) the Superintendent escorting Shaw and his crew along the corridor back to their vehicles in the back yard of the nick. Later that afternoon, Mr Goulding was enjoying a coffee in the typist's office, when Jill Carlton a Traffic Warden came into the typists bemoaning the fact that her hero Shaw, had been into the station and she'd missed him. She despondently told the assembled group that she would have loved to get Shaw Taylor's autograph and was upset that she'd missed him. It was then that Ken Goulding started to scribe something on a piece of paper and handed it to Jill as he rose to leave on his way back to his office. Jill read the note out loud to the giggling typists, 'To Jill, my favourite Meter Maid, sorry we never met in the flesh as it were! Yours very sincerely, Shaw Taylor. ' As the laughter subsided, Beverly looked at the 'autograph' Ken Goulding had forged for Jill and was amazed but not too surprised to find that Debbie's, Wendy's and her own authentic Shaw Taylor dedications had all been written in the same handwriting as Jill's dedication from the TV legend Shaw!

My 'oppo PC Doug Watson and I were sent one damp dismal morning to Windmill Precinct in Smethwick to 'assist' Shaw and his production team with the vast crowds that may turn up and attempt to interfere with production. The Post Office at Windmill Precinct off Windmill Lane had been robbed by a professional team of armed offenders, it was a nasty robbery to be honest and the Postmaster there was quite shook up by it. The robbers, threatening staff with a sawn off shotgun had got away with quite a haul of money, it being a busy 'pension' day. As it happened, when Shaw and his crew turned up there was not a soul about, as it was a bitterly cold day. Windmill Precinct was a small pedestrianised walkway that hosted a small shopping precinct between a main road, Windmill Lane, Smethwick and Thomas Street, which backed onto a sprawling 1950s, concrete mess of a council housing estate, preserved in terminal neglect and municipal ennui in the 14th most deprived area of Britain. To help you understand just how neglected and lacklustre it really was, the BBC used to use the location when filming Northern Irish conflict drama's because the flats on there were a copy of the Divis Flats in Belfast. The Divis flats were pulled down nearly 20 years ago. The last of their doppelgängers at Smethwick were pulled down in spring 2008! So, I think you get the picture of just how run down the area was. The Police Five crew set up their equipment in what was only a matter of; about ten minutes. Shaw looked into the camera to launch into his now legendary gambit. "Where you here, The Post Office, Windmill Precinct Smethwick last Thursday morning, a busy pension day, as four masked robbers, armed to the teeth, stormed and robbed the postmaster?" As the camera started to roll, Doug Watson and I held back the assembled throng of admiring Shaw Taylor groupies (three old ladies holding shopping bags and an inquisitive chap dressed in a security guard uniform walking a German Shepherd).

Shaw Taylor and his crew sometimes used local bobbies as actors to re-enact an incident at the actual crime scene (so the villain that petrified your Gran on *Police Five* was not a professional actor, but an officer from the local Criminal Investigation Department!) and the victim or one of the witnesses would also be local detectives, which at the time, must have brought a smile to the faces of all our local villains. Not to mention the entertainment they gave their police colleagues! On this occasion, four detectives from the CID at Piddock Road, Smethwick were dressed up in boiler suits with stockings on their heads. As the last 'robber', the head guy with the gun, came running out of the Post Office, and made for Thomas Street via the gap between the launderette and the public library at Windmill Precinct (What a very strange location for a Library! it was a little cul-de-sac between two roads, like a square, it was ideal for robbing shops there, but the thing was the offenders ran straight past the library (The unique thing about Windmill Precinct library was that every book in there was in pristine condition, no one in the area ever read, they probably wasn't even aware there was a library there! The robbers could have gone to ground and hid in the library. Nobody would have gone checking for 'em, not in that library!

Anyhow, as the portly gumshoes run off, as rehearsed, around the corner into Thomas Street and were getting their breath back out of sight of the camera, which still rolling, pans back to Shaw, standing on the library steps. He puts on his sombre face, and starts to say, "Were you in Windmill Precinct on Thursday 27th of Octemter, when, etc. He'd just got going, and was really buzzing along as this little old bloke, well he looked old, but he was a young-old bloke, an oxymoron? No just a moron! (Sorry couldn't resist) He was one of those pale grey men, with greasy, long, dishevelled hair. Who are in their late forties, but, dress like they're sixty-five, because they buy their clothes at the Salvation Army Citadel. This guy was a person who had completely lost any self respect he ever possessed, y'know, when self respect goes, it really goes and this guy's self respect had gone on holiday quite some time before, never to return? Years of booze, fags and bathroom neglect, had turned this guy, prematurely into an elderly figure, old before his time. An odd man, He was short, thin and wirey, wearing a see through, grey, three-quarter length plastic Pac-a-Mac that went easily four inches below his knees, over several layers of dark woollen tops. He wore a pair of plain black baseball boots with no laces in them, a baggy pair of brown corduroy trousers, tied with string at the ankles, at the tops of his boots. He wore a red beret covered in small metallic badges, including a Robertson's Jam golly musician playing a saxophone and was carrying two heavy looking, dirty, canvas shopping bags, one full of shopping the other filled to the brim with crushed aluminium cans. He had long whiskery sideburns and a Catweasle type, pointy beard. Oblivious to what was going on in the Precinct, he just walked (Through the police cordon!) straight up to Shaw, looked curiously at the camera, looked back at Shaw and says to him in an extremely strong, but sober, Black Country accent, " You'me Shaw Taylor aye yer?" grinning a wide, toothless grin. Shaw Taylor replies, "Well yes, I am actually, but", pointing to the crew, he says, "I'm just doing a programme here, we're doing a piece for Police Five", "oh sorry mate", he says, laughed about it and then repeatedly says "Sorry Shaw, mi old mucker" as he walked off around the corner where the bogus robber, CID men had just run to. Shaw, ever the professional, composes himself and says to his camera man, "Where were we?" His camera operator tells him, "We'll just roll from the last line you'd got to and we'll be able to edit it." Or words to that effect.

Shaw starts his speech to camera yet again. It is then that this extraordinary little man reappears at a rate of knots from around the corner, looking around the Precinct anxiously, with a worried look on his prematurely ageing face; he sees Dougie and me in our unmistakable police uniforms and makes a bee line for us, walking, forgetfully & stupidly straight through Shaw's camera shot! This time, thankfully, quietly, he alerts Doug and myself, grabbing me by the arm, he leaned towards my ear to softly speak out of the corner of his foul smelling mouth, "Officer, there are four desperate looking fuggs around the corner in Thomas Street, they were taking womens stockins off their 'eds and one of 'em's got a gun. I thought you might wanna know that 'cos Shaw and the telly blokes might be in danger like!" Dougie is grinning at me. Tears of mirth are forming in my eyes, as I, try to explain to this bloke, exactly what is occurring. In a road to Damascus moment, I think the penny eventually dropped and the light, albeit quite dim, came on, he'd understood!

Shaw went for take three. Thank God the crew didn't film it. Otherwise, Dennis Nordern or Griff Rhys Jones might have had a field day on ITV's It'll be All right on the Night! After Shaw had successfully finished filming he signed autographs for all the bystanders who had patiently stopped to watch him working at the sharp end, as it were. The perfect professional, he had time for everyone of them, even the toothless disruptive male shopper, Smethwick's own Albert Steptoe/Victor Meldrew lookalike, who still seemed totally oblivious to manners and breeding.

He just talked to Shaw Taylor as if nothing else was happing in the world, and the best of it all was, when it was his 'turn' to get Shaw's autograph, the guy didn't even have a piece of paper and he asked the great Shaw Taylor to autograph one of the packets of food that he had just placed in his shopping bag. I think Shaw wrote it on the back of a Vesta Beef Curry boxed meal, 'Best wishes, Shaw Taylor', which I suppose had pride of place on his kitchen shelving; until he got peckish one lunch time!

This only leaves me to explain the chapter's title. It's based on a joke that anyone who knows Shaw and Police Five will definitely understand: Q. How did Shaw Taylor die? A. He fell off the back of a lorry!

He didn't die, when chummy interrupted him in mid flow though. Nice one Shaw! Mr.Shaw Taylor MBE British actor and television presenter, you are sadly missed.

I sent Shaw a completed copy of this chapter. He liked the Ken Goulding forgery story and told me, "I trust your mother-in-law Pauline wasn't tempted to try the telephone number, what was it? The local massage parlour?" Shaw was kindly complimentary and genuinely supportive. Many Thanks, Shaw.

With regard to TV programming I am also reminded of a story retold to by a lad I worked with when I was a Crime Assessor at West Bromwich, PC Ron Groves, who, when he wasn't a Crime assessor with West Midlands Police was a member of a Agincourt re-enactment group that among other things went around the country dressing up like King Harry's away team for that particular French fixture, raising money for Charity etc.

I'm not sure how it came about but his group were invited onto the BBC children's TV programme 'Record Breakers' with the late great celebrity Roy Castle. They were going on the telly to try to break the world record for how far one of their number could shoot an arrow from an old English longbow, mmm, riveting, but hey, each to his own. I suppose you could write a whole chapter about what coppers get up to when they're off duty. Some take up sport, some amateur dramatics, some even paint and write books (See www. bryanconnor.co.uk if you don't believe me!). Also trying to break world records on this particular programme was a sword swallower from Ashby de la Zouch, a trampolining Nun from Scunthorpe, a record pie eater from Wigan, Mister Memory from Inverness, who could memorise a tray of over two hundred different items and remember them a staggering ten minutes later and finally, Diving Doris from Kidderminster, who was attempting to dive off a five hundred foot platform into a wet sponge.

After another successful 'wrap' cemented together by entertainment legend Roy Castle, Bucks Fizz singer Cheryl Baker and Guinness World Record editor Ross McWhirter. All the participants, apart from Doris who'd gone to the local infirmary with a splitting headache, had gathered in the 'green room' for post show refreshments. You know, a choice of Red or White Table Wine, Tea, Coffee and Fruit Juice (for Roy of course) and a decent assortment of butties and vol-au-vents.

Things were going swimmingly (Except for Doris) and Ron Groves' bow and arrow group, who incidentally had managed to brake a few bows and arrows but no records, were having a fabulous time helping themselves to the free menu. After a while, Mister Memory, got up and thanked everyone for the experience, then apologised stating that he had to leave early for another gig he'd arranged to do on the other side. No, he wasn't clairvoyant, not that other side. I meant he had a programme to take part in for Independent Television and off he popped to get his taxi. The frivolities continued (Ah the heady world of Sex,Drugs,Rock n' Roll and Children's Television), but then, about ten minutes later, theres a loud knock on the door, Mister Memory, the world record holder for feats of memory, pops his head around the door, surveys everyone in the room and screwing up his eyes in a perplexed and almost apologetic expression says to the amazed gathering, "Did I leave my overcoat in here?"

THE BEARWOOD
BIBLE BASHER

As I have already stated, there are people who always want to tell coppers or anybody in any kind of authority for that matter, how to do their job! Because of this, I am always more than aware of the fact that it is rude to do this and if I start lauding it over someone, I quickly chastise myself and stop 'instructing' them. Barbers are a good example, nearly everyone who visits the Barbers tell them how to do their job! When I visit the barbers shop and they say, " What do you want?" I always say, " I'll have a number two at the sides and the back please and whatever you think with the rest." I always tell the barber to just get on with it. They've done all their training and passed their exams. Who am I, a complete layperson, to start giving orders to them on how to cut hair? My barber always grins and says,'Yeah you're right', and then of course I then continue to pass comments like, "Can I have the sides a bit straighter or can you make the square neck a round neck!" We do all have the annoying habit of telling everybody else how to do their job. There's nothing worse than being told how to do your job, especially when you've done the job for quite a while and you've become quite adept at it. Policing is one of those occupations where everyone and I mean, everyone, fancy themselves as a bit of a Perry Mason or Hercule Poirot. Everyone knows a barrack room lawyer. There is always someone in the pub who knows what to do, because they saw it on The Bill or Holby City. When it comes to the police, you get it all the time. We are never off the telly! Its a strange paradox, that in the 'real' world, very few people are fond of the police. Journalists hate us. Documentary programme makers hate us. Trendy, well to do 'luvvies' in the entertainment industry hate us. Politicians hate us. Comedians hate us, we are always the butt of their jokes. Religious leaders hate us. Demonstrators from Left and right of centre hate us. Teenagers hate us. Almost everyone in the country it seems. So why, oh why are there so many police based dramas and reality television programmes in the world?

I can think of loads and loads of examples nowadays, where members of the public have a go at the police or try to tell police officers how to do their job. However, one episode that I always recall when people try to put me right happened at Yuletide. It was Christmas time and I was posted to a busy built up shopping area called Bearwood. The Bearwood Road, gets very, very hectic in the three weeks coming up to Christmas. There are many fashionable and popular stores there. Just like any other main shopping street, at Christmas, it is bursting at the seams with shoppers, brass bands playing carols, charity collection canvassers and criminals. The problem is, that on those gloomy wintery days, just before Christmas, the world and his dog, not only want to visit a gaily illuminated festive shopping area that is packed to the gunnels with fellow sufferers who also brought their dogs. They all want to go there in their motor cars, therefore requiring some place to park! So, invariably added to that list of seasonal visitors are Three wise Traffic Wardens and wandering groups of Police officers, shepherding the sheep that bleat aimlessly from store to store waiting to be fleeced of their Christmas bonuses. We're sent in numbers to these areas by our supervision because they expected us to make sure that traffic flows freely along the main Bearwood Road, an important local artery and a busy bus route. Because of the increase in pedestrians we have to watch for inconsiderate drivers that park on double yellow lines or the zig zag markings of a pelican pedestrian crossing. Ambulances, Fire Engines, Police vehicles, Buses as well as the normal through traffic have to use this busy thoroughfare, particularly when its busy with Christmas shoppers. So, the antisocial berks who park their cars on Bearwood Road's double yellow lines don't really think of emergency vehicles, commercial vehicles or bus passengers going about their business, they just want to rush into a shop, get their other half a box of chocolates for Christmas, nip back to the car and zoom off before anyone catches 'em illicitly parked. One particular busy, cold and fittingly misty pre-christmas afternoon, this guy comes up to me and introduces himself to me as an important member of the local Neighbourhood Watch, he's also a prominent member of the Rotary Club, was a Rear Admiral in the Royal Navy during the War and had been a part time General in the Scouting movement for the last sixty five years. Had seen action in umpteen different global military conflicts including the Spanish Civil War, you get the picture. These blazer clad, handle bar moustached, know-all's, seem to come out the cracks in the pavement whenever a copper appears anywhere near them. I think a police uniform catches their attention like an electromagnet! Nonetheless, this geezer comes up to me and says, "Officer, look at that car over there parked on double yellow lines, its scandalous officer, disgraceful,

Bryan Connor

what are you going to do about it?" I said, "Well I'll go and have a word with him and ask him to move it." He said, "Look, I have parked my car correctly. I pay my road tax and my council tax. You must go and do something about it. Put a ticket on it now, before he drives away, that's what you should do, I am a friend of your Chief Constable, play golf with your Chief Superintendent and mixed doubles in the Tipton and District Sunday Table Tennis League with his lovely spouse and I always attend the local police ball." You get the picture, dear reader. (I'm very tempted to tell you the great old joke, 'Firefighters may well have bigger choppers, but why have policemen got bigger Balls than Firemen? They sell more tickets of course!' I was reminded of this because it was the Superintendents wife who used to handle all the Policemen's Balls at our station. But, the Superintendent soon ended that by starting to handle them himself, Oooerrr!) Anyway I very much digress.

Getting back to the story, "No problem at all sir," I reply to the friend of the Chief Constable. I amble up to the car taking out a small black notebook held tight shut by an attached elastic band. I push down the end of my trusty biro and I start writing in the opened notebook, the smart aleck companion of the stars is in seventh heaven that I'm evidently carrying out his command. He was gratified to see that he'd told me how to do my job. He's grinning from ear to ear and now off on his merry way, knowing that he's aided the police service in all it's mighty power, to knockoff this poor bloke, who has nipped in to a local shop to grab a late pressie for his missus. A short time later, the driver comes back and he's enormously apologetic. He is just like you and me, he's an ordinary bloke who is thinking to himself, 'Oh shit, I've only been gone two minutes, give me a break mate', he doesn't come it, he doesn't laud it over me, he doesn't tell me that he pays my wages because he's a tax payer, he just says, "I'm sorry, I just popped in the shop to get me missus a card and a box of chocolates. I've only got the....!" "Let me stop you there", I said, "You can see that I've already started writing, I will hand this paperwork to you immediately when I have finished, I was gonna place it on your windscreen, but since you have returned, I'm going to hand it to you personally. Let me hand it to you and I'll be on my merry way." The bloke sighed reluctantly shrugging his shoulders saying, "Yeah okay."

A split second later, I finish writing, tear off and bestow the scribed decoration upon the gentleman, then off I go on my merry way to whatever is the next exciting adventure, that awaits me. On the piece of paper I hand to the Mondeo owner it affirms, 'Hello mate, that bloke you saw me speaking to with the handle bar moustache, just demanded that I report you for parking on double yellow lines, but, this is the time of good will to all men, a time when we should all be nice to each other, your Christmas gift from the West Midlands Police is this little piece of paper make sure you dispose of it sensibly, Have a very Merry Christmas!". As he drove away he waved to me and beamed. I smiled and put my thumb up as I carried on persecuting the poor motorists of Bearwood. D'you know what, to tell you the truth, I had a thoroughly good Christmas, Mondeo Man had a thoroughly good start to his Christmas, and even the pompous prat who tried to tell me how to do my job, probably, had a nice Christmas too. Job done. Lots of people think that the police have league tables when it comes to knocking drivers off. Its not true, we don't. When we do get the members of the public like him earlier, who do remind us that they pay our wages and that we are their servants, I'm always very tempted to say, "Yeah, we have a quota. Two more tickets and my wife gets a Fridge Freezer!

Speaking about Bearwood Road, reminds me of the time I told a devout born again believer to go away, in the Sex and Travel type mode!

You really don't see this done much nowadays. Years ago, if the West Midlands Ambulance Service were running a None-Stop from anywhere on the Western side of the force to the Burns Unit at the Queen Elizabeth Hospital, then our Sub Division, who had the main A4123 cutting right the way through it would be the main route chosen. As a result, we would send a foot patrol officer to all the main traffic light junctions to aid its journey through Sandwell. On one such pre-Christmas Saturday afternoon I was sent to the busy junction of Bearwood Road and Hagley Road West. It was heaving. I had the key to the traffic lights control box. Hurriedly opened it, and switched all the lights to Red. Literally stopping everything that moved. I obviously had to get out to the centre of the junction quickly. It was then that the grinning, black suited, three-quarter length over coated, bobble hatted, white, clean cut, middle aged, bible toting, male approached me and said, "Excuse me officer, but do you know where you are going to spend eternity?" I said, "You'll have to excuse me mate, I'm a bit busy." I went out into the middle of the junction and just as I was trained, I first made sure that I was calm and in control. I steadfastly held up my right arm firmly upright with my flat palm firmly pushed out towards the already stopped traffic. I turned to all the junctions sternly reinforcing firmly that I wanted them to stay put. I remembered the training I received at Ryton on Dunsmore Police Training School. When two full classes of young police officers pretended to be motor vehicles whilst we each took turns to stand in the mini junction directing each other! I remember laughing as I recalled standing at the back of this queue of 'traffic', and stated humming a song loudly. The instructor Sergeant

Coslett, came over to me and asked why I was singing out loud and I told him, much to the amusement of my classmates, that I was an Ice Cream Van! Even the Sarge saw the humorous side of that. All the vehicles around the busy junction was now at a standstill. I was masterfully, in charge. Knowing by way of the crackling voice on my issue Burndept radio that the Ambo was close. I began beckoning the Birmingham bound traffic on against a red traffic signal. There were some doubting Thomas's who hesitantly and unnaturally drove against the red traffic sign at the behest of a uniformed police officer. I vehemently waved my arm, openly encouraging them to get a move on. My intention to 'free' that particular approach, knowing that a zooming Ambo would soon drive at a rate of knots straight through it, swinging a right along Lordswood Road and hurtle toward the QE. Everyone else in their cars were stacking up in massive queues of traffic but were impressively patient. Everything at a standstill, I was ready but what is more important, the junction was ready to receive the racing emergency vehicles. I heard the sirens approaching and as the adrenalin started to pulse through my body, I caught site of the lead motorcycle cop in the far distance.

The grinning black suited three-quarter length over coated, trilby hatted, white, clean cut, middle aged, large leather bound bible toting, male religious zealot, had remained rigidly standing on the street corner watching my exhibition of police craft with great interest and an inane grin across his chops. Whilst I was still doing my utmost to keep some semblance of order at the busy junction, the man with the book which I presumed was a bible, under his arm, started to defiantly walk out into the carriageway with his bible carrying arm raised toward to oncoming large metallic wheeled objects as if he was walking on water or parting the Red Sea. Moses like, he instantaneously halted the oncoming traffic whose drivers disbelievingly stared at this well cut man who continually grinning said, "Well officer, Have you really thought about where yow will spend all of eternity?" I irritably, unhurriedly and vociferously looked him straight in the eye and snapped, "Foxtrot Oscar, now!" (This of course being a euphemism for the Anglo Saxon phrase that I really used!) The man looked at me as if I'd just rammed a six foot spear through his chest, visibly shaken, he shrank in stature, obviously shocked that a Police officer even knew that sort of language, let alone used it! He scurried off back to his former vantage point and the safety of the road side gutter, bible tucked under his arm; he stared at me indignantly, like a scolded schoolboy who just had his catapult confiscated. His bottom lip quivered as he waited by the side of the road, presumably waiting for me to finish my point duty so that he could complain to me about my behaviour. Just then the unmistakable sound of the police motor cycle and ambulance sirens could be heard in the distance. Simultaneously I got a message on my Burdept radio telling me that the Ambulance escort had just cleared the Hen and Chickens Public House traffic lights on the Wolverhampton Road and would be at Warley Bowl junction in approximately one minute. My junction was the next main crossroads after the Warley Bowl Traffic lights.

A small crowd of people had gathered on the corner in the curious expectancy that if a copper had stopped all the traffic on a major thoroughfare like this then something must be about to happen type anticipation, close to where the Man of God quietly stood holy book in hand, his little beady unblinking lifeless eyes burning into me. His initial feelings of affection and anxiety over where I would be spending perpetuity had now obviously turned to indignant anger and he now knew exactly where I was going to spend infinity and it wasn't with him and I wouldn't need warm leather gloves and an overcoat! I had other things on my plate at that time, like where the poor sod in the ambo was going to spend eternity, but I did start to think, "Oh sugar, you've done it now Connor, swearing at a member of the public and him a man of the cloth too. The more I worried the more important in stature the man with the bible became. From being just an ordinary, door knocking, God bothering type of fervent believer, he moved through the Church of England ranks like quicksilver. I knew a lot about the Church of England, my Mum being a Born Again, member of the Parochial Church Council. I thought, 'He's too old to be a curate, too scruffy to be a vicar. He might be a Canon. No, Cannons go off don't they! What if he's a Bishop!'. Yes, a man very high up in the Church hierarchy, a personal friend of the almighty, whose complaint would be taken so seriously by the Chief Constable that I would be unceremoniously booted out of the Force! I started wondering how I would explain to my family, my friends and relations how I'd lost my job because I'd told a respected messenger of the almighty to go and do one! As Sgt Stan Roby the controller warned me that the Ambo Escort was coming towards me I saw the flashing blue lights of the lead motor cycle and heard the adrenaline pumping, ear piercing, combined blasts of the warning sirens of the police bikes and the Ambulance. I could smell the sweaty leathers of the police rider clad from head to foot in black sitting astride his dynamic hot searing police liveried BMW R80 motorcycle which screeched to a halt right by the side of me, looked around the junction at my handiwork, nodded his approval just as the Ambulance flashed through the junction at a vast rate of knots quickly followed by the second police motorcycle which was in the throws of overtaking the Ambulance, preparing to become the lead bike as the static scruffy next to me sped off in his new role behind the Ambulance continuing to hurtle towards the next hazard. The siren noise died down and dissipated as fast as it had arrived like a giant Doppler effect. It was literally over in seconds. The poor victim in the back of the Ambulance at least had a decent chance of surviving thanks to the skill and training of those fantastic drivers of all the emergency vehicles.

I quickly glanced at all the patient road users who had waited at my behest for what to me seemed like an age. It was probably only a matter of about 15 minutes tops. They in turn realising why they had been asked to wait seemed to appreciate that I was only doing my job and that after all it might have been one of their friends or loved ones in need of our assistance. It is one of those times that you realise that the job you do is one that is important and mighty satisfying.

Then there was the man with the book. Who, having seen the reason for my nervous outburst was again a devotee of mine. He shook my hand tightly and apologised profusely for interfering in what he described as a nerve wracking and critical event. I smiled and said, "It was worse for the poor sod in the back of the ambulance". He nodded in agreement and with a sufficiently pious and concerned expression said as we parted, "I'll pray for both of you!" I said to him, "Just limit your prayers to the patient in the burns unit mate, if you start praying for me that will take an eternity!" I was of course instantly reminded of the verse in scripture that reads, "The gate that leads to damnation is wide, the road is clear, and many choose to travel it. How narrow is the gate that leads to life, how rough the road, and how few there are who find it. [Matthew 7:13-14.] Yes, the roads of the West Midlands can be quite rough and very few bobbies find what that bible basher was peddling. Amen to that.

'St George'

A STAIN ON A SAINT

Saints play a big part in many peoples lives. Whilst driving up in the car to Blackpool Illuminations with my wife and Grandkids, my little grand daughter Teri, who was seven at the time, was reminding me that soon it would be her birthday. She reminded me that she was born on St Valentine's Day. I told her that Nanny Bev and I had St Valentine's Day to thank for us meeting. I then said to her, "Nanny Bev was born on a saints day, St Patrick's Day. Your brother Matthew is named after a saint, oh and so is your daddy." "What, St.Dave?" she replied incredulously!

When I'm not a police officer, not painting portrait paintings (Viewable at www.bryanconnor.co.uk at very reasonable Prices folks!) and not writing books, I love watching The Greatest Game known to humankind. Professional Rugby League, now better known as Super League, thanks to Rupert Murdoch and Sky television. I am an ancient and loyal fan of the greatest, *the* greatest, rugby league club on the planet. St Helens Rugby League Football Club, known more popularly to all their followers as 'The Saints'. They are known by the majority of our rivals as the stains, for anagrammatic reasons and this story sort of supports that argument! The St Helens supporters have always had a friendly rivalry with Wigan RLFC supporters, our bitterest rivals, who recently moved into the new JJB Stadium. and even though they share the ground with the local successful Premier League football side, the pitch always seems to have a beautiful, rich, grassy surface for the simple reason that every fortnight without fail during the summer months they put manure on it (I've cleaned that up folks!). One of my favourite Wigan stories is about the car full of saints fans that were visiting the JJB for the first game there and they were lost on the new ring-way in Wigan. So they stopped and asked a chap walking his dog, "Excuse me mate, how do you get to the JJB?" He had a quick think and then replied, "My Uncle takes me in his Reliant Robin!"

St Helens, Lancashire, happens to be the town that I was born in, well, quite a few years ago now, I'm being mendacious about my age of course, but I was born in St Helens and I'm a life long Saints supporter. I've lived in the Midlands for thirty-five years, but I'm still a St Helens supporter, travelling north along the M6 motorway every chance I get, with my long suffering wife Beverly, to watch my beloved Saints. I saw my first game when I was six years old and I've been watching them ever since. It's a rugby story I'm about to impart now. I can't remember where it took place (which you may, when you've read this, agree is probably just as well) I can't remember the date, other than, it takes place one wintery Sunday afternoon in West Yorkshire. Many rugby league matches take place on a Sunday in West Yorkshire, but I'm sure it was somewhere like, Wakefield or was it Featherstone, but then again, it could have been Castleford thinking about it! OK, we have established, it was a rugby league venue in Yorkshire and the mighty Saints were playing there. It was a terrible wet winters day, bone chillingly cold and windy, the icy rain chucking it down in 30 degree stair rods. Before the game, the home club's antique tannoy public-address system, I think during the eighties most old rugby league venues still had those huge trumpet shaped funnels, that were a poor excuse for a public address system. They'd probably have better off just cupping their hands together and hollering at the top of their voice. Because when they used the tannoy systems, voices seemed to echo two or three times around the ground before the sound rebounded into your ear drum and you'd see people screwing their faces up, as if in agony, you know how they do, with their hand cupped around their ear, trying to pay close attention to whats being said.   On this occasion, a small group of well dressed, but obviously non rugby folk formed along the touchline as the tannoy announced the very sad bereavement of a local club official who, had either been a director of the club or a local government official in the locale or both, but fundamentally had been an enduring servant of the East Pennine based club and had passed away. His widow and close family lined the wing that their loved one had often scanned like a hawk from his seat in the stand during his days as a spectator, to possibly dispute the bounce of a ball going directly into touch. Now, his remains hovered over it, in a small receptacle that looked vaguely like a rugby ball, nestled in the non-fending arm of his widow. The echoed announcement was made. After ricocheting off the main stand it sounded something to the effect of, 'According to Councillor Blenkinsopp's final wishes, his ashes will be scattered on the ground of his much beloved home town team.' The group then solemnly walked across the hallowed turf and reconvened under the black dot, the point directly beneath the posts at the popular end of the stadium. His widow then opened the urn containing her husbands remains and started to disperse some of them, very tenderly and ceremoniously with a great deal of dignity underneath the sticks. Followed in turn by each member of the little group of family members as they passed the urn one to another. A civilised, respectful and polite silence accompanied these proceedings.

The small, but reverent curtain raising event was soon over, everyone in the ground finishing their pies and cups of steamy Bovril along with their pre-match reviews of how they thought their lads would perform today. They gave their undivided attention to the main event of the afternoon. The two teams ran out of the tunnel to a tremendous roar of anticipation from both sets of unsegregated supporters. The unmistakable telltale scent of the wintergreen that covered the lower limbs of the gladiators wafted into the nostrils of the away fans; packed like steaming sardines under the meagre rusty corrugated cover supplied by the rickety old stand that stood down wind of the players, who now lined up reverently around the centre of the pitch for the minute's silence, just before kicking twelve cans out of shite out of each other! Remember, it's a freezing cold, winters day and the rain is still sheeting down relentlessly, drenching the players. The sides trembled, half with nerves and half because they were almost naked, standing against a wind chill factor that must have dragged the temperature gauge to well below freezing. Proof, as if it was needed, of the way that Rugby League players show their own impeccably observed silence as a mark of respect for someone who loved their great game. One of the things that Rugby League does do well, is; respect. It's a bloody hard game, but it's also a family game and everybody involved in the sport is always respectful during a minutes silence. The away fans, on this occasion, respecting a fine yet anonymous stalwart of their game. Not like bloody football, where people just shout out moronically during a minute's silence, it's pathetic really, no respect. You hear the same sort of morons at England internationals, booing the opposing fans during the playing of their national anthems. Enough of Association Football. Which I do like by the way, in spite of becoming a follower of West Bromwich Albion! Come on you Baggie Boyz!

Anyway, back to that Yorkshire day in the mid eighties, when a younger and much hardier (to the inclement weather) me watches the game being kicked off by the home team's stand off half. The ball, wet and slippery flies through the bitter, wind swept, floodlit Yorkshire sky, towards the advancing line of immaculately soaked but cleanly blue clad saints and straight into the arms of a stocky prop forward called George Mann. Mann, was a rugged, unbreakable, New Zealand international front rower. A truly great rugby league footballer, who, with ball in hand sprung into action driving straight at the oncoming defensive line of rock hard tykes. The first would be tackler tries to grab George, going high, George hands him off as if he wasn't there. He trips and slides on the wet slippery surface, unintentionally ducking under another high tackle attempt from the second wave of tacklers. George Mann had quite a turn of speed, considering he was a prop forward. As he slithered along the muddy surface he handed off the next opponent; springing himself forwards from his adversary's upper torso and into the clear! The defence opening up like the River Jordan in front of Moses. Saint George, our 'Chosen One', the gigantic antipodean, forges through the opening and scampers straight up the middle of the muddy playing field, unopposed virtually. The trailing Egyptian army in pursuit. He eventually decides to dive a good five yards short of the try line but slides, wonderfully, his momentum carrying him effortlessly across the mud-covered surface, like a water slide at a swimming pool, towards the try line and grounding the ball under the posts, the away supporters in unison chant,

TRY! As George opens the scoring for the Saints, straight through the ashes of Councillor Horace Blenkinsopp!

George Mann gets up, surrounded by his team mates who are congratulating him on a fine solo effort. It is then that we catch sight of an out of breath prop, grinning from ear to ear, with a modified wide, broad greyish white band of ash down the front of his predominantly blue kit. A bit like the 1970s Birmingham City shirts, that were Royal Blue with a broad White band running straight up the front of it, if you remember the days of Trevor Francis and Bob Latchford. Saints had played in their Royal Blue away colours, not their usual all white with a red vee, that wouldn't have looked so bad in retrospect. So now most of the remains of Councillor Blenkinsopp was resting in part, down the front of George Mann the St Helens' Antipodean prop forward. I've always thought how discomforting it must have been for his widow and his loved ones that Councillor Blenkinsopp's final resting place was the washing machine in the laundry room at Knowsley Road, the home of the mighty Saints. That would suit me no end, there is no place I'd rather be, when I've thrown a seven, than the home of my beloved Saints! I don't suppose the dear old Councillor would agree. Looking at it philosophically, it could have been a lot worse. They could have been playing Wigan. What an epitaph! It brings a whole new meaning to the term, 'A Bluey Whiteness!' There is no truth in the rumour that St Helens RLFC use a washing powder called 'Bugger', If Bold won't work, If Aerial won't work and if Persil won't work, then Bugger it!

Dear reader, if you're reading this book now, or listening to this on a recording. I'd like you to stand, for just a couple of seconds silently and if you've got a pot of tea or summat a bit stronger, I'd like you to raise your glass or mug; joining me in a toast, to a true rugby league legend,

Councillor Horace Blenkinsopp and all those other great rugby league patrons, who have graced the terraces of the greatest Game, both past and present. Well done all those people that have gone before, all the best! I'd also like to take this opportunity of letting my loved ones know that when I jump off the perch, as it were, I would much prefer to have my ashes spread over the Saints pitch on a very dry day please and preferably not on a match day. I'd also like to remind you all, especially the pie eating Wiganers, of the pertinent lyrics of a famous religious song, which states that ALL of us 'are trav'ling in the footsteps of those who've gone before and we'll all be reunited, on a new and sunlit shore. When the saints go marching in, when the saints go marching in. I want to be in that number. When the saints go marching in! Amen to that Brother, Amen

BEATING BILLY THE BURGLAR

This chapter is not about gratuitous violence nor does it relate to the time I was victorious in a game of snooker with my brother in law. At several times throughout my police service I have worked with quite a few Crime Prevention Officers. Some good, some, not so good. I've even worked with one Crime Prevention Officer that got the sack for shoplifting while he was still in post as a Crime Prevention Officer! Talk about pot calling the kettle! He got done for stealing items from a very well known pharmaceutical retailer. He half inched a pair of womens tights and a ballpoint pen! Items he obviously couldn't afford on his Thirty Grand a year salary.

In fairness, he'd been having domestic problems and was separated from his kids. Living in a pokey, rented, box room in a dingy inner city suburb! There cannot be any excuse for stealing other peoples property, other people go through stressful situations without stealing. What was worse was that he'd been advising stores how to protect themselves from store thieves! He gave up a well paid profession, a fabulous career with a marvellous pension because of one obtuse moment in his life. Because of which, he had been suspended from duty pending a decision from the Director of Public Prosecutions about his future with the force. As a friend, I kept in touch with him, I not only worked with him, we were both members of the same Cricket team, we were close. I tried to understand and be supportive, where many of my professional colleagues predictably turned their back on him. The last time I saw him over a pub lunch, he was critically putting down the police service. A service I loved then and still love now! This great job has been good to me, has fed and clothed both me and my family, it has got me a house and will supply me with an adequate pension when I finally hang up my helmet. I told him that I didn't agree with him, but he cynically carried on making critical and hurtful remarks about the police service and the men and women that carry out the duties of that office. Sadly, that was the last time I saw him. I wonder if he is still bitter and twisted as a result of what was, at the end of the day, his own stupid actions? Life is too short you know.

If by any chance you are reading this Craig, I hope you and your loved ones are well and life is treating you benevolently.

Why do shoplifters do it? Its got to be the weirdest offence on the legislative books. Most shoplifters, like my old mate Craig, don't require or need what they steal! It's true.

My first shop lifter was a Fifty-Two year old West Midlands Travel Bus Driver who, during a scheduled break at work, had parked up his double decker bus at a local Bus station at and had taken the two minute walk along the High Street to a well known local Department store on that busy thoroughfare. He'd entered and walked around the aisles of the sort of store that invites its shoppers to place their selected items into a wire basket, before paying for them at the checkout, before leaving the store. The Bus Driver selected a multi pack of Cadbury's Double Decker chocolate bars from a stand and placed them into the inside pocket of his jacket, then leaves the store without offering to pay for them! A Passenger Service Vehicle Bus Driver swiping a packet of Double Deckers. You can't make it up can you? Its a journalists dream headline.

Under the eagerly observant eyes of the store detective, who duly followed him out of the store into the High Street, making sure that the full offence was committed before challenging him on the pavement outside the store about not offering to pay for the goods he'd taken from the store without offering payment.

When the smartly suited, sad, pallid grey, embarrassed figure of the bus driver stood in the dock before the local magistrates he pleaded not guilty and claimed, in his defence, that recently he was suffering from temporary mental blackouts and that he had medication prescribed from his General Practitioner for them!

Now how dim-witted was that? That was a good bit of advice from his solicitor wasn't it? A Bus Driver, claiming as part of his defence for stealing a packet of chocolate bars to a Court full of people, including several members of the press, states publicly that he suffers from mental blackouts that cause him to momentarily lose consciousness! Only for a few seconds though, he adds, in mitigation. Was it wise deciding to tell the world and his dog, possibly on the advice of a well paid solicitor, that he suffered from blackouts! Considering most of his working day was spent carrying large numbers of passengers on his bus, all of whom put their complete trust in him to get them from one part of the West Midlands to the other safely? Result, end of a long and until then, unblemished career as a Bus Driver, with little or no prospect of getting another job at his age or receiving his company pension! Crime really doesn't pay does it.

Bearing in mind that we police the United Kingdom upon the consent of its populace. Our primary duty being to Protect life and Property and then to Prevent and Detect Crime. Noting that Prevent, comes before Detect. That means that, when we get to the Detecting part of that phrase, then in some ways we have failed in our primary task.

When I was involved with crime prevention initiatives I loved speaking to new groups of Neighbourhood Watches at their primary set-up meetings. The Neighbourhood Watch projects introduced by the Home Office during the 1990s were very popular, some of the meetings would be held in function rooms of Churches, Community Centres, School Halls and the like.

I attended and spoke at many of these meetings assisting the Smethwick Neighbourhood Watch Officer Martyn Flannery. I had known Martyn all my police service. He had been a Zulu (Early Response) Driver on my first operational unit, 'A' Unit, a good lad to work with, in spite of his being a lifelong Dingle, a Wolverhampton Wanderers fan! I remember Martyn once managed to persuade a local Ford Motor Dealer to lend us a top of the range Granada Saloon car fitted with an up to date Alarm System to demonstrate the same at a Crime Prevention display at a local summer fair, which went a bit Pete Tong or totally pear shaped, as we say in the job. Now, you think that I'm now going to tell you the tale of the borrowed luxury saloon car fitted with a fantastic alarm system that was lent to the cops for a crime display that got half inched (Er, that is to say stolen) from the back yard of the nick aren't you? No, dear reader no! Martyn and I left the back yard at Piddock Road nick early on that Saturday morning heading for Langley High Street fête promptly. But not before the whole of the nick from the Superintendent right down to the lowliest probationary constable on the early response team had had a full guided tour of the shiny Ford Granada, with white walled tyres, it's fabulous alarm system, its heated seats, its electric drinks maker, tinted mirrors and built in Sky dish etc, you get the picture?

God was in his (or her) heaven, the sun shone, the sky was a clear azure blue and the little smog covered dickie birds sang their merry morning songs as we drove down the High Street, Smethwick towards the local Gurdwara. That is the name given to the Sikh Temple. The Smethwick Gurdwara is one of the biggest and best attended in Britain. As Martyn, a grade one police advanced driver, started to overtake some parked cars on the nearside, one of them, a huge Mitsubishi Shogun 4x4 monster truck thing, that at the time, around the late eighties was still a rare and hugely cumbersome sight on British roads, pulled out sharply from the nearside of the road just in front of us. It was obvious that the driver hadn't looked in his rear view mirror before pulling out and to be brief, the Shogun ripped the whole of the front grille and front nearside wing off the borrowed, top of the range, Ford Grannie! Ooooops! Martyn went ashen white!

It wasn't his fault, but, it is always a giggle listening to a cop you have always respected and admired for his driving prowess and professionalism start to rant and rave just like any other Road Traffic Collision victims do! I remained extremely calm, of course, I would, after all, I wasn't driving! Much more to the point, I wasn't going to be the one who would have to explain it to the Ford Dealership! We were both gobsmacked when out of the drivers side of the slightly scratched Shogun emerged a white guy in full Sikh attire, with a very long beard, wearing a turban, the bangle, the full five K's Sikh regalia! He was an American Sikh visiting the Smethwick Gurdwara. He was good as gold and accepted full responsibility, stating that he'd only been in the country a day or two and was still getting used to driving on the 'wrong side of the road.' I said to Martyn later, that not many police officers could state that a sponsored car they had borrowed for a police crime prevention display had been written off by a white American Sikh in a rented 4x4 in the middle of Smethwick or anywhere for that matter! It did't help that when we came back out to the back yard at Smethwick nick with the Superintendent, Mick Karalius in tow, to show him the damage, some wag had felt-penned the bold word, 'OUCH!' across the damage to the Granada Saloons front nearside! You never did find out who wrote 'OUCH' in Permanent marker ink (So that the Ford Dealer saw it too) did you Martyn?

Sorry mate, I couldn't resist it! I even wrote to the BBC TV programme Record Breakers to see if they were interested and some wag from the BBC sent a great spoof reply back to me inviting Martyn onto the programme. Which he strangely declined!

I attended numerous Neighbourhood Watch meetings with Martyn. Who, admittedly wasn't Gods gift to public speaking and so asked me to 'preach' to those new converts to the American idea of crime prevention. I used to start all my talks to Neighbourhood Watch Groups with the same story. It's not original,mind you, but there's nothing new under the sun is there? My thanks go to Inspector Dave Pryce who told me the following tale:

After being introduced to the group by Martyn, I would begin. "The other day ladies and gentlemen a young woman rang our office asking for some advice. She thought that she may have been the victim of an attempted Burglary. Somebody had been around the back of her house and had removed little bits of putty from the rear dining room window frame. Removing putty then lifting out the glass quietly is a well known Modus Operandi. Some burglars remove all the putty from around the window frame, neatly taking out the piece of glass, then reaching their arm through the opening into the property to undo the unlocked window catch." I then told them that I visited the scene and had a look at the back of the woman's house noting that indeed some putty had been scratched out from the window. However, nowhere near enough putty had been removed to take out the pane of glass. Nobody had gained entry into the house, so I explained the Modus Operandi to her, stating that on this occasion it looked like someone had had a go at the putty, but perhaps they had been disturbed by a neighbour or the householder returning so making good their escape. They had certainly not at all had got anywhere near removing enough putty to even weaken the fitting, let alone remove the pane, so I was bewildered. The next day, lo and behold, the woman rings our station again. Again, being a helpful police officer, I go around to look at the scene and for a second time, note that someone has had a go at the window like the first juncture, only insignificant particles of the putty had gone, not all of it, nowhere near any entry gained to the premises. It was very puzzling. Yet again, I try to set her mind at rest and took my leave. The next day, she calls again, same scenario! This time the woman is cheerfully smiling, revealing that she had solved the great mystery. The putty had been removed by next doors pet cat!

Which was employing its razor-sharp, but elegant feline claws, to score against the window pane, scraping dry putty from the windowpane as it did so!

I would then rub my chin, looking puzzled, directly into the faces of my now captivated audience, revealing that it was one of those sleek, slender, creme coloured moggies, with the brown face and almond shaped vivid electric blue eyes. By this time I would be doing my Marlon Brandoesque, puzzled frown look, scratching my dome, seeking their assistance, in an effort to try to identify what breed of cat it was. They would always start to shout out differing breeds of cat. Depending on whether your audience were thick or not. Some bright spark would eventually, if cajoled correctly, utter, quite loudly, but timidly, the word SIAMESE! I would then reiterate just as loudly, Siamese? No, no, it was a putty cat! I would powerfully state.

Foolish as that sounds. It always, always, got a chuckle! I even used it the other night at The Kingfisher Night Club in Kingswinford during a talk to the Brierley Hill Rotary Club, some twenty years later and even now it still breaks the ice with listeners!

Now remember, when it came to advice and protecting your home against a break in, I would ask them this simple question. You have returned home to find, for whatever reason, that you are locked out of your house and your spare keys are locked in that house. How would you get into it? Like the vast majority of opportunist burglars, you would go round the back of the house, you don't wanna break in the front of the house because it's too public, makes too much noise, attracts attention, you don't want people seeing you break into places, neither do burglars. So the obvious place to go is around the back of the house! First, again just like an opportunist Burglar, you would check for insecure windows or doors. We all leave home leaving windows open, especially in warm weather. If there aren't any insecure doors or windows, the next best thing to do is to look at where you can make the least damage, now remember this is you getting into your house, burglars could really not be bothered about how much damage they cause. The easiest way for you to get in your house if you're locked out and you haven't got a key, and there's no other way in, is to break a window, one small pane of glass is cheap and relatively easy to replace, compared to having to replace a whole door. If burglars decide to break in through your back door, its because on a cheap back door, any universal key, used on the lower back door panels, will always secure entry. A lot of back kitchen doors, have panels that are about, quarter of an inch thick, if that! Any door with these thin type of panels can be opened by any size ten universal key, that is genuinely true, it can be opened by any size ten universal key. What is a size ten universal key? A size ten universal key is a boot, my friend. A boot on the end of a foot. You may have a size nine or a size eleven or size seven universal key on the end of your foot, but whoever you are and no matter how large or small you are, there is a universal key at the end of your foot that when wrapped in a tight laced leather container, can be forced to break that quarter inch panel, permitting you entry, by climbing through the broken panel, consequently gaining the free run of that house, that's what people do when they burgle houses, they kick the back door panels in. The biggest part of an average persons body, is their head! If the criminal head goes through, the criminal body will follow (Thanks again Peter Cook!). How can we stop this Bry? I hear you say? Will we have to replace the door? Hell no! You can get the door reinforced by securing an inch thick piece of wood or MDF over the vulnerable panelled bits! It won't cost much and when Billy Burglar tries to kick that panel in. He'll hopefully break the bones of his universal key! Its better than having your house screwed! Bry, I've got glass doors in my back door, what can I do? I could put bars up, but It will make my house look like a prison I hear you say. Well, why not splash out on some ornate ornamental steel frames and screw them to the frame of the door!

Now, the other thing about some back doors of houses, are their locks. I have found that many pensioners tend to have old fashioned single action back door locks on them. These locks don't even have any levers in 'em, if you've got a door lock that hasn't got any levers in it, replace it with a good British standard five lever or a seven lever mortice lock.

They are cheaper than the alternative - being burgled! Levers are flat pieces of metal, positioned in the barrel of a lock that move by the key being pushed into the lock. The belly of the lever is cut away to various depths to provide different combinations. A lever has pockets and gates through which the bolt stump moves during unlocking. If you wanted to replace a key for a single action bolt lock, you will find that the Key Cutting staff at your local store won't even have to cut a key! There are only four types of single action lock. If you have these four keys, and most opportunist burglars have, they want an easy life, so carrying four keys with them and trying them in every old back door they try is easy and if they try 'em and the door opens, then no problem at all, no noise, no mess, no damage, no injury, bingo they're in. If they are disturbed they go into bullshit mode, giving better waffle than a parliamentary candidate at a local election and thats good waffle! Stating that they are from the local council, the water board or one of the many gas suppliers. Folks, when it comes to being victims of burglary it even effects the sexes in different ways. The male of the species has the outlook that says; 'Hey, I'm insured, I'll get new for old replacement. So I'm not that bothered' Wrong boys! Your annual premium will go up (and up) because you've made a claim. In addition, please spare a thought for the women in your life! A stranger has rifled through her drawers! Ooooer missis! Joking apart Gents, women feel violated by the act of burglary, someone really has invaded their space and taken their possessions. Some women, believe me, never, ever, get over it!

If you haven't got decent window locks on your windows. Why not? Buy some and fit them. Some now cost the price of a packet of fags. Have a look at your door locks, make sure you've got levers in 'em. If you've got a five lever mortice lock in your door mate, great, it's something like 70,000 to 1 that a criminal will be able to copy that key or have a duplicate key on them to try by chance. Anything that slows Billy Burglar down is good, that's what we're talking about, trying to put Billy off burgling your home. Remember, I've had one particular question asked me hundreds of times, and I mean hundreds of times in my 30 years of policing. "Officer are you saying that if I spend all this extra money on my house, I won't be burgled?" If, listen to this, this is genuine, 'IF', the burglars wants to get into your home, they *will* get in, there's no two ways about it, if someone wants to get into your house they will get in your house, there is nothing you can do to stop them getting in, they'll cause a lot of damage, may cause a lot of grief but if they want to get in, they will get in. What you must do is try to slow them right down, make it difficult, the more difficult you make it for the burglar, the more chance that burglar will think, 'Sod this, I'll go where it's easier to break in', that is genuine. I've talked to burglars, and you can ask any detective, they will tell you. Even professional burglars will tell you; if house 'A' is an easier house to break into than house 'B', they'll go for 'A' every time, the easy target. Time is of the essence for them, they wanna be in and out before you can say HANDCUFFS. They will get into your house, taking items that will just go into pockets. 'They took my telly, they took my stereo, they took me computer, they took this and that', yes it happens, but the vast majority of burglars are fast, in and out, opportunist burglars who are extremely quick.

Okay, that's the advice over with. There's lots more advice you can get if you want it, if you need to get crime prevention advice, you're no dimwits, you know where you can get crime prevention advice, but I'll tell you what, if you do not have decent British Standard (You know, with the little kite mark) locks on your house matey, you are asking for trouble. Fit reputable locks on your home and though not cheap, they will bring peace of mind! Alarms are all right, but when you are at home on a weekend and an alarm goes off a couple of doors away from you. You look through the window, of course, you report anything suspicious of course. If things appear to look fine you ignore the alarm, in fact most activated car and house alarms annoy you, as the bloody thing keeps ringing! I've got two mortice locks on my front doors and I've got a dead lock and a mortice lock on my back door, I've got locks on all my windows, and touch wood (I'm touching me head) that's all I need, I've never been burgled, and hopefully I never will be. All you can do is try to make it difficult for the burglar, let them see that you've thought about it. Unlike the drama programmes that would like you to think that these people are stupid. Far from it, they are deviously knowledgeable. They are sharp opportunists who, if you give them the opportunity, will make you a victim of crime. Good burglars will turn their nose up at your 'Fort Knox' and go to pastures easier, not greener, easier.

There's no such thing as a unburglable house, it's like having an unsinkable ship, there's no such thing, ask Leonardo Di Caprio and Kate Whats her name! Unburglable. Is that a word? If you are in a Neighbourhood Watch, put the stickers on you windows. Some Burglars can read you know, well most of 'em! Anyway that's the crime prevention advice, if you need more, get some.

CAIN AND ABEL (A MODERN MURDER MISERY)

I had been the Permanent Beat Officer on Cape Hill for about four years. It was the mid Nineteen Nineties. I was on a late shift 2pm x 10pm and I'd just popped into the Bingo session run by school caretaker, Olive Element, at Shireland High School annexe in Waterloo Road, Smethwick. I always called in after the local Police Surgery, which my beat partner PC Doug Watson and I shared every other week with a local councillor in tow, usually Councillor Sid Pemberton (A genuinely well loved pillar of Sandwell Council). I liked calling into the main hall to see the Bingo women for a cuppa and a chat, the majority of the bingo women, worked at the school as dinner ladies and cleaners. They were my kind of people. Salt of the Earth, honest, working class folk. The kind of people I'd grown up with. I sometimes acted as the bingo caller but was more than a little frivolous with the calls. For example, I'd pick out a Number 27 and would announce to the expectant group of females, "On its own, Twenty-seven, Two Little Ducks, Forty –One or Key of the Door, Nineteen." To the uninitiated heathens who are not educated in the ways of the Bingo faith, this is sacrilege. It's like walking in Marks and Spencer's and shouting "Waitrose!" It infuriated some of the real Bingo stalwarts who really got wound up. The more I did it and the majority of women giggled at my antics the more distressed they got. I thought they were going to lynch me one night! They were an excellent bunch, who trusted me, even though I was a bobby and a bloke!

This particular evening, I left the annexe about twenty-five to nine. It was pissing down with rain, on a dark Wednesday night in October. I could hear fireworks going off close-by as I crossed the main drag on my way back to a warm dry police station. I never understood why people buy fireworks with their hard earned cash, just to let them off when it's bucketing down with rain. I suppose they're the same clowns that light them up in broad daylight. Reminds me of two lads we brought into the nick one night, Tom was sniffing Battery Acid and Dick sniffed the powder out of fireworks. We weren't sure what to do with them. So we explained the circumstances to the Duty Inspector, who said, "Charge Tom and let the other one off!" Sorry, they can't all be gems you know. As I trudged along the wet pavements of the dimly lit street. I thought of having a quick pint in the warm and cosy police social club before going home to watch Midweek Sports Special with Elton Welsby as I ate my fish and chip supper bought on route home. I saw a figure coming towards me. It was a Littlewoods Pools collector on his round. As he got nearer he said, "Mate, there's a bloke slumped in the entry down there, I think he might have collapsed." "O.K Mate, I'll go and have a look at him" I said. Thinking, 'Great, There goes the pint!" On the left hand side if the road there is a set of Victorian villa type houses that are approached through what might have been at one time an entrance for horses and horse drawn carriages. It led into a small courtyard that contained modernised flatlets. In the very dark, unlit, covered walkway entrance, sat a middle-aged white male, very scruffily dressed.   He was sitting up against the wall, arms, limp, hanging by his sides, legs straight out in front of him. He stank of fusty beer and stale urine, was extremely pale and slipping in and out of consciousness. I'm going to call him Abel. As I got closer I could see that Abel was bleeding copiously from a deep lesion in his stomach. I calmly spoke into my blue Burndept Radio. "PC Connor Kilo 3?" "Go head Bry" said Sergeant Phil Forber, the Smethwick controller. I asked Phil for an Ambulance whilst feeling for a pulse. I couldn't find one. I couldn't hear or see any signs of him breathing. To stem the torrent of blood gushing from Abel's stomach wound, I pushed my left leather gloved hand firmly onto the centre of his wound. These few minutes seemed like an hour. Not a soul about, just Abel, whose dimming life light was seemingly ebbing away quickly before my eyes and me.

A young lad ran hurriedly past through the rain and as he saw me in full uniform crouching over Abel he shouted, "Leave him alone pig, he's done nothing." I literally tried to kill time lingering around helplessly, vulnerably, waiting for assistance. I realised now, just how those people who call the emergency services on the nines for urgent assistance must feel as I waited for help to arrive. I tried to talk to him, whispering in his dying shell like, "Come On, breathe."   I'd not long seen the comedy film, The Road to Wellville, which tells the story of Dr John Harvey Kellogg (Anthony Hopkins) and his eccentric methods and beliefs as employed at the Battle Creek Sanatorium at the start of the Twentieth Century. A line spoken by actor John Neville in the film kept running through my mind. Upon wishing the leading protagonist farewell his character says, 'Follow your heart. It is the one organ that will surely let you down one day; so don't waste it while you are alive' I thought about that line as I whispered encouragements to the ever weakening inside Abel's chest. He had obviously wasted his own heart until then, but now, here I was urging it to beat,beat,beat. I started to realise that this was now a probable murder scene.

Keeping up a good rapport with Phil Forber, the consummate professional, I managed to pass all the required information the CID would need for the investigation. I clumsily fumbled around on my utility belt, past my expandable telescopic baton and my handcuffs for the small leather holder that contained a few pairs of medical gloves, a group of safety pins, a few plasters and importantly an airway breathing device used for performing mouth to mouth resuscitation. I looked at the ailing, blue lipped Abel, whose rotten teeth filled oral cavity was drooling gooey saliva and was not relishing the thought of having a stab (Bad choice of words?) at my first aid revival training on this lifeless drunk with halitosis! I'd only practiced on a rubber mock torso. Unfortunately for Abel, I hadn't passed my First Aid exam in my initial probationary training by many marks and that had been nearly fifteen years ago! Providentially (For the two of us), I heard the reassuring and melodious tones of the approaching ambulance. The Doppler effect of its siren growing louder by the second. It wasn't long before the entire cavalry troop had arrived at the scene. I was mightily relieved when the Ambulance crew told me that my possible murder victim was still just that. Abel was, at least, still alive. I must have done something right.

As they went to place Abel on the stretcher one of the Ambo lads told me that I would have to take my left hand out of the glove and leave it with the casualty as his blood had completely congealed around it. Not that I was bothered about losing the sodden, blood soaked apparel. I was very surprised at how easy it was to remove my hand from it, the glove refused to budge, it seemed almost to be super glued to Abel's torso. Off in the ambulance to the (luckily) nearby Dudley Road Hospital went the motionless, fading Abel.

I immediately began to write down a contemporaneous, chronological record of all officers attending the scene in my pocket book. The detectives that arrived where all briefed by me as they T.A.'d (Time of Arrival). Having made hurried initial enquiries it transpired that the injured man, was a well known inebriate in the area. He lived in one of the ground floor flatlets by the cloister under which he'd been stabbed and had fought for his life. He had a twin brother let's call him Cain, who had a flat in a nearby council block in Clough Street about ten minutes walk away. They were both alcoholics and were far from anonymous to the public at large. The scene was secured and at about ten fifteen, I was relieved by one of the lads who'd just paraded on the night shift. He took over the crime scene arrival log. DC Will Dagnall (Wilbur), drove me back to the nick at Piddock Road. Still laughing and joking with Will about our spoiled evening drink and snooker match. I followed him through the back door of the nick into the brightly illuminated main corridor intending to get my witness statement form underway. It was then I glanced down the front of my uniform and become fully aware that I was completely smeared, virtually head to foot, in bright crimson and dark red clotted blood. I immediately went into shock and passed out at the sight of so much blood. I looked like a cross between a cast member of Casualty and a Hammer Horror Dracula film extra. A proud, gold badge owning, blood donor of years standing, I blacked out at the sight of so much rich, red, cold, congealed, gelatine like set, human blood. It certainly is thicker than water, believe me.

I wasn't out long and was soon embarrassingly swigging down lashings of hot, sweet, strong tea with a large drop of strong liquid sedative, added by old Sam, the Police Social Club's Barkeeper, who had not long closed the bar upstairs. It transpired that Cain's meagrely furnished flat contained one, spare, uninhabited room; that contained nothing but upright, tightly stacked, empty green Bulmer's Woodpecker Cider bottles, that filled the room entirely, wall to wall. So much so, that you could walk across the top of the bottles to the window on the outer wall without touching the floor of the room or knocking over a single bottle. It was strikingly artistic in a smelly old discarded cider bottle sort of way. It would probably have won the Turner prize!

Cain and Abel, were apparently very close brothers when sober, which was undoubtedly a rare occasion, about as rare as an Albion away win in the Premiership! They fought like Itchy and Scratchy, when under the influence of any sort of alcoholic beverage. It reminds me of the legal incongruity that states that a police officer can only ever give their professional opinion on one particular subject in a court of law. That being, the state of someone's intoxication. Hence, the infamous phrase utilised by countless police officers giving evidence in the witness boxes of court buildings the length and breadth of the country: 'Your Worships, The defendant's eyes were glazed, his speech was slurred and his breath smelled strongly of intoxicating liquor. He was drunk. ' I wish the Police Widows and Orphans Fund received a pound for every time that phrase had been uttered in court. (They'd have a few quid!) It's amazing how many times you hear officers (Both real and especially the imaginary ones) who state that they could smell alcohol on the defendants breath. This cannot be true, as alcohol is completely odourless.

Abel was arrested on Suspicion of Attempted Murder and once sober, admitted that he had critically stabbed his brother with a broken beer bottle following a fiery argument over the tenure of a litre bottle of a cheap 'own brand' white cider! How poignant is that? It doesn't say much for modern Britain does it? Where its cheaper to buy a can of beer than a sandwich and the Cain and Abel's of this world prefer to exist on a liquid diet. Abel was remanded in custody by the local magistrates and sent to the Green (HM Prison Birmingham, Winson Green) awaiting his next bail appearance. Cain was operated on straight away and after being at deaths door for about a week, made an inexplicable recovery! Consequently, a recuperating Cain discharged himself from Dudley Road Hospital, against medical advice of course and hobbled directly to an off licence. He then continued on to Piddock Road Police Station. Where he spoke to the detectives handling his case, clearly now an intended Grievous Bodily Harm wounding. Informing the incredulous gumshoes that he did not wish to make any formal complaint of assault and flatly refusing to make a statement of any kind. His brother Abel was released from custody the same day and bound over to behave himself for the following twelve months for what became a Breach of the Peace! Amazingly, had Abel jumped off the perch and gone to join the choir invisible. Cain would have still been serving life imprisonment for a repugnant murder. Instead, They can still be seen outside the local Off Licences, within a short ambulance trip of the original crime scene, on most weekday mornings. To quote the Moody blues standard, 'Isn't life strange?'

According to the Book of Genesis, Cain and Abel were the first and second sons of Adam and Eve, born after the so-called fall of Man. Cain, a farmer, commits the first of many biblical murders by killing his brother Abel, a shepherd, after God rejects Cain's sacrifice but accepts Abel's. At least Abel didn't die over something pointless then! Interesting that in our modern day Abel forgives his tormentor!

'You know what that is?'

FOOT IN MOUTH and other DISASTERS

Many times throughout my professional life I have said and done things I wish I hadn't. Bobbies in particular, are not the most discreet people in the world sometimes at conveying information to the public in a clear and concise way. I remember an amusing report that I saw once in Police Review, where the head of a mental institution in the north of Scotland eager to allay public anxieties following the escape of a very dangerous patient in their care stated in a hurriedly issued press release:

'Reference the escape of Rupert 'Mad Dog' Soul. This man is not a public menace, he only attacks police officers.' The worst, 'I wish the earth would open up and I could jump into the hole' comment I ever regret making was on one dreary grey afternoon on the High Street, Smethwick. I was having a cuppa at one of my tea spots out on the patch, Audrey's Florists, a couple of doors up from the Police Station. This was a regular tea spot for me. On my patch and very close to the busy shopping area of Cape Hill, should there be any issues with shoplifters. I would be readily available. I was chatting away with the staff as they made up their orders for the afternoon van. A respectable looking elderly woman came into the shop and was chatting to Audrey, presumably about her order. I unfortunately, didn't hear what she was ordering or the reason, I only heard her northern accent. I regret to this day that I hadn't heard her order. Coming from St.Helens in Lancashire, I recognised an accent local to the North west region of England and told her that I'd recognised her accent and asked her where exactly she was from."I'm originally from the village of Rainhill near St Helens in Lancashire," she replied with a smile.

After explaining that she had moved down to the Midlands with her husband, who worked in the Chemical Industry and had been promoted in his job, down to the West Midlands some thirty years earlier. I then unthinkingly blurted out, "Ah, Rainhill, I know it well," informing her of my birthplace, which is only about seven or eight miles as the soot covered crow flies. I grew up in St Helens and knew the area well enough to know that Rainhill is best know in the area as the location of a huge hospital, in its heyday one of the largest psychiatric institutions in Europe. "Thats where all the fruit loops live, isn't it" I said cockily, adding, " "Rainhill, famous for the Railway Trials won by Stephenson's 'Rocket' and also the home of one of the biggest nut hospitals in Britain" I continued. "Yes, thats right", said the woman calmly, "My sister died there yesterday."

After a few tense seconds I nervously answered an imaginary call on my Burndept Radio, feigning an urgent incoming message in an effort to drag myself out of the slippery hole I'd just jumped into mouth first! "Yes, control, over, road accident you say, over, people injured, maybe trapped, over, better get there as fast as I can over", I ranted glibly as I looked for the way out.

Fortunately, my stunned, hushed, audience seemed to believe the self instigated communiqué and I made my exit stage left a là Basil Fawlty. More by luck than judgement, I chose the correct, main door of the shop, that took me into the safety of a dark street illuminated, bustling High Street full of busy shoppers and not Audrey's storage cupboard.

As I walked at a brisk pace away from Audrey's I chastised myself for the wicked and rude faux pas. I couldn't believe how stupid I'd been. The poor woman had come into the florists to order a wreath for her departed sister. I learned a valuable lesson from it though, boy did I learn from it. The famous adage about speaking when you are spoken to is a good one. I remember the very next time I related this incident was the second time I made an unforgettable faux pas!

It was a very hot afternoon and I was helping police the Sandwell Show at Dartmouth Park, West Bromwich. A group of us were having a drinks break in the back of a police carrier and a probationary constable was asking what folks most embarrassing moments were. The conversation eventually got around to witness statements and it transpired that this young officer had taken a statement from a witness where the witness had vividly explained a situation in just a phrase he'd used. It was that 'memorable', that I cannot remember what this 'vivid' phrase had been. Other than to say that I shared with that small group of officers in the back of that carrier, my most vivid statement.

I had not long been in the job when as a foot patrol officer I was sent to assist a couple of traffic officers dealing with a fatal road traffic accident, where an inebriated middle aged Asian male had alighted from a West Midlands Travel Bus on the main drag in a busy town centre shopping area, stumbled as he got off, fell under the front nearside wheel of the vehicle and was crushed to death. One of the scruffies (traffic motorcyclists) asked me to take a statement from one of the witnesses travelling on the Bus. This woman had been sitting on the lower deck, on the long seat situated on the offside of the vehicle behind the drivers compartment, just before the stairs, facing the nearside pavement. She saw the Asian male, a man in his late thirties, make his way down the stairs and stagger past her along the centre aisle toward the automated exit door at the front nearside lower corner of the vehicle, opposite the driver. She stated that he looked appeared a little the worse for wear and could smell 'drink' on him and his clothing.

The man was the only person alighting at that stop. No one got on at that request stage. She saw the man stumble slightly to the left of the door as the automatic doors pssssst shut. It was then that she saw the long seat opposite her, not being utilised by passengers and under which is located the vehicles huge front nearside wheel, rise slightly, and then fall back into the gutter as it drove over some kind of obstacle. It was then that the witness uttered the phrase, "I saw the mans brains shoot across the pavement like pips out of an orange."

My tiny audience in the rear of the van where as stunned as you are now. To top it all, Daz, a young Sikh officer, who had been a colleague of mine for quite a few years by then, says straight away, "Bry, that was my Dad."

I was flabbergasted, surprised and embarrassed. I couldn't believe my ears and thought Daz was joking. What are the chances, statistically of that happening for a start? He wasn't joking. I thought, how surprising it was for him to say that in front of other officers! Perhaps later, when we were alone, yes, he might have told me, but no, he told us all there and then. I was then and was for quite some time afterwards, embarrassed that I shared the tale with anyone, let alone a member of the poor chaps family. With time, I have thought it out as another grand example in life of always being aware of other peoples feelings and trying to glean as many details about a situation as possible before opening the orifice under my nose.

Coppers are masters of putting their foot in it. I accompanied one young probationer, who told a newly made widow at the front door that her husband had been fatally injured and when asked to elaborate, had explained that their he was now at the local general hospital so he was in good hands and had a very good chance of recovery, thanks to the advances in medical science! I remember quickly taking that particular lad to one side and explaining exactly what 'fatal' meant.

One of the best deliberate faux pas I ever heard was by a fellow PC Santorini, a lad of obvious Italian decent, who hailed from the Black Country's capital, Dudley! Santo and I were on nights in a marked panda driving around the mainly industrial area of Black Patch in Smethwick, when on some waste land we saw a small fire. Deciding to stretch our legs moreover find a god excuse to have a fag, we parked the car up and walked over to the small bonfire. As we got closer it was obvious that there was a human figure or mannequin at the centre of the flames. Santo ran back to the car and grabbed the fire extinguisher from footwell in the police vehicle. I could see that it was a human body, which sadly, was well beyond recovery. He or she had been there for some time and was badly decayed at the extremities. Santo, put out the remaining embers and we of course called it in. Before long there was the usual 'circus' of busy police staff. A hive of activity at and on the approach to the crime scene, with the arrival of numerous detectives, scenes of crime officers, dog men, pathologists and so on. Accompanied by the drones of the generators powering the temporary spotlights and small inflatable tent now protected the area.

The body was that of a young oriental male and was obviously not easy on the eyes. However, the most notable items in close vicinity of the unfortunate victim was, what appeared to be a perfect circle of silver and copper coins next to the deceased. The senior officers at the job discussing tentatively the possibility of a triad or organised crime connection.

That was when Santo, a Dudley kid remember and renowned for his dry sense of humour, points towards the enigmatic circle of small change and stated, in quite a matter of fact sort of way. "You know what that is don't you?".

It goes without saying that he immediately gained the full attention of everyone there, including the Detective Chief Inspector Ron Pimblett, who not only had been disturbed from a very deep and enjoyable repose but now stood in the middle of a piece of waste ground Black Patch at three in the morning, trembling, with only his three three-quarter length black Gannex obscuring his favourite Paddington Bear pyjamas. Everyone had their eyes and their attention now firmly fixed on Santo, I think even the dead bloke was waiting for Santo's enlightening insight into the mystery.

"Forty-nine pence". He said, straight faced.

That was the first time I'd ever seen a twenty-seven stone unfit, senior detective chase a uniformed constable across a crime scene, with intent to commit serious physical damage. I think Santo is still running now!

One foot in mouth moment that I always recollect is the day the new admin girl, Julie Howells, had been shown around the police station and by lunch time may well have wondered what kind of organisation she'd joined. For during our break in the TV Room, my shift oppo,

Bob 'Gobbo' Platt was devouring a huge mixed kebab and chips, when someone from the shift clocks that the new girl is in the corridor, by the open TV Room door and says something to the effect of, "I like the new girl thats started this morning, whats her name?" Another member of the shift blurts out, "Joan Howells." To which Gobbo with a mouthful of kebab says, "I bet she does!" Within plain sound and hearing of the young woman. I looked accusingly at my partner and said, "Bob, that's her in the corridor", to which of course he simply shrugged his shoulders, grinned, winked and finished his kebab.

Another notable, foot in mouth moment I can recall was one day when I was accompanying Martyn Flannery, I think I've mentioned Mart before in other stories, he was at the time the subdivisional Neighbourhood Watch Officer but I'd known and worked with him for donkeys's years. Martyn, a very experienced officer on the streets and a past master of the faux pas. On this particular day I accompanied him to a local co-ordinators address to deliver some Neighbourhood Watch literature.

After initially meeting all co-ordinators at the very well attended set up evenings that Martyn would host at a local school or church hall. Martyn would continue to stay in touch with them by communicating weekly by way of his office police landline (a telephone to you). When he got the chance to nip out and see one of them, he'd jump at it, as all these pro-police people would do a Test Match special on him, supplying him with gallons of tea and copious amounts of cake or biscuits. This particular co-ordinator lived in a mid terraced block of townhouses that had a long narrow pathway leading up to her doorway. Mart, had already rung the ladies doorbell and I was half way to the door carrying the said box of Neighbourhood Watch bumph. A dark mahogany shaded, tight permed, bespectacled, red faced, extremely rotund, possibly even perfectly round white lady, in her mid to late forties, wearing large gold coloured earrings and a humongously loose fitting turquoise patterned shell suit with blue trainers, flung open the door and in an over familiar tone said, "Hi Martyn, long time no see." It was a this nanosecond in time that Martyn Flannery entered the F.I.M. (Foot In Mouth) zone, he smiled an embarrassingly polite but cheesy smile and in a matter of fact way said, "Hi Wendy, Whens it due then?" Looking down at the vast expanse hung roughly between the bottom of her sagging breasts and then unceremoniously over the top of her elasticated jogging bottoms. Without a moments hesitation she innocently retorted, "Whens what due Martyn?"

I was immediately hit for six. I dropped the box of literature and had to swivel around on the back of my heels Anton Du Beke-like to conceal the fact that I had immediately got a fit of the giggles, so much so that I could feel the content of my nasal passages trying to force its way out! I ran to the car and was leaning with one arm on the cars rear wing for support as I bent over appearing to be vomiting into the street. I coughed and spluttered for air whilst at the same time laughing uncontrollably. So strongly, that tears were cascading down my face. How embarrassing, I thought, I was here at the FIM zone again. But this time as a sort of unwilling victim. Lets face it, I've got form for getting involved in embarrassing moments. Luckily for Martyn, it gave him the opportunity to rush away from the co-ordinators doorstep and to my aid, to render roadside assistance, like the RAC as it were. Wrestling me into the front passenger seat, he then made his way around to the drivers side of the car, shouting over to the co-ordinator as he did so, "Bryan's having one of his asthma attacks. I'll get him back to the office. His inhaler is in his desk drawer. Sorry Mrs ... I'll give you a bell later on." I sat with my head in my hands, shoulders rocking, literally sobbing with mirth. We got a few streets away and Martyn pulled into the side of the road. He turned towards me with a serious face of fury, obviously, intending to issue a bollocking. This was difficult at the best of times, ask any of the hundreds of gaffers I've had over the years! His mistake was he looked me straight in the eye. I saw his light, pale skinned, freckled face turn from that of a very serious look to a slight smile, he said, "Its your fault, you dickhead, if you hadn't started laughi" He couldn't finish the sentence. Martyn's smile became a grin, then the grin became absolute uncontrolled laughter! It was a brilliant F.I.M. moment between two mates. You can't buy that can you? With not a pint of beer in sight. Needless to say, the woman wasn't pregnant, she was just (very)full of life's rich rewards. I don't know if Martyn ever went back to that address. I know I didn't.

Speaking of Anton du Beke, did you know his real name is Tony Beak? I don't suppose it sounds the same on BBC, the announcer saying, "Now its time for celebrity Saturday night ball room dancing with Bruce Johnson and Tony Beak!" It doesn't sound the same. I think you can guess who Brucie Johnson is can't you? All right my loves, Nice to see you to see you....

'I curse you'.....

THE AMAZING SAGA
OF SOLOMON JERVOISE
GOMMORRAH

I'd been in the police about 12 months and had been 'Independent' (the term for walking the beat alone, without being wet nursed) for about 7 months. One afternoon, on late shift, I receive a radio message to return to the station to deal with a gentleman in the front office reporting an assault.

A local tatter (Rag and Bone Man) had been driving his hoss 'n cart past the old deserted ambulance station in Ross Street, Blackheath, and was making his way back to his yard in Rowley Regis, when he was hit on the head by a missile, viz, a piece of sharp metal (allegedly) thrown from the flat roof of the ambulance station by one of a group of boys who were on the roof playing 'tracking' (A form of the game hide and seek), intriguing eh?

The scrap gentleman was quite badly cut on the top of his balding pate. So, after being sent by the quick thinking office PC on the early turn due to finish shortly, to get it treated at the local Russell's Hall Hospital, the tatter, (lets call him Mr Trotter) arrived back at the station to report the matter to the young PC Connor. The main problem, identified at the onset even by me, the most green of sprogs, was one of communication. Mr Trotter unfortunately was encumbered with a hare lip, or cleft pallete to give it its proper name, where his upper lip had been congenitally divided into two parts only to be partially reunited by surgery, causing him an embarrassing speech impediment that of course he had learned to cope with. Luckily for me, at the time of the assault he was accompanied by his young teenage assistant, who had not only 'gazelle like' chased the group of miscreants from the roof, but had managed to catch hold of two of them, obtaining one of their names by confiscating his West Midlands Travel bus pass, that didn't just have his name but also had his photograph!

Clifford, the tatters mate, a tall gangly youth who was the spitting image of a young spotty Peter Crouch, grinned broadly, exposing a large gap where his front teeth used to be, as he handed me the confiscated bus pass, stating, "You'll get both on 'em from that officer, as I think them's twins like". "Doppelgangers, eh?" I said. "No, Identical twins officer" said the misunderstanding Clifford who grinned proudly as I praised him for his detection skills and urged him to take the entrance test for joining the police. "My future's with my uncle Terry in tat," replied the young retriever, who was able to provide me with enough information for a witness statement. I told his uncle Terry (the Injured Party) that I would come and visit him at home for his statement.

PC Les Sculthorpe a very gregarious Black Country bobbie with a wickedly sarcastic sense of humour, accompanied me to the scrap yard in Rowley Regis the following day to obtain a full and in-depth statement from Mr Terry Trotter. Mr Trotter's 'office' was also his front room. Mrs Trotter went off to brew the tea as we made ourselves comfortable in the very cluttered living room.

It was a contemporary mish mash of useless items, really it was other people's garbage! Old broken lampshades, gramophone players, ancient vacuum cleaners, tainted bird cages, ageing sewing machines, wooden cased televisions, bookcases, electric fans, rolled-up rugs, boxes of assorted paper back and hard backed books, a badly stuffed ram, with only one horn in the middle of its head, standing over a small heap of leaking sawdust stared at us both with a very bewildered look on its face from a huge dusty glass case. In the bay window was a white baby grand piano, which took up a third of the room. On top of the piano was Mr Trotter's office paperwork, a black Bakelite telephone, a huge grubby well thumbed rolodex and a genuine, very revealing, 1978 Pirelli calendar. On the walls were old dusty, faded, framed oil and watercolour paintings of mainly lakeland scenery. From the ceiling hung a very insecure blinking fluorescent strip light that looked as out of place as the stuffed ram. It was bizarre, like visiting the Black Country version of Harold Steptoe's front room. A large hot coal fire roared in the hearth and in front of it lay an old white (formerly golden) Labrador Retriever Dog that snored loudly, slightly raising his rump to emit sporadic pungent farts in our general direction as he snuggled closer to the heat source.

As Mr Trotter rolled another cigarette in the Rizla fag machine on his lap, Scully asked him the mundane stuff like 'full name please?', 'occupation?', 'date of birth?'. At any other time this pre-requisite to the obtaining of a witness statement would be quite uneventful. But through the lips of Mr Trotter, every word created a titter from both protectors of justice. "Name?" "Troughpher, pernouhsed Troughpher, T.R.O.T.T.E.R. Troughpher!" "Christian Name Scully asked?" "Perrie". "What?" Said Scully, "Perrie! Perrie Troughpher. Perrie, fought for Perranthce are you beff!" "Oh,Terry short for Terrence?" I interjected in sluggish apprehension. "Yeattttthhhh" replied Terry infuriatingly, raising his eyes toward the ceiling as he spoke, whilst under his breath (so as not to cause offence) adding the short anglo saxon phrase, "Puffin' thwath." Fighting back the titters I carried on scribing as poor Scully tried to ascertain the actual location of the incident.

"Where were you assaulted?" "Here", said Terry, pointing to an obvious grubby bandage wrapped and safety pinned around his head. "No, where were you, er, geographically when you were assaulted?" asked Scully. "On my Sephon handth Carthe in Both Beat, Blaggheef", Terry hurriedly opening a local A to Z and pointed to Ross Street, Blackheath. We ascertained that he was driving his horse and cart along Ross Street with his assistant Gliffherd (Clifford) and that Gliffherd lived in Bimblebill Bode, Smebbick (Thimblemill Road, Smethwick) just down from the Bimblebill Bublick Owse. It went down hill from there!

From the outset Mr Trotter spoke the Queens Anglo Saxon quite freely, if you get my drift. The problem was trying to understand what he was saying without smiling let alone laughing right out loud. Thankfully, I did the scribing for the statement as Scully asked the questions.

When I got to the main part of the statement, covering his assault, Mr Trotter's venomous anger had reached fever pitch and to the close of every sentence he would add his own short burst of swear words, for example, He would add the epithet, "Puppin Bapsterds (No translation available!)". OK, yes, it's funny, but spare a thought for the poor officer having to write this soliloquy down, sitting in PC Sculthorpe's eyeline as he, unbeknown to poor Mr Trotter was pulling faces trying to extract a laugh from me. Everytime Mr Trotter uttered a word I was, I will admit, in my mind, rolling round on the floor laughing out loud with tears of joy cascading down my rosy cheeks. But on the outside I was the model professional, we Brits are like that, never wanting to cause offence to anyone, especially in their own home, so inwardly I have literally fallen apart but the interesting humorous paradox is on the outside I was the caring professional trying desperately not to smile in the presence of Mr Trotter.

At this stage Mrs Trotter, a small, frail, demure middle aged lady, who dressed older than her years, entered the room with a tray containing a hot pot of tea, some cups and saucers and a small plate of Jammie Dodgers. Her curler covered grey hair was hidden by a headscarf that curiously had a picture of Blackpool Tower on it. She was accompanied by an old grey (once golden) Labrador dog. The dog slowly walked around 'his' visitors, eyeing them up, sniffed them in the crotch, circumspectly looked up at each one, still sniffing them, then slumped himself in front of the old fashioned wood stove that was remarkably hot and was blazing away. The hound immediately started to quite rapidly knock out a loud snoring noise. Scully, a dog lover, sitting only feet away from the old slumbering growler, that by this time was also knocking out the odd, 'silent but deadly' that wafted across the room directly towards my nostrils, was sitting on the edge of a large leather arm chair, only about 12 inches off the floor, so he was sort of squatting precariously on the front edge of the seat. The dog looked up at him and went towards him, presumably for another sniff of his crotch. Misreading this approach as a sign of friendship, Scully reached out his right hand to stroke the dog, at the same time saying in a low friendly tone, "Hello mate." Mr Trotter shrieks, "Bo! Stoff! Beeve him abome. He'll abb yer." Which roughly translated would read; 'Officer, the animal is not a pet, he's a security guard dog for my scrap yard. He's extremely ferocious, not very people-friendly and likes the taste of human flesh, that of young masculine copper's especially'. This is of course a rough translation but I think you get the point. Scully certainly did! The sharp points of the canine incisors, that is, the friendly pooch, was anything but burying his teeth deep into the thick blue serge of Scully's tunic sleeve, easily ripping it apart with a loud ripping sound whilst simultaneously swiftly and violently shaking his head from side to side, as if to kill his prey, as it were. Like a gun dog instinctively does with any quarry it gets it fangs into. Scully's arm being shook around like a long narrow serge bean bag as he tried to pull safely away from the rabid hound. Scully's face was a picture. He went white with his eyes standing out on stalks! The geriatric growler tore virtually the whole of Scully's tunic arm off! This was the green light I required to enable me to release my restrained hilarity - I began to uncontrollably laugh out loud. Raising my eyebrows towards Scully with a sort of, 'It xxxxxxx serves you right' expression on my self-satisfied fizzog.

Now reader, you think that is bizarre, You have heard nothing yet and I swear its all true and remember, I'm a copper, coppers don't lie, do they? If they do their noses grow! The tatter's wife hears the commotion and re-enters the room with a large leather belt in her hand. She walked calmly over to the dog, who was still holding the 'dead' tunic sleeve tightly in his victorious jaws and proceeded to inaccurately aim a kick towards the pooch and his guild halls (The testicular region that is). This resulted in the beast releasing his catch and scuttling out of the room at a fast rate of knots to avoid a scolding, yelping loudly as if apologising, his stiff motionless brush like tail folded firmly between his briskly pumping hind quarters as he ran like the wind! Mrs Trotter commenced pouring the hot steaming tea from the pot as if nothing untoward had happened. So we carried on taking the statement from Mr Trotter in the same 'surreal' vein.

I finally obtained a witness statement from the Injured Party. In the same standard way that all probationers have been instructed to collect the recollections of eye witnesses of police related incidents for over a century of policing in Britain for time immemorial. Remembering that the basic phrase for taking witness statements went thus, I Was, I Saw, I Did. At a certain time,day, date the statement taker (always written the first person) was at whatever location, for whatever reason, doing whatever act they were doing. You would then record whatever they 'saw' and what they 'did' as a result of what they witnessed! Sounds simple and if you try to keep it simple, it is just that, simple!

It transpired that on the specific Time/Day/Date in question the unfortunate Mr Trotter, in company with his young assistant Clifford had been 'tatting' for second hand goods in and around the Rowley area and were riding the horse drawn cart (Like Albert Steptoe) along the road making their way back towards Mr T's scrap yard in Blackheath along Ross Street, when a small metallic 'missile' was projected from the roof of the old flat roofed ambulance station, Striking and badly cutting Mr Trotter on the head. The piece of metal had been thrown deliberately at him by one of a large group of young lads who were taking part in a game of 'Trackin' (Tracking was a team game not dissimilar to Hide and Seek where your caught team mates would be held in a 'den' and could only be freed by a fellow team member, still at liberty, who had managed to evade the clutches of your opposition searchers) on the flat roof of the old, derelict, two storey, Victorian building. At seeing the missile reach its intended victim so accurately the group of miscreants scattered and ran away from the building in all directions. Clifford chased and caught one of the group, making a 'citizens arrest'. Remarkably unlucky for this 'suspect' was that at the time he had his West Midlands

Travel bus pass, containing his photograph, in his pocket, which Clifford confiscated in the name of justice! The said document gave the young Sherlock Connor his first lead!

With my still fresh witness statement in hand I ventured out into the world of criminal investigation. I interviewed the suspect or 'Bipple Basberb' as Mr Trotter put it, that Clifford had apprehended in the presence of his parents, let's call him 'Malcolm', but his actual name was Dwayne! Dwayne's parents were remarkably normal Black Country folk and upon hearing their son, naturally, denying all knowledge of even existing, let alone, being anywhere near the old ambulance station at the time of the assault, his dad, persuaded him to tell the police officers everything that had gone on! Which he did! With no requirement for the wrack, knuckle dusters, no sleep depravation....nothing! It transpired that he was playing 'tracking' on the roof with a cast of thousands of his mates and proceeded to supply me with a long list of their names and addresses...numbering about twenty of his cohorts!

I eventually, after numerous enquiries, believe me they were numerous, managed to interview all the lads who had been trackin' on the roof that afternoon during the summer holidays, very time consuming but a great way of learning how systematic the investigation process can be. Every one of the youths I saw, in company with their parents, said that the lad responsible for throwing the lump of metal from the roof at Mr Trotter was a young Dudley lad by the name of Solomon Gammorrah. All the youths I had interviewed were all told that the facts would be reported & that they may be summonsed for any offences disclosed. They were all duly told to return on bail pending a decision on what judicial action would be taken by the Crown Prosecution Service.

So into her Majesty's Custody came the young 13 year old Solomon J Gommorrah, in company with his genuinely dutiful parents. Solomon was what would now be classed as a 'Special Needs' child. Always getting into trouble with teaching staff at his local comprehensive school, with his peers and with neighbours. Four foot six inches tall, but a bonnie lad, as my Auntie Brenda Crosby would have said (he was a stocky barrel), very easily led and very much the kind of lad who carried out 'dares' if provoked by his contemporaries to win their friendship. Unfortunately these goaded challenges usually led Solomon into breaking the law, stealing, damaging public or private property or more commonly fighting (more like bullying) other youths at the behest of his acquaintances.

Mr and Mrs Gammorrah were both in their mid to late fifties and had obviously had Solomon late in life. God Fearing, Born Again Christians, these proud West Indian émigrés were not only adamant that their son was innocent, but that he did not require a solicitor to be present during his interview, as he was not guilty of any misconduct. Solomon had by this time been interviewed by the police on numerous occasions for numerous reasons and on each occasion his parents had dutifully and respectfully attended the police station, each time pleading with the authorities to be lenient with their blameless and innocent son who was of course always 'unwittingly' involved with the wrong crowd of youths who had led him astray.

In spite of the overwhelming evidence I had already amassed demonstrating Solomon's guilt, he denied the personal accusations in the presence of his humiliated protectors just as he always had, blaming several of the other youths for the assault. The difference on this occasion was that my Inspector decided that because all were denying the offence, no one could be cautioned for the offence and so I would have to compile a report for the Crown Prosecution service to decide on how to proceed with Mr Trotter's alleged attackers.

The decision came back. Charge Solomon Gammorrah with assault and take no action against the other 'trackers'. In fact, their statements taken under caution would now be used as Section Nine witness statements in the Prosecution Case against Solomon Jervoise GOMMORRAH!

Almost twelve months to the day that Mr Trotter had been assaulted the cast of a thousand trackers all re-assembled to discuss the incident again. This time at Old Hill Juvenile Court, Cradley Heath, a relatively small assembly room next to the main courtroom in the small homely Black Country town. The court room was packed to the rafters full of witnesses along with their collective parents or legal guardians! The Three Magistrates sat at the small front table, as did the Prosecuting and the Defence Solicitors, Probation Officers and Social Workers. A freshly bathed Injured Party (Terry Trotter) sat, front row centre, wearing the suit reeking of moth balls, that he was either probably married or de-mobbed in, sitting appropriately next to the woman he bought the suit for, minus the hair net & curlers, joined by the original 'arresting officer,' Clifford and his girlfriend. The accused sat in between Mr and Mrs Gammorrah, the trio dressed in Sunday best. Solly, paradoxically, glancing over his shoulder to ingenuously smirk and pull faces at his 'so-called' friends and acquaintances, the very people who were about to bear very negative and damning witness against him in an assault trial at a public court. Ah, Ignorance is bliss some would say!

After hearing so many of these juvenile 'witnesses' perform their under rehearsed and nervously performed 'tale' in the dock, one after the other retelling the same damning and somewhat unconvincing story that Solomon Gammorrah, alone, picked up that small piece of metal, boasted openly that he could accurately hit a moving target from a distance of fifty feet or more and then, totally unprovoked (of course), formed the intention to senselessly lob it at the head of the unfortunate objective, the modern day Steptoe, splitting the head open of same! At that time, I don't think Solomon Gammorrah could have even fastened a pair of shoelaces by himself, let alone hatch a plan to assault a passing Tat man driving an 'Oss and Cart. In a nutshell, Solomon's public defence solicitor went through the judicial motions, as did the prosecution solicitor and the other social 'professionals' employed by the state to ensure justice for all the vulnerable Solomon's of this world. The Magistrates seemed also on this occasion to have decided that this was a situation where one boy had denied an offence and cried 'Wolf' or rather denied all knowledge just that once too often! All attendees had decided that there was sufficient 'independent' evidence to convict Solomon and invoke a custodial sentence (if you call the testimony of approximately a dozen badly rehearsed street kids' interpretation of events, accurate evidence). At one stage, a nine year old 'witness', lets call him 'Liam' (you can always replace the 'm' with an 'r') stands in the witness box. Well I think he was standing, but you couldn't tell as you could only see the crown of his head above the front carved wood facade of the witness box. In a high, squeaky, unbroken, nervously shaky boy soprano voice, this scruffily dressed, red headed, speckledy faced, recently scrubbed up angel, promised the court that he would tell the truth, the whole truth and nothing but the truth. Truth? This was a nine year old street urchin from a lower working class West Midlands council estate, who, if he found a crisp new £5 note in the street would do exactly what any normal nine year old council estate child would do with a found £5 note . Spend it on fags and sweets!

The prosecution solicitor looked without purpose toward the void from where the squeaky voice had emanated and after confirming that Liam and Co, including Solomon where actually on the roof that afternoon, asked Liam who had thrown the piece of metal at Mr Trotter. Liam whispered, "Solomon Gammorrah did it" pointing a small right handed index finger, wrapped in a grubby blue sticking plaster, in the direction of the accused. At that Mrs Gammorrah jumped to her feet and stormed up to Liam in the box, pointed her right(eous) index finger accusingly and shouted at the top of her voice like a modern day american television evangelist performing a kind of judicial exorcism , "I curse you, in the name of Jesus!" she ranted in a strong Caribbean patois accent. She repeatedly danced around the witness box like a cross between a professional boxer and a voodoo dancer, reproachfully pointing at the diminutive, petrified, copper headed witness, cursing him, in the name of our Lord and Saviour! I, like everyone else was totally shocked at this critical religious outburst.   The senior magistrate, in the centre of the judicial trinity (how apt) told the magistrates clerk taking notes to strike that remark from the official records and beckoned me to remove Mrs Gammorrah from the room, which I did, amid the obvious pandemonium from bemused court staff and parents of the bands of witnesses. I asked the seemingly hen pecked Mr Gammorrah to climb out from under his wife's thumb and calm her down. The female messenger of the Almighty eventually condescended to leave the room and the case was restarted.   Mrs Gammorrah still ranting her Old Testament Fire and Retribution on a terrified nine year old Black Country child. The Pros Sol (Prosecuting Solicitor) continued the cross examination of the now calmed copper pate. Having confirmed who had thrown the missile from the roof of the ambulance station he asked the twitching red dome, "What did Solomon Gammorrah do then? " After a pregnant pause the Ginger cranium aimed its reply towards the learned enquirer, again in a squeaky young

Black Country accent announced, "Solly laughed his Bollocks Off Sir!" The court erupted into hoots of laughter. It was my first not-guilty trial, bear in mind. Where all not-guilty trials like this I thought? Like a cross between a Billy Graham Evangelical Crusade, an episode of Jerry Springer, a Cattle Market and a Punch and Judy Show? Back through the double swing doors rushes the blinkered light heavyweight from the Old Testament stable, Mrs Gammorrah. Enormously enraged and ranting piercingly at the top of her voice that Jesus (and more importantly, his Dad) would castigate all those other wicked young boys from the rooftop incident who were all lying to negatively influence the magistrates' view of her pampered offspring's leading part in the event. She seemed to be doing a brilliant job doing exactly that herself! The senior magistrate looked straight at me and boomed across the court, "Officer, remove that woman from these proceedings". He then repeatedly shouted above Mrs Gammorrah's unwarranted biblical curses from the almighty that she was very much in danger of losing her own liberty and being arrested for contempt of court! Mrs Gammorrah, eyes now tightly clamped shut, was visibly shaking, both arms stretched skyward, praying aloud (an independent observer may have described it as ranting and raving) in the centre of the room surrounded by the heathen unbelieving, mocking parents and guardians of the lying witnesses, who found her antics embarrassingly hilarious. Fanatically, like a television evangelist on crack, she screeched at the top of her voice pointing at son Solomon, who seems bemused at her actions, as she literally repeatedly blurted out, " I am FREE....I am FREE ...... Jesus Christ, Lard God Almighty I am FREE, Lard, give me the righteous strength to assist my precious child, Oh Mighty Jesus Christ Lard, help me in my time of need!" During this holy tirade I managed to persuade the Pork Pie hatted

135

Mr Gammorrah to physically carry his harridan of a wife out of the proceedings. I think even he knew that his wife's actions might not be seen in a positive light with regard to his son Solomon receiving some sort of fair justice from their worships! I remained outside with Mr & Mrs G and it took quite some time to calm Mrs Gommorrah down enough to go back into the court room again, where proceedings by then, had got back to some modicum of order. We entered the 'ring' in time to hear the Magistrates Clerk announcing to the court that the Magistrates had found the case against Solomon Gammorrah 'Proved'. Everything was fine - no pandemonium....and the Social Workers and Probation Officers started to discuss young Solomon's very near future, if you get my drift. Everything was fine that was until Mrs Gammorrah asked me to explain what was currently happening! It took some time but as I did so, the dimly lit bulb in her head gradually came on to full beam and we experienced the second coming & the unholy pandemonium returned to the proceedings!

It was then that the 'cursed' child's Dad went straight up to the Magistrates and smacking their highly polished desk with his clenched fist demanded that the biblical curse from the almighty rendered by Mrs Gammorrah be lifted immediately or have her arrested. Amid this chaos, the Magistrates Clerk brought a swift end to proceedings and the courtroom was cleared in seconds, leaving Mrs Gammorrah to chastise only Solomon and her long suffering hubby, as they were the only people left to listen to her religious dogmatic diarrhoea. I spoke to the cursed victim's parents and explained that as the case had been proved against Solomon, it would make all christian curses from his lovely mater null and void, but that if they noticed that their son had any peculiarities in the near future that they should ignore the 'heathen' police station and take him straight to the local vicar to let the professionals deal with it. I think Mrs Gammorrah, that perfect example of christian tolerance is still outside the Courts now, complaining her sons innocence in the middle of the car park built on the location of Old Hill courts that were torn down nearly twenty years ago! So, a local bully, torment, thief and general anti social browbeating yoblet, aka Solomon Gammorrah, was sent away to a Youth Detention Centre in Mid Wales where he would learn new things, like, reading Janet and John, breaking into estate cars and How to improve your fraudulent IT skills. The whole of Sandwell, except Mrs Gammorrah, sighed an extremely huge sigh of relief as he was (alas only temporarily) taken out of general circulation. But it doesn't end there. A few months later I get to work one Sunday morning to be informed in the local briefing that one, Solomon Jervoise Gommorrah had escaped from the Detention Centre in Caerwys or whatever. Escaped meaning that he walked off, through the unlocked main gate of the underesourced Home Office holiday village in Cymru.

OK, so you are a desperate young escaped fugitive convict on the run from Wales. Where do you go? St Tropez, Costa Del Sol, Montenegro, Rio de Janeiro? No, Solomon runs straight to his mum and dad's upper storey council three bedroomed maisonette in the Black Country of course. When I visit the address with my oppo Doug Watson to check to see if Solomon has arrived home yet, we are left waiting on the first floor landing for an inordinate amount of time, even for Mrs G. Eventually, the door opens and there is Mrs Gammorrah, who is dressed in her Sunday best ready for church. She looks nervous and is shocked to see that the officer they sent to do the 'routine' check happens to be yours truly. The officer responsible for sending her 'innocent' young son away to the Godless land of the Druids.

She didn't invite us in and was very defensive, which of course was not surprising but she did seem very nervous at my presence and left the door ajar, looking through the four inch crack in the closed doorway. Normally, she'd be shouting at me, nose to nose as it were. I asked if Doug and I could come in. Strangely, she didn't ask why. She just said "No, stay at the door". I explained that her precious Solomon had done a runner from the Welsh Detention Centre and that as a matter of course Doug and I would have to check the address to see if Solomon was there, as we were worried about his safety. After reiterating that she was a Born Again God fearing woman she quite rightly stated that Solomon would be stupid to do that and I readily agreed. But said, just for the record you understand, that my gaffers would check that I had done my job properly, unless she had something to hide that is. That did it, the Christianity reared its head. "I'm a born again christian God fearin' woman, I don't lie officer." Again, she reverted to form, repeating the phrase, "I am FREE Jesus Christ, Lard God Almighty, please give me the holy strength, Oh Mighty Jesus Christ Lard,help Me!" I whispered to Dougie, "How do know when a Born Again Christian is lying to you Doug?" "I dunno," he says. "Their lips move!" I said. Mrs G, who you would have thought would take umbrage to my remark embarrassingly condescends to let us stand in the hallway of 'chez Gommorrah'. An extremely nervous Mr Gommorrah, still wearing his pork pie hat, asked us if we wanted a cup of tea. I said, "Thanks, but I get the impression you and your lady wife want us to get going as soon as possible. A nervous Mrs G said, "We will be late for church. As you can see Solomon is not here." It was then that I clocked an inordinately large lump underneath the coats hung on the rack in the very narrow hallway of the property. I leaned against the coats as we carried on small talk with the Gammorrah's. It was obvious that there was someone hiding under these coats. That someone was holding onto the wall hooks of the rack but had bent their knees raising their lower limbs up under the bottom edge of the hanging coats! Of course you know who it was. I then noticed a grubby Puffer type coat, popular with teenagers at the time, hanging on the coat rack. I asked Mrs Gammorrah, "Is that Solomon's coat?" She replied, "No, he's in Wales serving his sentence officer, as God is my witness that is my husbands coat". I narrowed my eyes, looked at her sceptically and said to her "Mrs G, being a Born Again lady you wouldn't lie to me, would you?" "Of course not", came the worried reply. "Do you know where Solomon really is Mrs Gommorrah?" "No, as Jesus Christ is my witness". Looking at a very guilty looking Mr G, I said, "I can feel a body under these coats Mr Gammorrah" and as I leaned on the lump with a bit of weight I heard a slight 'Humpff' sound coming from under the coats hanging on the rack. I wink at Doug and say to the Gammorrahs, "You don't want to be late for church, I'll pass Mr Gammorrah his coat". She replies, "Thank you PC Connor, he's not wearing that coat today, he doesn't don't need it". I removed the three-quarter length gents overcoat from the hanger and passed it over to Mrs Gammorrah. Only to reveal a doubled up, fugitive, hanging onto the coat hangers for grim death. Still dressed in the Home Office Bib and Brace denim uniform that he'd been issued by the staff at the Welsh Detention Centre. I shouted loudly, " Solomon!" We were just talking about you sunshine, but of course, you heard every word didn't you!" I looked at the Bad Samaritan, the shamed Mrs Gammorrah, again the not so innocent victim of her son's stupidity, and said to the mendacious follower of her creator, "Mrs Gammorrah, 'There are two paths you can go by your sons or your makers, it is truly a miracle, we talk of the beelzebub and he appears! Say bye bye to your mummy Solomon." Solomon was taken straight to Piddock Road, with the quieter parent in tow, awaiting a car from the Probation Service to take him back to the Detention Centre. It was then that young Solomon told me he was going to kill me. Do you know, I have received numerous threats from disgruntled customers (offenders) over my thirty years of police service but you could see in Solomon's eyes that he meant what he said. I told him that his mum wouldn't like him talking like that. He was definitely an odd fish and it wasn't the last time our paths would cross. Solly went off to serve the remainder of his Welsh condemnation but I did cross swords with Solomon again, five years later. When he tried to kill me!

I was still a permanent beat officer on Cape Hill, Smethwick with my partner Dougie Watson. Our Sergeant at the time was Sergeant Roy Mantle. Roy called us into the office and told us that the BBC were to film a drama exploring themes of race, gender, nationality, and sexuality against the backdrop of the Irish Troubles in the Windmill Lane area of Smethwick, where apparently one of the local blocks of flats was an exact copy of the Divis flats in Northern Ireland. Among the actors in the production was Michael Kitchen the English actor best known for his role as ITV Television's Detective Chief Superintendent Foyle in Foyle's War. An enjoyable enough programme, which incredulously depicts a Police Chief Superintendent actually performing operational police work, albeit in the early 1940's. Now that really is a work of fiction! Most very senior detectives nowadays couldn't detect a fart in a colander.

The Beeb asked for Trafalgar Road, Smethwick to be closed for filming the entrance to the flats in Windmill Lane. Dougie Watson and me were to 'police' the closed off street, keeping back the vast hordes of film buffs that just might turn up on this bitterly cold, dark, winters evening in Cape Hill to watch the production team as they beavered away to produce more chewing gum for the eyes of the watching, licence paying masses, hungry for culture.

Problem was that in the preceding days to 'shooting', word had got around the streets and the majority of the locals believed that they were about to get a visit from the American actor Michael Keaton. Known for his early comedic roles in films such as Night Shift & Beetlejuice, and more to the taste of the resident film fans, his still then quite recent portrayal of the famous comic book superhero co-created by artist Bob Kane and writer Bill Finger, Batman in the two Tim Burton directed feature films of the late eighties.

So by the time Dougie and me arrive at the location in Trafalgar Road, by Ron Tibbetts' Taxi Cab office, where the BBC crew were setting up their filming equipment, there are about a thousand, I'm not exaggerating, well behaved, but noisy, Batman groupies, gathered on the pavement, some even dressed as the Caped Crusader, eagerly awaiting the famous Hollywood luminary. When Dougie and me tried to enlighten these excited aficionada that it was Michael Kitchen, that's Kitchen, as in a room or part of a room used for food preparation including cooking, and sometimes also for eating and entertaining guests, NOT Keaton as in er, Buster. That they still thought we were pulling their legs. As if uniformed guardians of justice would lie to a members of the great British public! So they continued their vigil.

At about five thirty that evening a bemused Michael Kitchen was filmed, first walking towards the flats and then walking away from the flats. He repeated this arduous acting task numerous uneventful times and was in Smethwick for about oh, fifteen minutes? Then he was whisked away in a big impressive Jaguar saloon car with blacked out windows.

As the evening went on and on and on, most of the the crowd astutely drifted off home, beginning to get a smidgen bored waiting for Mr Keaton and had gone back to their domiciles to watch Batman on their own pirated Betamax videotape machines instead! Only the diehard morons who hadn't the sense to see that their Hollywood hero wasn't going to appear hung around in the cold dark street.

It was then that I clocked young Solomon Jervoise Gommorrah amongst the now dwindling crowd of enthusiastic Batman devotees. I noticed that had his hands were always, peculiarly; firmly thrust into the side pockets of his baggy jeans, so I kept an eye on him, just in case he was concealing something, a weapon of mass destruction maybe. Solomon soon noticed that the dashing young officer scrutinising him was none other than yours truly and almost at once went from being a tranquil, shivering, bored, Keaton-spotting moron into a quaking troglodyte, who'd remembered his intimidating threat from all those years before, post-the swinging from the coat-hanger episode in his mother's hallway that fateful day that he'd done a runner from the Valleys of darkest Wales straight to his Black Country home. I think we heard a penny drop, ooh several minutes later, when, like a caveman possessed, he made a beeline straight towards me, his wild gawking eyes steadfastly fixed on yours truly. Now by this time Solomon had grown a little bit taller (a good two foot taller to be exact), but fortunately his stocky frame had also become acquainted with fat and sugar based products as he was as broad as he was tall.

He must have been about six foot, six inches tall, three feet wide and easily a good twenty five stone in weight, more than a little porky, Solomon was a big, big lad. He half walked, half waddled, half ran towards me, shouting, "Connor it's time for you to die!" I fumbled toward my peg pocket to make sure my trusty 'Simon' was with me. 'Simon' being my old wooden truncheon, I called him 'Simon' as a joke really based on the children's game Simon Says. Being a friendly neighbourhood beat officer, I only took my peg out with me when I attended any public order events, like football games, riots or national front marches. So I nervously fumbled, in case I hadn't got him with me. Thankfully for me (Not Solomon) I had Simon, in the long narrow righthand truncheon pocket of my police issue trousers, it's right next to the handcuff pocket (they think of everything don't they). A lot of bobbies gave their staffs or pegs (truncheons) a nickname. Mine was called Simon, as I say, because of the children's nursery rhyme Simon Says. If I had to use Simon, which was I will admit rarer than someone in a toyshop finding rocking horse droppings, I would first make sure that the would be recipient, for example, a gobby belligerent drunk at a pub showing off to the Junction 9 he was with, would hear me loudly say (well within listening distance of all the gutless morons he was drinking with, "Mate, this is my friend, Simon and if Simon says, sit down, stop swearing and be quiet, you will sit down,stop swearing and be quiet!" If you get my drift. I think educationalists call this approach, Nuffield creative expression! Simon is a fantastic old truncheon, and must be over a hundred years old. He had been handed down by generations of retiring Cape Hill Beat officers and I am the latest and probably the last owner. I received it from PC Roger Anderton, my Cape Hill beat predecessor who was a living legend on Cape Hill, but that's another story.

Back at the filming sesh (as we luvvies call them), the shaven headed Solomon had seen me and I was clearly in his sights! Pleased and not a little flattered of course that he'd remembered me after all those years. I now saw this huge lump racing toward me and I could hear Dougie shouting up for back up on his Burndept Radio. Solomon, obviously forgetting his christian upbringing, looked a little upset, his enormous 'Shrek' like face was screwed up with hate as he charged like a rhino towards me. Luckily, none of his associates joined him, they were morons too, so chanted the usual verbal encouragement, repeatedly, something like "Kill the Pig, Kill the Pig," As Solomon got closer, only a matter of feet away from Simon and me, he dragged both of his shovel sized hands out of his deep trouser pockets and held them in front of him like a contemporary Boris Karloff in the role of Solomonstein er, I mean, Frankenstein. I actually grabbed Simon's handle, something I had never done in anger operationally, no tell a lie, I had broken quite a few windows with him, but he'd never struck a living sole, not whilst in the safe keeping of his current incumbent anyway. I felt something hot and wet run down my leg and hoped it was sweat as the roaring hulk dove towards my gulping throat. Then blessed redemption came:

A van load of bobbies squealed round the corner in a Gene Hunt 'Starsky and Hutch' type two wheeled cavalry charge? Dougie rugby tackled the giant Solomonstein? Jesus appeared to Solomon in a sort of road to Damascus (or Windmill Lane) type way? Or did Simon brake his duck?

No. None of these dear reader. The ambling colossus thundering toward me wasn't wearing a belt around his waist (or anything else to keep his jeans up for that matter) and he'd had his hands firmly hard-pressed into the pockets for a very important reason, that of physically holding his keks up! His trousers were too big for him and even though fastened up would have fallen around his ankles had he not held them up! So, thanks to gravity, Solomon's trousers immediately plummeted earthward, settling, timely; around his galloping huge calves, tying up his huge plates of meat (his feet) and causing the bare hairy legged man-mountain to lunge headlong with alacrity into the coarse asphalt directly in front of me . He hurtled face first into the ground, so no real damage was done. It left him with a face that looked like a bloodied blind cobblers thumb. Dougie was clicking on Solomon's brand new bracelets before he'd started to bleed profusely, bless him. In fact for a short time he did a very passable impression of his former victim Terry Trotter (who said there isn't justice in the world)! The ugly mob, they were from Cape Hill, Smethwick, so lets say, the uglier mob. Still craving a spectacular event, were instantaneously disappointed, silenced, then instantaneously burst into hysterics as they too realised that Solomon was not wearing anything to support his trousers and was also wearing a strange set of underclothing for a young Black Country lad in his early twenties. Big hard Solomon Gammorrah, the terror of Sandwell, was wearing an outsized pair of middle aged ladies Pink frilly lace three quarter length satin cami-knickers! I can only presume that he had borrowed these 'delicates' from his god fearing protective Mother or stole them from her bottom drawer? Well it beats seeing the unmistakable Michael Keaton or is that Kitchen? Doesn't it? I've never seen Solomon Gommorrah since. I don't think anyone has. He probably left the area in total embarrassment and shame. If by some slender chance you are reading this Solomon, and it is slender dear readers, as Solly always had trouble with his reading. Solly, we have both grown a little older and perhaps wiser. I bet you always wears a belt with your trousers and always check that you are wearing the appropriate underwear nowadays....... don't you?

IN BETWEEN you AND THE BADDIES

"There are things known, and there are things unknown,
And in between are the Doors"
Jim Morrison

The British actress Elizabeth Taylor once said, "I feel very adventurous. There are so many doors to be opened, and I'm not afraid to look behind them. " As one closes, another opens, or so they say. In the famous painting by Holman Hunt, Jesus knocks at one, saying that whoever opens it, he'd come in and have some of their food and wine, charming! What I noticed about that Holman Hunt painting is that there is no latch on the outside of the door. Bit of thought there. The person inside must want to open the door. Some managers have an open policy when it comes to them. Those hinged barriers, that are basically used to cover an opening in a wall, or partition, leading into a building or space. Simply known as a door. A door can be unfastened or released to give right of entry or securely closed allowing more security.

Doors are widespread, common, they are universal, you find them in all kinds of structures. They allow us access to the inside or the outside and yes there is a choice folks! There are very expensive ones and rock bottom, bog standard cheap ones. Having entered through one they permit us access to progress from room to room. Doors allow aeration, illumination and of course draughts!

There are an awful lot of Doors involved in Police work. Apart from the obvious, 'as one door closes another opens' quote, we make endless enquiries at them, revisiting many, completely smash some! We are sometimes sent to the wrong ones! Sometimes unfortunately, there are dutiful visits to addresses where we literally call at deaths door on a daily basis. We have the satisfaction of slamming some to keep offenders locked behind them. Doors play a big part in the world of policing.

I recall knocking particularly hard the front door at an address in West Bromwich. I was re-visiting the address for about the fourth time that day with a huge six foot two inch tall bobby named Graham Gorley. A enormous Black Country man, who upon seeing the same acerbic, mocking, sarcastic, gobby mother of a young anti social lout, who had, on previous sorties lied to 'cover' for her progeny (Lets call him 'Tarquin') and portrayed him as, innocent as the driven snow, smiled broadly at her and said, "Hello Missis, remember us, we'em the Police". She instantly remembered us!

One summers day I was on mobile patrol out of Old Hill nick with a bobby called Lloyd Atcheson. Originating from the Black Country stronghold of Quarry Bank, Lloyd retired from operational police work a few years ago when he joined the Central Motorway Patrol Group! A good sniffer for crime and criminals, Lloyd was driving the marked police vehicle and I, as the ever vigilant observer, was thinking about what I was going to acquire for my lunch break. We are stopped at the traffic lights on Foxoak Street, Cradley Heath when Lloyd sees a little weasel, lets call him 'Lance', a local dizzy (Disqualified) driver, who had been continually banned from driving from when he'd been tall enough to reach an accelerator pedal at about the age of twelve. He collected points on his licence like Stanley Gibbons collected postage stamps. Problem was , like many teenage morons who fail to learn to drive the legal way, by the time he'd decided that his young joyriding days were over and he'd like to ring an insurance broker and go straight, as it were, Lance rang the nodding Bulldog that eats curry with comedian Roy Walker and when he explained his driving history the dog said, 'Ooooooo Yes! Give us five grand and we'll give you the minimum possible motor insurance cover!' To which Lance replied, 'Ooooooo No No No No.' Deciding to risk running over your loved ones with not a penny of insurance to pay for their funeral expenses. Lance is one of those recidivists who buys a nice car and unlike you, has no documentation at all. I can here him laughing in the pub now showing off to the other morons who condone him driving a lethal weapon at speed around the same streets as their loved ones! Anyway, you can obviously see where I'm going with this.

On this particular day Lance was driving along St Annes Road towards Dudley, in broad daylight if you please, only days after being charged by Lloyd for driving whilst disqualified in the same car. A little red Fiat something. It was a cheap tatty thing, I PNC'd the plate. It wasn't nicked. But it was a nail. Bad enough that it was a Fiat, which I am reliably informed is an acronym for Fabbrica Italiana Automobili Torino (Italian Automobile Factory of Turin) I believe, after having the misfortune of owning one, it stands for Fix It Again Tomorrow! I used to own a Fiat Tipo, the only car I ever bought from new, it was the worst car I ever owned, forever breaking down. I used to tell people that my Tipo must have been made on the weekend of the Turin football derby between Juventus F.C. and Torino F.C. with the Fiat workers putting it together during the match!

But yet again, I digress, Lance was driving (Well, trying to drive – bear in mind he'd never taken a legal driving lesson in his life and was now in his thirties with kids of his own) along as if he hadn't a care in the world! Lloyd immediately recognised him as a 'Dizzy' and he saw and recognised us as the 'Bizzy'. We followed him along Halesowen Road, Cradley Heath towards Netherton, in a sort of strange lowish speed track! After a few deviations, Lance saw sense and pulled over safely into the side of the road in Cradley Road, quite uneventfully. As we parked up and got out of the car to speak to him, he suddenly bolted out of the drivers side door of the crappy Fiat, leaving its thin metal door flapping open as he ran like a gazelle up the front path of the semi detached house opposite and vaulted clean over the side gate of the house with a single bound! Followed closely by Lloyd, who also cleared the back gate in one single superhero type leap. As I ran around the front side of the house I could hear raised voices and the makings of a brawl going on in the rear garden, Lance and Lloyd obviously getting re-acquainted. I took one look at the height of the gate in front of me (It was a standard sized back Gate – Whatever that is) Er, I'd guestimate about seven foot by four foot and after computing all the relevant dimensions of the various wooden barriers and the ratio of my speed and weight parameters (My old Physics teacher 'Smiler' Rowden would be extremely impressed) I ran headlong straight through the back gate which burst off its retaining fixtures. When I got into the back garden the two 'friends' were rolling around on the grass. Unfortunately I spoiled the fun by handcuffing Lance. The owner was not best pleased when I said,"Look what he's done to your gate old mate. We are ever so sorry". I apologised remembering the words of the clergyman Thomas Fuller who said, "All doors open to courtesy" He was right of course. I remember Lance complaining that the cuffs were too tight. I told him, "Relax, the handcuffs are tight because they're new. They'll stretch out after you've worn them for a while". the old un's are the best!

President Lyndon Johnson said, "We must open the doors of opportunity. But we must also equip our people to walk through those doors." As police officers we are highly trained to deal in various aspects of policing. What trainers cannot prepare officers for are the psychological effects that going to some police tasks bring. One such task is having to tell a loved one that a close relative has unexpectedly died. Such a situation always starts with a relative, friend or neighbour asking questions about the whereabouts of someone who has failed to stick to their normal routine. One of the worst sudden deaths I have ever attended involved a young school girl in Rowley Regis who had gone home for school at midday for her lunch to find herself locked out of the family home, with no key to get in. Fearing for the safety of her mother , who had been receiving treatment for depression, she called the police. I attended and having ascertained that there was no other way of getting in quickly I put the front door in. It was a flimsy, single action yale lock on the door; therefore a piece of cake to force. As I have said before, it's always the last room in the house that you are searching that gleans the answer to the initial query made by a caring family member or friend regarding someones safety and whereabouts. The schoolgirls mum was hanging behind the bathroom door, having fastened a mans plastic trouser belt her neck and the coat hook on the back of the bathroom door. It was one of those hangings where the victim had raised their feet only inches from the floor by bending their knees. All the mother had to do to survive was to place her legs firmly down on the bathroom floorboards! She obviously hadn't given any thought to the fact that the person finding her dead would be her unsuspecting daughter coming home from school at midday for her lunch. This only fired my anger and confirmed my personal theory, that suicide victims were selfish folk who don't give any thought at all for their loved ones, the people who have to learn to live, not only without that person but with the guilt of thinking that maybe they could have been the reason or contributed in some way to that persons decision to end it all. But the despair and hopelessness of clinical depression is an extraordinary illness. Unlike the obvious blatancy of a broken limb or a bandaged wound, we can't see a persons depression. You can only see its consequences. It's very sad that some folk in society don't even try to understand the pain of depression. Life really is a marvellous experience and is not a rehearsal. Why anyone would want to get off this ride before its natural end I will never know. Having said that I remember a bobby named Derek Frodsham tell me of a lady who had OD'd (Overdosed) her medication. In response to a family members concerned call. He had forced his way into the house and alerted the medical services in time to save her. Feeling very pleased with himself her went to the Hospital Ward she was recovering in to see how she was. She was fine and as a result cursed and spat at him, livid that he had interfered with her attempt to leave this mortal coil.

I once put a door in at a council maisonette where neighbours had heard babies crying. Having made enquiries I gathered the Parents had gone to perform an ancient Anglo Saxon ritual called Bingo. I forced the door by just leaning on it a little too hard. I jest not. Council doors in the eighties were, thankfully for us, easy to break into. I found two little ones, a boy aged about three and his sister about eighteen months, in a small cot upstairs. There were no lights or any form of heating on in the house. I placed the children in my little panda car and asked for back up. WPC Kath Kielowski 'KK' to everyone at Smethwick nick came to my aid. She looked after the children while I repaired the door with the screwdriver on my swiss army knife.

Back at a warm place of safety the children started to thaw out drinking seemingly gallons of pop and numerous bags of crisps and sweets from the bar upstairs. The parents visited the nick to complain that someone had broken into their house and abducted their brood. I introduced myself and then introduced them them to a cozy cell, slamming its door firmly shut! About a week later the gaffer Inspector Cook called me into his office and told me that he'd had a letter of complaint about the incident from the local council. Why? Because I'd fixed the broken door myself and not waited or asked for a council repair worker!

I went to an address in Bearwood with a colleague named Adrian Holding. Both young in service, we were members of A Unit at Smethwick nick. We had had a report from a concerned neighbour that they hadn't seen the occupant of this particular mid terraced house an elderly lady who lives alone. We knock the front door, nothing. We go around the back. There is no response and we decide to put the door in. We tell Sgt Stan Roby whats going on and I rush the old looking back door that hasn't seen a lick of paint for quite some time. I break through the door as if it is dried cardboard. It literally crumbled apart it was that old, dry and powdery. Flakes of rotted wood was blowing into our eyes. We searched downstairs. It was like walking into the fifties. We found rotted food and unwashed plates in the kitchen sink. A sign that something might be awry. We both slowly climbed the darkened stairs, it was a little like the scene in Psycho where the Private Detective is attacked by the 'mother' at the top of the stairs on the Bates' house landing. So I let Ade go first, after all he was the senior man ,by four whole months! Having checked all but the front bedroom (It's always the last one!) Ade, as senior man, made a management decision and said, "You look first". As I glanced around the door I saw the old lady. She was sitting upright, arms by her side. Her eyes were closed and she looked peaceful. Ade spoke into his Burndept radio," PC Holding Three control, can we have an undertaker for this job please?" As Ade finished speaking and Stan Roby answered him in the positive. The old dear hearing the voices from the blue box opened her eyes from her light sleep and said to us, "Officers, is there a problem?" Immediately, I looked at her and said,"Bab, somebody's smashed your back door in!" As I made a pot of Tea, Ade was given the task of explaining what had really gone on.

That brings me to the jewellers door at Cape Hill. Its 1982. I'm paired up with PC Francis (Frank) Cunningham, a stocky, green and white Glaswegian, who, once you had gained his trust, would run through walls for you. We were sent to an attack alarm at a Jewellers shop in Cape Hill. The sort of shop where you had to buzz a button at the front door and the staff would press a button that allowed you to open the clear glass door that bore a huge shiny stainless steel ornate handle half way up it on the right. We virtually flew to the location in our little mini metro panda car and TA'd first at the scene. Frank ran up to the door, grabbed the polished handle and pulled. Nothing. The door remained firmly closed. We could see jewellery strewn all over the shop floor and the freshly shocked staff looking distraught. It was a genuine Robbery. A perplexed and exasperated Frank pushed,pulled,tugged and shoved the door all to no avail. The poor young lady in the store gathered enough of her shredded wits together and pushed the entry button. This coincided with Frankie giving this enormous door handle a huge yank. Resulting in a small cracking sound. The sort you hear just before a windscreen shatters at seventy miles per hour on a motorway. An experience I have unfortunately had twice. The door then totally disintegrated, cascading into thousands of tiny chunks of float glass that descended into a huge pile of sparkling door in front of a semi cowering Frank who hopelessly groped the huge stainless steel ornate handle in both hands! In this bizarre, almost surreal scenario, I walked past Frankie and stepped over the pile of glass into the shop. I heard Frankie mutter something under his breath which I assume must have been contemporary gaelic!

Then there was the job that involved a door that I went to on FA Cup Final Day with my Tutor Constable Mick Benyon. The cup final was an all-London tie between Arsenal and West Ham. Arsenal being the strong favourites, playing in their third FA Cup Final in a row. Alf lived on the patch, in the Bearwood area of Sandwell at the time. We were on lates and had gone to Alf's directly from the parade for a snatch of the TV coverage.' Be sure, your sins will find you out', is as true a phrase then as it is now! Within ten minutes of the kick off Alf's radio burst into life urging us to attend a ground floor flat in the Black Patch area of the sub-division. An address that Alf instantly recognised as that of a local weirdo, Tommy Tomkins. Who not only had severe eczema, but was also the proud possessor of genital herpes! He was a borderline mental patient who was being cared for in the community thanks to caring politicians who wanted to save tax payers money by keeping poor sods like Tommy to face the daily ridicule of an ignorant forgotten populace. He was known to officers at Smethwick who had often brought him into the nick for Drunk and Disorderly offences and minor thefts. As passed the front gate on the way to the motor we both heard the unmistakable Wembley roar following a goal. Alan Devonshire beat Talbot and Rice out on the left and crossed the ball over towards the far post. Pat Jennings got a slight touch on it, Cross's shot was then blocked with Pearson's hard drive from the rebound neatly nutted into the onion bag from directly in front of goal by Sir Trevor Brooking's bonce. But Alf and I wouldn't learn of this and West Hams One-Nil victory for another couple of hours. We got to Tommy's flat to find that some local kids had nailed his front door on with six inch nails! Tommy was crying and very upset. We kicked the door in and got the claustrophobic and somewhat encrusted, flaking Tom out into the open air where he took great gulps of the stuff as he bemoaned his misfortune to us. He noted that Benyon the long in the tooth street wise cop had heard it all before and so concentrated his sob story on the young proby (Probationary Constable) viz, moi. I was having it big time. He told me that he had been broken into over a dozen times and that on the last occasion they had stolen all his Christmas decorations, his scrapbook of the Royal Family, his portable black and white TV and his framed pictures of Jesus. As he mentioned the Saviour he began to sob pitifully and I put my arm around him and said "It's alright Tom, we'll get them back for you". Alf sarcastically added,"Tom we must try to forgive them for they know not what they do, it's what Jesus would want". At which Tom growled through clenched teeth, "They'll fucking burn, the little bastards". To which Alf replied, "Thank you the Archbishop of Canterbury, next week's pause for thought comes from Charles Manson live from his prison cell in California. " Oh, by the way. We missed the footie waiting outside Tom's insecure flat waiting for the council worker who came to fix the door who said, "Sorry I'm late lads, I was watching the game!"

One misty September morning on earlies, I went to a sudden death at a block of flats on the Oldbury Road,Smethwick, christened by the locals as, the concrete jungle. An old man who in these modern times, merely subsisted in his fourteenth floor cell, with little or no human contact, for donkeys years, had broken out of his Jacob Marley-esque earthly shackles, luckily, passing painlessly in his sleep. His 'neighbours', a couple of young migrants from Iran that hardly spoke a word of English, had plucked up enough courage to ring 999 to inquire if the old gentleman that lived next door could be visited and asked to turn down the volume on his bass droning television. Which, during the early hours of the morning had been blaring away for at least the last six weeks. The number of weeks the young couple had been living in the flats.

My shift partner, PC Bob Halsall and I could smell the 'tell tale' disgusting odour, permeating the whole of the landing outside. It easily subjugated the smell wafting from the lift, that was supposedly fitted with urine proof floors by the local council. That distinct smell we experienced on the landing has only one source, well known mainly to Emergency service staff and Military Combat Troops.

It was the smell of human demise.

As the callers had not seen the old man for some weeks we both feared the worse as I lifted up the flat of the letter box on the front door. I could hear peoples voices in conversation. My early optimism was swiftly weakened as I heard the green goddess, Diana Moran, vigorously putting magician Paul Daniels through his physical paces, in a BBC Breakfast Time TV broadcast. The sound of which was being amplified from the overheated television set located somewhere in this dark momentary mausoleum.

We easily broke down the door of the flat to enter. The clinging smell of bereavement was almost over powering, it hangs in the atmosphere and is sickening to most humans but somehow emergency service workers seem to get used to it. Whilst very tempted to open windows and 'air' the place out. We couldn't because of course the site was a possible crime scene and had to be preserved as such.

Why is it that the sudden dead are always in the last room of the building you search? Incongruously, the corpse was waiting for us in the 'living' room at the end of the depressing hallway. In the sparsely furnished, Black fly filled room, lay the remains of an elderly white male, who looked to be in his late seventies. He was lying on his side on a small grubby two seater settee in a semi foetal position, wearing the vestiges of a tattered pair of tousled pyjamas. He was badly decomposed and it became instantly apparent that most of his face and parts of his upper and lower limbs had been brutally torn off. The lesions on the carcass were roofed by a thick stratum of writhing worm – like insect larva. You know, the average household dustbin produces around 30,000 flies a week from eggs laid in the rotting rubbish it contains. So given how long our man had been lying undisturbed, the flies in the vicinity had had a field day.

As Bob took a few steps forward, pointing his illuminated maglite toward the gruesome sight, we both heard a restrained but seriously hostile growling noise coming from underneath the bed settee he lay on. Emanating from the four inch, darkened gap between the settee and the bare wooden floorboards, we could make out a small pointed black crusty snout, followed closely by two healthy, shiny black, beady canine eyes. Which belonged to the dead man/past masters best friend and solitary friend, confidant and companion. A little Jack Russell dog, who we later learned was humorously and bizarrely named, 'Spot'. Why? Because apparently he hadn't got any! His owner shared my kind of sense of humour.

Following his Masters deep sleep and as days turned into weeks and weeks into months, Spot had become so hungry that he had decided to become a Cannibal literally wolfing down the hand that fed him. Normally the idiom of biting the hand that feeds you means you have turned against a friend or supporter and repaid their kindness with a wrong. But I'm sure on this occasion this worthy little companion was just surviving and I'm sure by the way he was willing to defend his master that Spot fully appreciated his owner. I looked at the remaining piece of Tomato Ketchup soaked Egg McMuffin that I'd been stuffing my face with ever since we'd had our Breakfast disturbed by being sent to this job and threw it in the direction of Spot who seemed to enjoy it. Not long after this we were joined by the Police Surgeon Doc Wang, a great guy, a small thin oriental man. He joined us outside in the corridor and could already smell the subject. With a massive frown on his face he sniffed through the letter box of the flat, took one look at Bob and me and said, "Oh he dead Boys" I said, "You'd better go in and check Doc" He reluctantly had to agree and with a handkerchief wrapped tightly around his nose and mouth he did the business and confirmed this very sad and meagre life extinct. One of the lads on the shift adopted Spot, who had a good innings for a Jack Russell home. Spot only joining his former master some eleven years later. I think he retained the name Spot but, I would have been tempted to re-christen him 'Caliban' after the Shakespeare character in The Tempest, whose name is an anagram for Cannibal.

Another door story I remember happened to a young officer I knew named Lee Moses. He joined the job in about 1981 or 82, he was only in the police a few years, deciding after a couple of years to move to the States with his Connecticut wife. I remember two Lee stories, the first was when someone had brought a small World War One handgun that they had found in their loft into the front office of Smethwick nick. The said firearm sat momentarily on a desktop with a found property card attached to it with string whilst the front office PC got the safe key from the key cupboard. It was then Lee pick it up and said the classic phrase, "It won't be loaded". Needless to say shortly after that, the still warm revolver was safely nestled in the safe awaiting an inspection from a firearms officer as a red faced PC Moses started to type a report for the Superintendent to explain how the small hole in the ceiling of the front office had been produced. Thankfully, it was mid Sunday afternoon so there was no one in the TV room upstairs having their lunch break! The other Lee story involved a pre Christmas visit, with Frank Cunningham who I mentioned earlier, to a B&E (Burglary) at a very large mid terraced Edwardian house in Bearwood on an incredibly windy Sunday morning. These traditional two storey houses were absolutely huge, housing a basement cellar, two large rooms and a kitchen on the ground floor and then three bedrooms and a bathroom on the 1st floor, with an room in the loft space of the dwelling. With the old fashioned wooden front door opening into a small coat, umbrella and wellington boot laden vestibule and another large frosted full glass panelled door that led to a narrow hallway that ran the length of the house. Half way along the hallway would be another full sized approximately six foot by three foot glass panelled door leading to the dining room and kitchen. This house, like many at the time, had louvre, slat type, windows above the rear facing casements. They were ideal for ventilating a steamy kitchen or bathroom, however, their thin aluminium frames made them easy to prise open with a screwdriver, allowing thieves to slide out the two narrow

12"x4", panes of glass from their panels reaching an arm into the premises, to open the large window below that of course had not been fitted with a window lock. It was like shelling peas to an experienced house breaker. Removing these panels allowed the intruder entry to the whole house, which of course was full of rich pickings, which; at this time of the year included the children's christmas presents around the christmas tree!

It was this incident that actually made me, from then on, place false gifts under our Christmas tree at home and keep my girls presents locked away upstairs. I had just TA'd at the address in the Zulu with Bob Halsall and was walking up to the front door. I saw Frank and Lee speaking to the lady of the house as they stood in the vestibule. As Lee pushed open the inner door the lady said, "Wait till I've closed the Front", before she could say the word *door*, Lee opened the door leading into the corridor allowing a sudden gust of wind to propel down the hallway blowing the partly open middle door, causing it to slam shut at a considerable rate of knots. The safety glass of the access door shattering instantly into a million pieces with an extremely great crash! After a fleeting, pregnant pause. A mortified PC Moses inanely winked at the IP (Injured Party) and said assuredly, "Don't worry missis, you can claim for the damage on the household insurance". I went back to the Zulu to get the brush, normally used for clearing glass off the road surface at an RTC (Road Traffic Collision) from the boot. As I passed Frank, I looked at him, grinned and whispered, "You're beginning to have form for damaging doors Frankie" (It was only a few days after the incident at the jewellers shop)! A true Glaswegian, Frank brusquely replied with some unrepeatable, but colourful, colloquial phrases in his native gaelic tongue. Incidentally, we later caught the Bearwood Burglar responsible for this break in. It was a professional brummie burglar by the name of named Robin Banks, who's arrest is mentioned in another part of this book.

I'm now reminded of a story involving the catch on a Yale locking front door. PC's Dave Bullman and his then probationer, Paula Newlove, were at Paula's first Sudden Death; an old man who had passed away of natural causes in his armchair watching television. What did he die of? I think he died of a Thursday or was it a Wednesday! Having taken all the required details for the Sudden Death forms, the two law enforcers were awaiting initially, a doctor, who would declare the suspected deceased's life extinct followed closely by the black clad undertakers, who would take the by then confirmed departed body away to their local chapel for a much deserved rest. Now, for whatever reason; Dave, an ex army Guardsman, who for the majority of his Army service played trombone in The Regimental Band of Her Majesty's Coldstream Guards. A notorious practical joker with a coppers sense of humour, was without explanation, mysteriously 'called' away to another job. Dave could see that young Paula was particularly uneasy about being left alone with the late lamented Mr So and So, but reassured her that he was only dead so wasn't a risk." Anyway Paula, I'll be back in two shakes of a lambs tail and you need to familiarise yourself with being around the dear departed, it's a police training 'must' really. Will you be OK?" said a sensitive and compassionate Bully. She anxiously but courageously acquiesced, nodding with a hesitant smile. "Thats the spirit," Said Bully as he left via the living room door into the hallway of the former pensioners flat. Before leaving, sliding the small catch of the Yale type, cylindrical pin tumbler lock, across. This action temporarily retracted and held back the locking bolt of the lock. So that as he closed the front door behind him it would 'appear' closed but really was still totally insecure. He drove the police panda car around the corner just out of sight of the premises and sneaked quietly back into the premises without being seen. Through the gap in the jamb of the living room door, which he'd left slightly ajar, Bully could see that Paula had hardly moved an inch from the same spot in the lounge that she had occupied when he'd left the flat, on the reverse side of the living room door. So he got down on all fours. Crouching down on his hands and knees he reached an arm around the bottom of the door and with a eerie ethereal groan, tightly grabbed hold of Paula's right ankle. She immediately screamed frenziedly like a banshee and was more than a little unnerved as the smirking, moustachioed trombonist popped his beaming face around the bottom of the door! Mr So and So really didn't see the humorous side of this blag, remaining quite cold and insensitive in fact, but I think Paula did. Well, eventually, when she'd come down off the ceiling. Paula later became a very good detective and saw much more gruesome sights than Mr So and So, peacefully dead to the world in his armchair . I think she learned a very good lesson in policing that day though. When you are paired up with Dave Bullman keep your wits about you, be prepared to be a victim of his 'strange' sense of humour or go sick!

Some doors are frequently used symbolically as objects that hold distinctive importance, with a custodian or administrator of the keys to those particular doors, being granted special powers. The austere reinforced soundproofed concrete cells with moulded furnishings at Smethwick nick are the responsibility of one such custodian, the Police Custody Officer, generally a Sergeant, is responsible for overseeing our temporary guests known more generally as prisoners; allocating them a cell and ensuring their welfare during their brief stay at Smethwick Police Station. Our special visitors are fed hot microwaved stodge, watered down with a choice of numerous flavours of dehydrated hot or cold beverages and if need be even washed and changed in accordance with the Police and Criminal Evidence Act! Cell doors in the custody block are huge cumbersome opaque hinged steel affairs, containing a small serving hatch with a sliding lockable steel cover. My cell door story begins with a very large drunken Irishman one St Patricks night in the nineties. He was a big 'un. Seventeen foot two and thirty eight stone in his stocking feet. Like anglers, coppers do tend embroider the truth, but he was about six foot two and built like a brick shithouse. After imbibing a few snakebites he had fought the majority of the pub succumbing eventually to six of our number, with the help of the pub bouncers and bundled unceremoniously into the rear of an Austin Metro two door saloon driven by yours truly! Whoever the senior officer was that agreed to accept a full fleet of those tiny two door motor cars for the force, designed initially to replace the Austin Mini, to use as operational police cars must have been totally raving mad or had shares in Austin Rover! Austin Metro Police Panda Cars were to operational police work what Dame Kiri Te Kanawa the full lyric soprano from New Zealand is to professional underwater Yak strangling. On either side of our outsized Celtic guest was PC's John 'JJ' Jenkins and Pete Connolly who sat either side of the man-mountain to keep him still! In the front passenger seat knelt Mick Unkett, a keener than most bobbies, Special Constable, who, facing the rear seat of the car leaned over the back of the front passenger seat helping to hold down the hefty Hibernian by his very broad shoulders. In spite of the close attention of the custodial sardines, the guy continued to physically jump around in the back of this Mini Metro which bounced all over the carriageway, jumping in and out of the kerbside. It was funny watching JJ and Pete hanging on to him for dear life bouncing up and down in the rear view mirror like a pair of cowboys riding an out of control bucking bronco. His head continuously banging against the thin padded roof of the police dinky toy as his beery breath frothed and bubbled out of his foul mouth! As I turned left into up the sloped entrance and under the automatic barrier of the back yard pulling up outside the caged entrance of the ramp leading up to the custody block door, I thought, 'How are we going to get him out of the car?'. Mick Unkett got out of the car and pushed his seat forward allowing Pete room to safely jump out. Simultaneously, I left my door wide open and pushed the seat forward permitting JJ to spring out of the drivers side. OK, the officers were now safe, but chummy was still in the car and refusing to budge. He sat in the centre and on the edge of the rear seat with both hands pressed against the sides of the inner roof. Then he started rocking. Not like Chuck Berry or Elvis you understand. Smethwick's answer to Bono was rocking from side to side and the little car suspension didn't like it very much, obviously preferring garage or middle of the road stuff!

Question: How do you expel a corpulent drunken belligerent celt from a small two door hatchback motor vehicle when they decline to egress of their own accord? Answer: With great difficulty! My colleagues tried brute force, threats, enticement with sweets, logic, reason and even good old fashioned bribery. No dice, he was having none of it, still being influenced by the copious amount of liquid medication. he'd imbibed. The great American comedian Milton Berle said, "If opportunity doesn't knock, build a door." I decided that it was time to try a different tack. We were looking at this situation all wrong. It was time for the unconventional approach. Thinking completely out of the box I thought. There are mainly four kinds of drunkard. The

Violent 'Want to scrap everybody in the world' Drunk, the Gobby Loud Argumentative Drunk, the Sleepy Comatose Drunk and the Cheerful, Jovial, Happy, Giggly Drunk. This guy of course was a violent 'fight the world' drunk. However, Professor Connor of the University of Life had a theory that perhaps this man could be a schizophrenic drunk and therefore capable of displaying other drunken traits as well as this vicious aggressive one. He had exhibited signs of loud garrulous intoxication along with confrontational quarrelsome instances. So I thought I may be onto a winner here. I approached the car unaccompanied, my colleagues admiring my complete lack of common sense. I smiled at this pink hulk. He disturbingly smiled back at me. Interesting I thought. I stared to laugh quietly. He started to chuckle too. Progress I thought! He still had both arms pushing against both sides of the roof, but had encouragingly stopped his rocking motion. I decided to go for it. To advance my advantage I started tickling him under his arms and around his tummy. He started giggling hysterically like a baby. I jest not. Then came the pièce de résistance, I did a Bruce Forsyth. Long before anyone at the BBC ever had the idea of Strictly Come Dancing I asked this Irish violent drunk if he cared to dance. Pointing towards the dance floor, aka, the concreted ramp leading to the Custody Block doorway at the back of the nick. To mine and everyone else's astonishment he accepted my offer, climbing out of the car and embracing me. Easy Tiger! I led of course, being the sober man. I was a perfect gentleman of course, no roving hands. We commenced our Waltz up the ramp all the way to the back door as the amazed choir of gobsmacked onlookers hummed the Blue Danube Waltz by Johann Strauss one of the most consistently popular Waltzes in my dancing repertoire I think you'll find! Len Goodman would have been proud of me. Having got him into the

Custody Block he became quite compliant answering all Sergeant Roy Mantle's questions. He only started to play up again when it came to placing him in a cell. So this time we did the Hokey Cokey! I swear. Following the instructions given in the lyrics of the song and prompted by me. He did the actions, first putting his left leg into the cell and shaking it about. We went through all the verses but when it come to the bit where, You put your whole self in your whole self out. He put his whole self in the cell and I slammed the steel door shut with a fantastic clanking crash! Continuing to sing and performing the actions to my flabbergasted and stunned dancing partner I pointed first to him in the cell and then pointed to myself with a victorious grin on my face. I sang, "In (Pointing to him) Out (Pointing to me) In (To Him) Out(Me) shake it all about, you do the hokey cokey and you lock the cell, thats what its all about!" To the collective applause of our live audience. Shortly after this he began to head butt the cell door. Thud,Thud,Thud, rhythmically striking his thick scull into the steel cell door. Again ignoring all appeals. I offered to come into the cell and try a Cha cha cha, but this time instead of readily accepting my offer he remembered what happened last time he'd agreed to such a request and turned down my offer. I was a wall flower! This resulted in him making a more frenzied and repetitive head banging attack of the cell door instead. Step in Professor Connor with his next incredible theory in reverse psychology. I told Roy Mantle the Custody sergeant of my plan and he thought we had nothing to lose by trying it. I approached 'Tiny' in Cell One and once he'd stopped butting the door to actually listen to me I said. "Mate, I've got to guard you all night. But I want to watch the Football on the Telly next door. Can you do us a favour and keep banging the door with your head, then I'll hear you and know you are ok, so I won't have to keep checking up on you. OK?" Result: He told me to enjoy more sex and travel as much as I could, then lay indignantly on his three inch thick waterproof mattress, covered himself in his thick wirewool type blankets and began a deep abstemious slumber. My reward for this positive result? A steaming plastic cup of dehydrated soup or was it coffee?. It wouldn't be my last utilisation of this ploy!

EDWARD THE CONFESSOR ONCE LIVED IN ROWLEY REGIS

It had just gone half past seven on a warm and sunny Wednesday evening in July when the open collared, short sleeve shirt clad Police Constables Steve Chisnall and Dan Joynt from Oldbury Police Station raced up to Darley House in response to a message from the Force Control Room that a man could be seen dangling precariously from an eleventh floor balcony by just his finger tips. Darley House, being a grim, grey, uninviting, concrete, nineteen storey council tower block in Wallace Road, Oldbury a small town, in the Middle of England once the cradle of British industry, home of Jack Judge, surprisingly, the Englishman who wrote the famous traditional Irish song, It's a long Way to Tipperary and the well known West Bromwich Albion supporter and part time funny man Frank Skinner (Who, wisely, now lives somewhere in London counting his money), located in the Metropolitan Borough of Sandwell in the West Midlands, the sixth most deprived metropolitan borough council district in the United Kingdom. Mind you, it really is a long way to Tipperary from Judge Close in Oldbury. Three Hundred and Fifty Seven miles to be exact. The road gets a bit damp between Holyhead and Dun Laoghaire but after that it's all plain sailing down to Tipperary!

Chris Collins (Real name of Frank Skinner) was nine years old and still (Injudiciously) living in Bristnall Hall Road in Oldbury only a ten minute jaunt in a fast car from Darley House and its sister ship Malton House (Which later sank after striking 300 pounds of TNT) which were approved in 1966 as part of the Wallace Road & Newbury Lane building project to improve the area. Supplying spacious high rise, but, affordable, homes with all the conveniences required by a booming populace. Completed in 1969 they were an impressive 52 metres high, the same height as nelsons column. By the eighties only Darley remained. Malton being one of the first high rise blocks in Sandwell to be blown down. I was one of the officers on that blow job; in fact it was my first. Being a young inexperienced officer at the time, I was a little nervous but once you get used to being covered from head to foot in white dust it. But I digress, Darley House, like Oldbury Town Centre had, by the mid eighties, fallen into decline. As the marked Austin Metro panda car approached the block, the familiar opening notes of the Coronation Street theme tune breezed through the aerated gaping windows of the surrounding flats. A small crowd (At least twelve people) had gathered in Wallace Close, craning their necks and pointing skywards at a white male in his mid thirties, wearing a tight fitting short sleeved, but baggy trousered dark grey suit that made him look a little like Norman Wisdoms Gump character, without the cap that is. This man was, as the radio message had reported, swinging off a small balcony hand rail, about thirty metres up from terra firma. Steve immediately recognised the dangler and said to his partner, "Bloody Hell Dan, its Edward the Confessor. Now what's he up to?"

It is difficult to calculate exactly which floor to go to at an incident such as this as he was too high up to hear the officers shouting questions from below, their cries being drowned out by Len Fairclough noisily asking Ken and Deirdre Barlow if he could take young Tracy with him to the swimming baths! The two officers noticed on the floor plan in the foyer that the block had nineteen floors, so fearlessly decided to eschew the twenty two flights of steps going up instead in the lift to the tenth floor. Luckily, the lift smelled of Jeyes fluid indicating that it must have been cleaned that very day. The lift at Darley House normally had the scent that one would normally associate with a council lift. That of Stale urine, saliva, waste foodstuffs, used condoms and fag stumps all intermingled to create the familiar reek of a Tower Block lift. Add to that the miss-spelled graffiti liberally sprayed, daubed and scraped across the walls and doors and you have an elevator with the overall ambience of a darkened lead lined coffin with a capacity for up to six persons. A claustrophobic sadists' dream. I personally try to avoid using lifts in Tower Blocks, since being trapped in one with five hairy arsed bobbies one hot sultry summers day. My ordeal only lasted about 20 minutes. When you get trapped in a lift you hope there is enough 'supplies' for survival. On this occasion we had half a packet of polo mints between us! Which reminds me, what's the difference between a Police officer and a Polo mint? People like Polo! (For you young ones, that used to be the TV advertising slogan for Polo Mints). When I'm in a lift council lift, I feel like a balloon in a greenhouse full of cactus. You can't sit down; you can't lean against the walls. It's hell on earth, but again, I drift away from the point......Our brave officers took a deeply held breath, entered the electronic hoist and ascended the centre of this man made volcano, Mount Darley. They hurriedly spewed out of the lift on the tenth floor, took a fresh gulp of air and knocked the door of the nearest flat. Having gained entry to the balcony of that flat, they could see the man dangling from the balcony above, unfortunately just out of reach to make a safe attempt at grabbing him. As they were only one floor down they ran up the grotty stairwells and luckily chose the door right in front of them to smash in. Running through to the balcony they saw Edward (the Confessor) Smith (Only the surname has been changed to protect the guilty). Eddie was a well known CRO. CRO is the title given to our regular customers, who upon receiving a conviction at a court of law in the United Kingdom, would be allocated a Criminal Record Office number. Sadly,for the majority of law abiding Britons, a high percentage of Her Majesty's CRO's become recidivist lawbreakers, Eddie being a prime example. An ineffective criminal who was forever getting caught due principally to his own stupidity! A slightly obese, stocky little bloke in his mid thirties, but surprisingly quite fit for a toe rag, Eddie was holding tightly onto the rusting overhanging balcony rail for dear life. It was angled in such a way that there was nowhere for his short stubby legs to get a footing.   Straight away, Dan Joynt instinctively clapped one end of his handcuffs onto Eddies left wrist and the other around the balcony rail. So at least the nastiest injury Eddie was going to get now was a broken wrist. Unless, the crumbling balcony went with him of course. Chissy, who knew this miscreant only too well said, "OK Eddie what's the story then?" Edward the Confessor told him that they were actually standing in his mate, Duane's flat. Eddie actually lived three floors down and had climbed up the outside of Mount Darley to 'Surprise' him. You would have thought he would have checked to see if Duane was in first to witness this amazing feat of foolhardiness wouldn't you? Unfortunately Eddie had bitten off a hell of a lot more than he could chew and by the time the officers had arrived he was completely knackered, his strength draining and his bottle starting to go! Eddie as I say was a portly lad and a difficult fish to land. The crown representatives took an arm each, made a wish and pulled him back onto the balcony to safety. As Steve and Dan struggled gamely to pull him up and over the four foot balcony he still had the sense of humour to shout, "Hey lads be as careful as you can will yer, I've got my best suit on!" It was his ONLY suit of course.

Why the moniker Edward the Confessor? Well, I don't suppose you would be surprised to know that his real name wasn't Edward. Steve had arrested Edward at his home address on suspicion of a minor theft one Sunday morning on earlies, taking him to the cells at Old Hill. After a brief interview Eddie was bailed for seven days to appear back at Old Hill the following Sunday morning, giving Steve seven days to make a few more enquiries into the matter. On his way out Steve said, "See you soon Eddie," "Not if I see you first" says Eddie, smiling and folding the 47(3) bail form into the inside jacket pocket of the shabby grey suit he always wore. Sunday morning of earlies only came around once a month on the shift rota at the Hill and was always the shift's communal Breakfast morning. Everyone would chip in from the Inspector down to the youngest sprog on the shift. Gobbo (PC Bob Platt) and me, was usually the cooks on our unit. I don't know who would have cooked it on Steve's shift but I would guess it was Liza Bishop a little stout (Sorry Liza I'm being too nice) Fat and loveable WPC who worked at Old Hill for about sixty four years! She's a legend at the Hill. She was as tough as any of the blokes and had a tongue to match. She would with assistance from her minions, cook up a veritable feast of Bacon, Fried Eggs, Sausage, Black Pudding, Hash Browns, Beans, Mushrooms, Tomatoes and Fried Bread. liberally covered in Brown Sauce, accompanied by four rounds of medium sliced white bread with copious dashes of salt and pepper. To make up for the moderately high fat-content of this breakfast, the meal is generally topped off with a mug of heavy-duty 'stain the mug brown' tea or of course there was a bottle of Camp coffee for those officers with the more discerning palate. With enough cholesterol there to soften even the most resolute of arteries it was fodder fit for a king, ideal cuisine for keeping any athletically minded protector of justice in good physical shape. Jamie Oliver would have had severe palpitations, mind you, the mockney sparrow would have been about eight years old then…. It was bostin' fittle ar kid, great when you was fair clemmed (starving) leaving just enough room in yer bally for your lunch! As Steve and his shift companions were appreciatively wiping their plates clean with the remnant rounds of sliced bread, a call came over all the radios in the Rest Room. Auto Alarm at the school across the road from the nick! No need for cars, everyone tear arsed out of the back of the nick and across the road to the school. It was surrounded by police. Steve found a broken insecure window in one of the Infants classrooms. Everyone waited for the key holder who fortunately lived right by the school entrance. Steve and other officers checked the premises with the caretaker and all were happy that nothing was missing and it looked like whoever broke the window may well have been disturbed by the alarm activation and had cleared off prior to the arrival of the freshly fuelled up boys in blue. The following morning, Steve and Dan are pushing their Panda around Cradley Heath when they see Eddie who actually flags them down from the side of the road. With a cheeky grin on his face he says, "Yow coppers at Old Hill aye very good am ya? "Why is that Ed?" says a curious Steve. "Yow went to that alarm at the school yesterday mornin' day yer?" Says Eddie. "Yeah Why?" Says Steve charily. "Did you check that classroom where the window got bost?" says a grinning, almost arrogant Eddie. "Mmmm Yes" says the now inquisitive Steve. "Well, yer day find me hiding in the classroom cupboard did you?" says a tactless Eddie! Edward the Confessor instantaneously received his new nom de plume and of course a free complimentary tour of the cell block at Old Hill where naturally he did not pass go, did not collect two hundred pounds and went straight to jail, directly to jail as he was remanded in custody to Her Majesty's Prison Blakenhurst for an unexpected vacation! What a Pillock! You know, one of the main virtues that a criminal must possess is the ability to keep their trap firmly shut and be economical with the truth i.e. Keep your gob shut. If you do open it. Do what ALL villains and politicians do, Lie! Mind You, Eddie couldn't lie straight in bed. Not the sharpest knife in the canteen of cutlery that lad. I have had a drunken driver flag me down to ask for directions and then breathalysed him but I can't say I have known of many crooks who had actually flagged a marked police car down to gloat to the officers inside about their wrong doings! It's like a shoplifter going to a Store Detectives Convention to give them an impromptu speech on how to conceal items about your person in an effort to avoid incarceration! Poor Eddie, he was as dim as the torch he forgot to take with him to burglaries!

Steve also told me a story about the man from Rowley Regis who claimed to have a Portal to the Nether World in his late Father's 1940's bedroom wardrobe.

Now before you start to scoff, can I remind you that I personally know a man who, to demonstrate to the nation that he is quite a extraordinary individual, dresses from head to foot in gaudy highly coloured silken regalia as a symbol of his vocation. He also puts on a big pointy hat, carries various ceremonial objects around with him which includes a shepherds crook. He claims that not only does he act for an invisible almighty omnipotent eternal being that he claims created the Universe you reside in. He converses with the same both privately and publicly on a daily basis, receiving instructions from him! Nuff said? OK. The man I refer to is John Sentamu FRSA the 97th Archbishop of York, Metropolitan of the province of York, and Primate of All England. The second most senior cleric in the Church of England, after the Archbishop of Canterbury. My wife Beverly used to be his secretary when he was the Bishop for Birmingham. A very friendly and approachable bloke, I think he'll go places that lad. The other man, I referred to earlier, the one with the Portal in West Bromwich, was a chap known locally as 'Mad Maurice'.

Maurice was a former store manager with one of the largest chains of food, clothing, toys and general merchandising retailers in the world. This job, with its awesome responsibilities, was the source of his mental breakdown. Following his illness, the poor man would often ring the police reporting that 'beings' were trying to break into his home and that he could hear voices coming from upstairs in his house, attributing them to the four horsemen of the apocalypse.

They appear in the Christian Bible in chapter six of the Book of Revelation. The four horsemen are traditionally named after the verses that depict them producing: Strife, War, Famine and Death; though, only Death, is directly named in the Bible. Those enigmatic jockeys have been interpreted as being representatives of both good and evil and based either in the present or the future. The interpretation most commonly used is the basis for the modern Rock culture's uses of the Four Horsemen concept that sees the first horseman riding a scabby, putrefying horse, or 'oss if you are from the Black Country, he represents Pestilence, the instigator of decay, foretelling the ultimate destruction of all global food supplies (Don't tell Tesco's will you). Followed, consequently by Famine. An overfed, obese rider. Riding an emaciated and unhealthy mount (Similar to the one I backed in last years Derby), denoting insatiability and starvation.   Owing to the growing hostility over the remaining global food supplies, comes War, who rides a blood red horse, brandishing a humungous sword, which he uses to butcher millions who cross his path.   Bringing up the rear of this cheerful bunch, comes the black rider, Death. Oooooooooooooo. His horse is jet black. He is followed by the populace of Hell carrying all these residual souls to their final destination, Birmingham? Hardly the runners and riders for the Lou Siffer Invitation Stakes at Towcester are they? Mind you,the four 'Ossmen sound quite tame compered to some of the dreadful fiends you can encounter on an x box,Wii or Playstation 3 computer games nowadays! It makes you wonder what forms of transport the writer of Revelation (The Disciple John?) would have chosen today if he'd foreseen the coming of the widely worshipped games packages with their wholesome family message of global destruction coming through a home cinema surround-sound system with a powered subwoofer! They are certainly the most modern worshipped icons, followed by millions of believers who part with their hard earned cash and they don't even boast that they impart the 'truth'. Obviously the harbingers of doom would now ride motor cycles or pilot mighty star ships or even wield a Guitar Hero 3, moulded plastic legends of rock guitar! When Jesus makes his 'Second Coming' World Tour supported by U2 with Billy Graham as the warm up man he'd be executed after his Central Park gig by the largest empire on earth via humane injection. The Bishops and Clergy would have chains around their necks with a gold syringe pendant hanging off it? Much better than a small gold electric chair I think. Jesus' agent, will hold onto the full interactive rights the global audience would be huge getting more viewers than the Mike Tyson v Evander Holyfield 50 year anniversary ear lobotomy re-match! The early christian church really blew it when it come to holding on to the copyright. Fancy selling them to Hollywood Film producers!

Steve and Dan went to Maurice's home in West Bromwich, a quite unobtrusive detached house on a new estate on the then K1 police sub-division. The door was opened slowly and there stood a tall white male, about 6'04" tall, slim to the point of being anorexic, wearing a blue bath towel, having just bathed. He went on to report that he had just discovered wet footprints in his kitchen that led to, would you believe, yes, his bathroom! He then took the young protectors of justice upstairs to his Fathers bedroom telling them that he had found a portal to the nether world lodged in his dads walnut armoire, a wardrobe to you. It was a good sized double wardrobe that would easy hold within its capacity, a large pack of rugby forwards. You may have heard of the Chippendale, Sheraton and Hepplewhite schools of fine cabinet makers. This particular monstrosity was of the Arkwright school of cupboard building where the front had been made of American walnut with its contrasting highly polished finished look that your Gran would have liked. The back and sides of it had been shipped to the UK directly from the African Sub Continent. Not in a box, it was the box! For donkeys years such cumbersome pieces of furniture overtook the nation's bedrooms. Their well-carved fronts with poorly cast brass coloured handles, were mass produced in their thousands; the gradual attenuation in the use of timber for cabinet-making led to a change of fashion in favour of the more popular chipboard and glue, fix it together yourself and have one panel left over at the end, built-in type wardrobes, that you see everywhere nowadays.

All three men traipsed up the stairs to view the wondrous 'portal'. As he opened the wardrobe, err sorry, 'portal' door, which by now had large rounded green plastic handles. With his left hand, he beckoned the officers forward, wiggling the index finger of his right hand as he whispered, "Behold, the four riders of doom passing through the mighty portal". "The two officers, eyes as big as stainless steel soup ladles, leaned forward to get a better view of the interior of the 'portal' that had the familiar odour of naphthalene (Moth Balls to you). Inside the darkened portal they saw an ancient salmon pink coloured Electrolux stand up vacuum cleaner with its plug removed and four large demi-johns of a dark, amber coloured, liquid that looked suspiciously like what it was, stale urine. Steve slowly turned his head to look at Mad Maurice and in astonishment announced, "Bloody Hell Maurice, you're absolutely right. Look at the detail, it's astounding. "Steve turned to look at the dumbfounded Dan, who, as a mere mortal, was simply staring at what appeared to him, to be, an upright vacuum cleaner and four outsized bottles of piss! "PC Joynt, Can you get me the bright red, pressurised BCF portal sealer from the boot of the police vehicle please?". Dan left and very shortly returned from the panda car with the red BCF Fire Extinguisher from the back of the panda car. Steve earnestly looked Maurice directly in the eyes and said, "Now Maurice, this is totally top secret, the authorities have known about these portals for quite some time now. The last thing we want is a mass panic on our hands, so I am now taking you into our confidence. This may look and feel like a normal fire extinguisher, but it's not. I will now seal this portal. Do you wish to stay in the room?" A wide eyed, open mouthed Maurice, nodded quickly in total agreement. Steve leaned into the portal and very liberally sprayed the extinguisher into it. Covering the Electric broomstick and the bottles of amber fluid in a thick film of fine white powder. Dan, who, by now had had his own road to Damascus experience and picked up the plummeting penny exclaimed, "Look it's beginning to close, its closing, its closing!" Maurice quizzically addressed the two law enforcement officers, who he now saw in a totally new light purely because they'd believed him, "I can't believe it officers, its beginning to close, will it be secured for good?" Steve re-assured him that it would be and sealed the doors fast with a portal sealing clamp (a bent coat hanger, which had formally hung on the rail inside the portal). Maurice has never rung the police since. So one can only presume that the portal remains undisturbed. It also seemed very logical to use a fire extinguisher, as I believe naphthalene is highly flammable. I am informed that modern mothball makers use dichlorobenzene instead. Steve and Dan kept in touch with Maurice for quite some time afterwards, who unfortunately showed very little improvement. I wonder if the wardrobe is still there or if the four horsemen found a more appropriate medium, perhaps an antique effect Aspelund portal from IKEA. Understandably, if such important and illustrious religious representations as the four horsemen of the apocalypse should choose to announce their dramatic emergence to the whole of Christendom, from the back of an old dusty wardrobe in a box room located somewhere in the West Midlands. Who are we to question it? A burning bush was once used by a deity I believe. Incidentally, the officers never did ascertain if Maurice actually held a current licence to own a portal in the first place! I believe you can even get Japanese portals in High Definition now you know.

Another great story from Steve, took place in Tipton in a midsummer, sometime in the eighties. Now, snakes are fascinating creatures and with regular handling can become quite tame house pets, I believe. However, snakes, although cold bodied and limbless are obviously not goldfish. They have unique care and handling needs and should only be looked after by responsible people who can appreciate and meet those needs. A snake is not just for Christmas! Some serpents, like the one in our next tale, grow very large and can of course be extremely dangerous, so any potential snake owner needs to carefully research the scaly creatures before acquiring one. Tiptonites are notoriously known for their eccentricities, this story involves such a pet reptile that one unconventional troglodyte from Tipton decided had become too large to look after in his council semi. The outsized Boa Constrictor, let's call him 'Malcolm', that Mr Blenkinsopp noticed sun bathing in the front garden of his council semi at Princes End on that sunny afternoon was huge. Who does the finder call for help? Bearing in mind there is a Zoo with its reptile experts a couple of miles up the road in Dudley and an RSPCA office, four miles away in Rowley Regis? Of course he rings the West Midlands Police! Steve and his newly recruited crewmate, let's call him Ralph, are turned out to the call. When they arrive at the address a large brood of locals have already gathered by the dwarf wall marking the edge of Mr Blenkinsopp's garden, watching Mr B fearlessly holding back the passive looking reptile with a kitchen stool a bit like a brave lion tamer surrounded by tired, elderly, toothless and clawless big cats at a politically incorrect travelling circus. The boys in blue arrive to a round of applause (It was Tipton remember). Steve, without showing a morsel of fear bravely turned to the young probationer he had in tow and said, "Ralph, put the snake in the car, son". Malcolm was a young snake, only about five feet long. As he sunned himself on what Mr Blenkinsopp optimistically called a lawn, Ralph decides to tell Steve that he, like Indiana Jones in the cinema was ophidiophobic. The fear of snakes. It comes from the Greek word 'ophis' which means snake. The fear of snakes is a common phobia. A typical ophidiophobic, Ralph not only feared snakes when in live contact but also dreaded to even think about them or even see them on television or in print. Ralph's face went rather pale and he started to physically shake at the sight of Malcolm. A slightly annoyed but amused Steve told Ralph to go back to the car and wait there. After rejecting the black plastic bin liner initially offered by the expert 'lion tamer' to house Malcolm, Steve then accepts Mr. Blenkinsopp's alternative suggestion for a temporary Snake carrier, a canvas sack. The unemployed father of seven from Tipton instantaneously became the world's foremost authority on reptilia, in particular their suborder Serpentes, based purely on the masterful abilities he exhibited during his garden antics with a kitchen stool! Steve courageously popped the quite weighty tongue flicking Malcolm into the small hessian sack for his transportation into police custody. After thanking the great white hunter for his assistance,he took him over to the car, again, uncannily, to the madcap applause of an appreciative group of admiring Tiptonians. He dropped the sack into the lap of the horror-struck Ralph who upon apprehension of the situation held the sack containing Malcolm tightly at arm's length averting his gaze, much to the amusement of Steve who chuckled as he walked around the front of the police car and into the driving seat. The top of the sack was securely knotted so there was no way Malcolm could break away from police custody. Ralph eventually grew in confidence lowering the loaded sack to the floor, sitting with the bag resting in the passenger side foot well with a writhing beast between his legs, ooer Mrs! The marked Allegro was pointed in the direction of Dudley Zoo and off drove our heroes. Steve had already explained the 'Malcolm' saga to the controller at K1 who had arranged new digs for Malcolm at the location Mr. Blenkinsopp should have called in the first place, the Zoo. Much as the supervision at Wednesbury wanted to see Malcolm in all his glory. Steve was directed to drive him straight to Dudley. As they drove along an already fretful Ralph started to get quite agitated, increasingly sweaty and uncomfortable, he realised his worst dread was becoming fact, "The bloody things trying to get out the bag" he shouted anxiously looking ominously across at his tutor. With that, Malcolm's head pops out of a hole in the bag between Ralph's legs and the unmistakable beady eyes and flicking tongue of a dangerous boa constrictor settle on the cringing probationer. Ralph's eyes in return are quite beady, bulging out widely as he utters an understatement of boa constrictor proportions. He breathes deeply as if it was his last breath and utters with a trembling timid squeak that used to pass for a voice, "Steve, I think he's trying to escape!" Without a moment's hesitation and not even waiting for Steve to slow down. Ralph opens the passenger door and hurls himself out of the moving vehicle. A flabbergasted Steve is still driving along at thirty miles per hour with an uncontrolled Boa Constrictor called Malcolm squirming around freely somewhere in the same car. Steve looks down in the foot well were Malcolm had been travelling. He wasn't there. That's because he was in Steve's foot well wrapping himself around the foot pedals of the allegro. A traumatized Steve checked that the vehicle behind him was a safe distance away, then performed an emergency stop right there in the middle of the carriageway. Because a child had run into the road and the path of the oncoming car like the driving test Scenario? No, because a four stone boa constrictor called

Malcolm was out of the bag and exploring his new mode of transport! This caused the busy Saturday afternoon traffic to stop sharply behind the police vehicle. Bearing in mind the following vehicles were also trying to avoid a rolling Ralph who had darted across the carriageway under their wheels. Steve got out of the car and burst out laughing at the whole mayhem that had occurred. He glanced at a flustered Ralph who by now had made it to the safety of the central reservation and was dusting himself down and inspecting the damage to his former pristine police uniform. The bewildered motorists were just that, waiting for some direction from either the laughing policeman or his young bedraggled trainee. Steve, pulls the panda over to the nearside of the carriageway, composes himself, turns on the flashing blue beacon and then signals the waiting motorists inviting them to continue their routine excursions. Ralph hobbles over to join Steve at the police vehicle then both officers begin their search for the missing Malcolm. In trepidation, a nervous Ralph examines both foot wells, the mats and under the seats, nothing! Steve slowly and apprehensively checked the engine compartment and the boot. No signs of Malcolm." He must have got out during all the excitement" said an uncertain Steve." Ralph go and look down the road, and see if you can see him". "Why me?" said Ralph. "You lost him", said Steve, "Anyway, Driver drives!" After a thorough search of the road, down both sides for a hundred or so metres. The bobbies presumed that Malcolm must have slithered out of the police car and found a lovely damp drain to live in, ideal. Think our two pillars of society. They both get back in the car and drive off. Steve's brain was working overtime trying to think of an explanation to give to the supervision for Malcolm's disappearance. He needn't have bothered, a short time later the roof lining just above Steve's head began to move. All of a sudden, Malcolm's head appears through the half opened zippered access panel close to the panda's windscreen. Only this time Malcolm seemed more than a little irascible, hissing loudly and striking out repeatedly when disturbed by the presence of the startled officers, for the second time the vehicle is evacuated. Ralph also thinks of evacuating somewhere else too! The disinclined Ralph and Steve have a brief conversation to discuss a plan of action. Steve once more turns Masai Mara Ranger and without thinking of the danger recaptures Malcolm who accommodatingly submits and I think even he was relieved to get back into the sack. All this overlooked by a frozen Ralph who did his impression of a statue. The Keystone Cops finally deposited an exhausted Malcolm at Dudley Zoo, who; having been primed by the controller at West Bromwich decide to get their own back for all the April Fool's Day phone calls received from rookie police officers the length and breadth of the Midlands. All Fools' Day is that extraordinary day in the calendar celebrated in the UK on April the First. It is marked by the playing of practical jokes on friends, family, workmates and neighbours. Sending them on fools' errands with the aim of embarrassing the susceptible. The jokes only last until noon. If you play a trick on someone after this time you are the April fool. Historically, every April First a probationary constable or two, or even more in the West Midlands Police will receive a note in their paperwork basket to ring DC Lyon at Dudley CID. The note will include the telephone number of Dudley Zoo! The staff at Dudley Zoo must get sick of coming to work on April Fool's day when they get calls from young bobbies genuinely asking to speak to DC Lyon, which is usually met with the retort, "He's balancing a ball on his nose at present can he call you back?" So it was payback time. The staff good-naturedly listened to the whole saga about Malcolm as retold by the lads.

Then, with a totally straight face one of the Zoo Keepers says, "We can't take him boys, he's a deadly Patagonian constrictor. You haven't touched him have you?" "Why?" says Ralph gormlessly. "Because the Patagonian has small poisonous glands on the sides of his body that secrete when they're frightened." "Is it fatal?" asked the trusting Ralph. "No, but you'll probably end up sterilised for life". A smirking Steve, who'd been a copper long enough to know bull shine when he heard it, said to the keeper in his most somber voice, "It sounds really bad... is there an antidote Doctor?" The smirking Reptile house keeper who couldn't keep a serious look on his face any longer burst into uncontrollable laughter as he said," A couple of pints of Banks' Best Bitter at the nearest pub should do the trick mate!"

NORMAN's DOGGIE BAG

It was a surprisingly bitterly cold Sunday morning in the Black Country, the sort of cold snap that we don't seem to get any more even in the last few days of January in the UK until January 2010 that is. In those early hours it was Cold with a Ker Ker capital 'D'! A gibbons moon glowed in the night sky as I half slid, half plodded, along the glistening white parapets of old Smethwick town, past the Tollgate Shopping Precinct just off the High Street. The lone tyre marks left by the Gritting lorry left in its wake newly gritted roads that were freshly covered in a fine twinkling mesh of deadly ice particles. It was f-f-f -freezing, about minus 8 or 9 degrees! Mind you, I may well be exaggerating the temperature to some extent. I often remind myself. Millions of times a day in fact, not to overstress or embellish. But, I digress, I had just finished my one o'clock refs break and had not long left the station, making my way towards the Oldbury Road, intending to check the Industrial estates along Spon Lane that had sprung up on the former location of Chances glassworks. It's a sign of modern times I suppose. You have a site where literally thousands of local Black Country folk once plied their trades replaced by thirty odd Industrial units where a few hundred commuters from other parts of the West Midlands now ply theirs. Spon Lane was the main drag that marked the invisible divisional boundary betwixt us, the Kilo 3 sub division with the K1 sub division, our divisional Headquarters at West Bromwich. The M5 elevated motorway bridge spanning the road also sped high over the ward boundaries connecting the Sandwell Metropolitan Borough towns of Smethwick and West Bromwich of course. Most unimpressively, the West Midlands has most miles of elevated Motorway in Europe. I bet you're glad I shared that with you aren't you? I glimpsed at the £1.49 cheap alloy watch that I'd not long splashed out on at the 24/7 petrol station on the Oldbury Road. Ideal for operational police work, they had been churned out by the thousand somewhere out in the far east by an exploited labour force no doubt. But, If you were rolling around wrestling on the floor of a Function Room at some local hostelry, trying to slap a pair of cuffs on an odious twenty stone troglodyte from Birmingham covered in *Old Spice*, during a grab a granny night and smashed your watch in the process, it wouldn't matter. I once lost a rather nice Seiko watch early in my police career doing exactly that. So now I was glancing at a tacky, but none the less,reasonably accurate timepiece. Which came with a lifetime guarantee. When it broke the mainspring would uncoil and slash your wrist! My new inexpensive chronometer disappointingly indicated that it was still only quarter past two in the morning!

Spon Lane. Now there's a funny name for a road. What is a spon? A spon, was a holy relic brought back by Black Country Crusaders visiting the Holy Land in the Middle Ages. It's true. A good example of a spon would be a small sliver of wood, sold by some entrepreneurial market trader from a lively bustling bazaar in the ancient city of Jerusalem to one of our early English 'Tommy's,' English soldiers on the Crusades, who called this part of the Midlands, 'home'. One of these heroes, let's call him 'Enoch', would be told that the lump of wood he was holding was an indisputable portion of the blessed saviours cross and available to him for a paltry sum. Yes, there's one born every epoch! Apparently, there had been just such a relic displayed at the junction of the main thoroughfare between Smethwick and Oldbury. That part of the main road becoming distinctively known as the Lane by the Spon, developing into Spon Lane in latter times. Spon Lane also once held the dubious distinction of having the most public houses in one street in Britain, fourteen of them I think. This dates back to a time when this tiny part of the world was factually the hub of British industry and a great deal of thirsty foundry workers would quench their dehydration not only before and after, but during their work period. But, I'm going off at a tangent again.

A not quite full moon, shimmered on the surface of the solid, refrigerated puddles.in the pavement I walked on. Luckily, I didn't have to work in the gruelling hell on earth that was the upshot for those hardened foundry workers. I was a soft palmed copper. To protect myself against the harsh arctic, sub-zero conditions, I was wearing my pair of size ten 'Dockers' (Doctor Marten Boots – Black), two pairs of socks, one of thin polyester covered by an ultra-thick pair of woolly hiking socks. My pale sky blue *'Damart'* long johns were hidden under my thick blue serge heavy uniform trousers. I'll let you into my confidence, I'm sure you'll keep this to yourself. I was also wearing two old pairs of the wife's tights under the damarts! They were, to my amazement, unexpectedly snug albeit somewhat laddered because of my heavy-handed dressing technique! I also wore a string vest, a thick tee shirt, a uniform issue 'Rael Brook' blue shirt and regulation navy blue woolly jumper underneath a tightly belted tunic. Finally a Payne's grey three-quarter length Gannex Macintosh (Made famous by former Prime Minister, Sir Harold Wilson a real fashion statement of the time for a young man in his twenties...not!) dangled awkwardly on my lagged frame. There are some blokes in any uniformed organisation that look fantastic in a uniform. There are those who will always look like a Bag of shit. I always fell into the latter description, even when my boots were perfectly bulled to a finish that would easily please the harshest Regimental Sergeant Major! To finish the ensemble, I was wore a thick pair of 'issue' black leather, pure wool lined gloves and of course what every British Police Constable is recognised by, the world over, a Custodian Helmet (A Tit Hat to you). The helmet is supposed to be held on by a thin highly polished chin strap, but the only time you ever see one used is by uninformed members of the acting profession on televised dramatic cop shows (The entertainment profession get lots of things wrong when it comes to police work. Film makers: You only need ask a bobby, don't be shy. P.S. Don't ask a retired Detective Chief Superintendent either. They get a higher pension than a front line operational bobby earns! .While I'm at it, Why do you always have octogenarian former cockney wide-boys masquerading as senior detectives?). Custodian Helmets have two chin straps - one for normal usage which no self respecting bobby ever wears and one seat belt material type double strap fitted with a plastic chin cup for more arduous activities, which is folded up inside the helmet when not in use. When I was young in service I hated to wear the bloody thing. But, not only did I get used to wearing this headdress, I grew proud of wearing it. It's a traditional symbol, an icon of re-assurance to all Britons, everyone on the globe in fact. Whether they be in trouble, confused, a little off course, totally lost or just enquiring for the time! That hat singles us out, we are men set apart for the purpose of helping their fellow citizens. Approachable, trustworthy, reliable, upright. Just like our female counterparts, who unfortunately have to wear a sort of bowler hat, that doesn't really merit anywhere near the same authority and character as a Custodian police helmet.

Now that I was feeling sweaty with the significant heaviness of numerous layers of textiled insulation wrapped around me, I was still absolutely bloody freezing in the extremities! It was that cold, I could feel icicles forming on the tips of my newly grown and tidily trimmed goatee beard (Which I'd grown on the last set of nights, as per Police Regulations). My numbly anaesthetised freezing ears, could just about make out the crackling hullabaloo of voices that emanated from the prussian blue Burndept Police Radio I had pegged onto my synthetic left lapel; with its two inch, screw threaded, bakelite aerial and the diminutive yellow transmit button on its apex. The shaft of light originating from my green, moulded plastic, forty five degree angled torch, looked lukewarm as its glowing beam hurdled from building to building, doorway to doorway, but I can assure you it gave out no warmth whatsoever. I was walking vigorously, in an effort to get the cold blood circulating around my well lagged system. It was the 'Q' word. Bobbies are suspicious buggers at the best of times, if it's quiet, they will not use this term, as this may invite unwelcome policing activity! So, It was the Q word and as a result, was contemplating having a crafty fag in a shop doorway. I could feel the Benson and Hedges' fag box inside my Custodian, drumming out a message against the top of my noggin, like morse code, as if to remind me of their presence. A custodian helmet was a decent place to hide cigarettes. In fact it was a good place to hide anything! A mate of mine, Andy Armstrong even hid his chips in his....See my Tribute to Andy for the details! There was another reason for concealing my ciggies in my hat. It was because one particular shift Sergeant, who will remain nameless, would approach young probationary constables (and there were quite a few of them on the shift – certainly enough for that tight sod) and scrounge fags from them. He would tour around in the supervision car, 'meeting' up with probationers out on foot patrol on their designated beats. He'd give them a little warm in his car, have one one of their fags, sign their pocket book to record his 'meet' with them, before kicking them back out to face natures extremes again. So, I used to hide the remainder of my twenty *Bensons* under my hat and told this particular pillar of society that I'd left my fags in my locker back at the ranch! Mind you I can understand why he had to cadge so many cigarettes. Sergeants are only paid about double the wages of the Probationary Constables!

Anyhow, I was contemplating lighting up another coffin nail by the steps of the local Sikh Gurdwara when in the distance I could see the small figure of a man walking towards me. The fag would have to wait; I concealed myself in the shadow of a shop doorway, so as not to be seen by the shadowy figure that was getting closer to me. It was a white bloke, extremely thin, he looked to be in his late thirties. He was hardly dressed! He was only wearing a white vest,white-ish underpants and a well worn pair of brown carpet slippers. He was carrying a large tatty canvas black and white cross-word chequered, zip topped, ladies shopping bag. The kind of bag your mother used to take to the market when she was shopping for loose potatoes or fresh vegetables, with large arched handles, that he gripped tightly in his right hand. I'd only been in the job about a year at the time, but even me an inexperienced young sprog could spot that he was obviously an 'All Saints Job'. All Saints being Birmingham's largest Mental Hospital located (ironically) next to HMP

Birmingham, better known locally as Winson Green Prison. I immediately radioed my controller and asked for a police car and some blankets, explaining the circumstances. The panda car, with its more than adequate heater, was winging its way towards the pair of us. Anytime now, we would be making our way to All Saints, in a toasty warm, marked, Austin allegro panda car. The man, bizarrely, demonstrated no signs whatsoever of being affected by the harmful weather conditions. He was clean shaven, with collar length, long dark wavy brown hair. His thin but strong muscular arms were covered in tattoos. As I got closer to him I could see evidence of self abuse scarring on and around his wrists. Incredulously I said to him, "Who are you then?" He tells me his name his 'Norman'. I had no reason to disbelieve him, as he bore a crude self-inflicted tattoo at the top of his left arm that spelled out the word 'Worm'. With closer scrutiny; I suppose it could have said, 'Norm'! "OK Norm, this is a funny time to be out and about, where are you going?"I asked. "Work!" He replied curtly, in a soft but very broad Black Country accent. "Where do you work then?" I asked. "At a Foundry in Tipton" he brusquely retorts. Now, although there were quite a few foundries in the Tipton area in October 1980 and foundries are tremendously hot places were the foundry men remain quite warm even on the coldest of winter nights. Tipton was in totally the opposite direction from where chummy was heading and he was somewhat underdressed for the Sikh Temple! "What's in the bag then Norman?" said the intrepid young law enforcement officer, in some feeble attempt at engaging Norman in conversation. Whilst at the same time expectantly glancing down Smethwick High Street for a glimpse of the deployed mobile heater, err, I mean, car! Norman frowns at me, holds the bag tightly against his chest and counters very snappily and self-protectively,"Dogs!" "Dogs?" I say. "DOGS!" He growls (Sorry, couldn't resist). I can then see the lights of the longed-for approaching panda car. Doug 'The Thug' Froggitt was the driver. 'The Thug,' an old-school nickname that rhymes with Doug, doesn't sound very politically correct in these modern times of policing diversity. But hey, it's better than his other nickname, which was 'Thrombo,' Why? Because he was a slow moving clot!

But yet again, I digress, Doug turned on the blue beacon, which flashed just once, to sort of announce his arrival. I then said to Norman, "Lets have a look in the bag then mate". It must be the copper in us that asks questions like that of blokes who are obviously not criminal types. Anyhow, just as the panda pulls up at the kerbside. On the spare of the moment, Norman unzips the bag, holds both handles in a vice like grip, raising the bag roughly just six inches away from my face and quite unexpectedly and speedily opens and closes the zip end of the bag in a sort of clapping motion but more, knuckle to knuckle, whilst blaring, in chorus, down me ear hole, with a very loud imitation of a dog-barking, "Rerr,rerr,rerr,rerr, rerr,rerr,rerr rerr,rerr, rerr,rerr RERRRRRR!!!!" Well...I recoiled, for what seemed like six foot into the air! To say I was startled would be an understatement. I remember when I was a student in Birmingham. I went to the Odeon Cinema in New Street, to see the new release everyone had been talking about. It was a film called,*Jaws*. I sat in the centre seat of the front row circle. Next to me was my college roommate, Paul Singh. Paul was about five foot four inches tall and woefully thin, he weighed about six and a half stone wet through. When the scene came, where the fisherman's head shoots in a flash, out of a hole in a wrecked boat at the bottom of the ocean. Everyone in the cinema was instantly startled, except Paul. Who, not content with simply being 'startled'. Literally jumped forwards at a vast rate of knots, straight out of his seat, making a bee line for the the stalls below, but without using the stairs! I instinctively reached out at him with my right hand and grabbed the back of his jacket reeling him back in, like *Quint* sea fishing angler from the film, back into his seat! Now that's how bloody startled I was when Norman barked at me like a dog! Incidentally, I have remembered another odd thing about that visit to the cinema that day. At the end of the movie, when the Great White was dispatched by Amity Islands police chief, everyone in the flix, celebrated with a round of spontaneous applause. Something I had last experienced at the Minors Matinee at the ABC Capitol Cinema in North Road, St Helens when I was eleven years old. I have never seen such a response to a film before or since.

Back to Norman. Upon regaining my composure on the High Street, believe me, I was entirely delighted to find that my underpants were still surprisingly, uncontaminated. However, there was a peculiar smell in the air! Doug, was already walking over towards us and with a massive smile across his face at the scene he'd just witnessed he threw a couple of blankets over Norman and said to him. "Get in the car son, we'll get some colour back in yer cheeks." Now fully recovered from my sudden jolt, I sat next to my eccentric assailant in the nearside back of the warm cosy cop car. As I joined him and looked into his bag to search it properly, my glasses steaming up instantly in the warm Allegro saloon, which again brought a smile to Normans face! When the thin film of steam had cleared from my glasses I saw the thawing Norman, wrapped in the blankets, his eyes now sparkling and full of life. "I got you didn't I?" he said, smiling broadly at me, with a big toothy grin. "You got me alright, Norm" I answered. "Will the voices in your blue box tell you take me back to the hospital now, I'm fuckin' freezing?" he said, audaciously. Norm was referring to the blue Burndept Radio strapped around my neck and the constant messages that came buzzing from it. When we got to All Saints, it was still dark as we drove along the long misty driveway. With a heavy ground frost and the low hanging swirling morning mist, it reminded me of a Hammer Horror film set. I'm tempted to say that I heard an owl hooting in the distance, but you don't get many owls in Winson Green! The huge imposing Victorian building had an impressive set of steps leading up to an enormous, ostentatious pair of black, highly glossed, painted double doors. I went to knock, then saw a small, circular flush fitting doorbell with a porcelain button that had the inviting word,' PRESS' written on it. I wish I hadn't pressed! Just as Norman was about to say, "Just give the door a little tap. " The doorbell, which sounded like one of those bells that used to resound below stairs when the Duke or Duchess wanted another lump of coal putting on the already blazing fire, was at this time of the morning a tad loud. Like the toll of the bell that a town crier would peel off before shouting Oyez,oyez,oyez at the top of their voice! The door eventually creaked open slowly and the unbutton coated, slipper wearing, night security guard holding a pot of brewing tea in his hand, popped his head out of the gap in the door, looked at the assembled trembling trio, saw the blanket covered wanderer and said, "Hello Norman, do your new friends want a cup of tea?" We re-housed Norman, who, it transpired, had stopped taking his medication, an act which usually led him to explore the cold streets of Warley, his old home town.

What was in the bag? I hear you ask. Well, Norman wasn't lying. The bag, that went everywhere with Norman, had belonged to his dear departed mother. It contained about twenty 'dogs' of varying shapes, colours and sizes. Some were small decorative porcelain ornaments, doggie curios, bits and pieces of doggie type jumble. Some were small (toy soldier type) moulded plastic dogs. Some were those solid, garishly painted chalk characters (probably smeared in carcinogenic lead paint) figurines that fairground stalls used to award to punters as prizes for getting three darts in three separate playing cards or knocking down five or more targets on the air pistol ranges. He even had a small soft rubber 'squeaky' toy dog, toddler type plaything. So you see, Norman really was carrying dogs in his bag!

PEGGY MOUNT
VISITS OLD HILL

I like this story. It takes place in the Old Hill Front Office sometime in the very early 1980's. I say that because Old Hill nick is an old building that existed in the 1880's, so I couldn't just say 80's! It's a quaint old fashioned building that has a welcoming ethos that most of its visitors take to immediately. I say most for the obvious reason, that some of our more regular clients may not agree with me about its 'friendly' character! I don't think anyone now knows when it was actually built! Originally a Staffordshire Constabulary Station, it was certainly around by 1884, as it is shown on the local maps of the time. The year that saw a siege at Khartoum, against its defenders led by British General Charles George Gordon, in the same year the cornerstone was laid for the Statue of Liberty. Around that time came the introduction of domestic electric lighting in wealthy homes the UK and it we was still three years away from Queen Victoria's Golden Jubilee and Jack the Ripper was four years away from becoming the most infamous killer of all time! Nowadays, 'The Hill', as it is affectionately known, is still an operational satellite station on the K2 (South Sandwell) operational command unit, which is the modern term for 'division', of the West Midlands Police area. Another interesting fact about this particular area is that it encapsulates an area where once three different County Boundaries (Thus Including 3 Police Forces) once met. Those counties being, Staffordshire, Warwickshire and Worcestershire. There is a thoroughfare in the Bearwood area of Smethwick called Three Shires Oak Road where these three shires once met! Piddock Road Police Station in Smethwick was a Staffs County nick. Whereas, Oldbury Town just up the road, was policed by Worcestershire Constabulary! This area, as a result became known notoriously as an area for punishment stations! One bobby I knew, Derek Frodsham, a tall, erect, ex- guardsman was initially employed as a beat officer in the City of Worcester. Joining the old Worcestershire Constabulary Force upon his release from the Royal Army. Derek told me that he'd crossed swords with a particular gruff Sergeant who took an instant dislike to him. The sergeant always got his way in those days and it ended in tears with Derek being transferred to what was then a punishment station for Worcestershire Bobbies. Derek found himself leaving the leafy glades of the beautiful City of Worcester to become a beat officer on the Lion Farm Estate in Oldbury. A then, brand new 1960's inner city housing estate , a small concrete village! He'd never seen a tower block and now he had to police half a dozen of the bloody things!

The architect who designed the place has was given an award recently...a new guide dog! Another bobby I knew who was moved for disciplinary reasons was a bobby named Brian Stockley. "Stocky" was the collator at Smethwick or Smerrick, as the locals call it, when I joined in January 1980. The collator was a PC who administered local intelligence and formulated the daily briefing reports to the various shifts as they paraded for duty. Do you remember the grey haired old geriatric copper in the 'Frost' ITV Police programme with Detective Inspector Del Boy, who looks about seventy years old even then and Del always go to for intelligence reports? Well, He was the collator, that's what "Stocky" was. Mind you, the bloke in Frost was one of those super cops who Del Boy would approach by saying, 'I've found a tyre track at the scene of the crime' and he'd say, 'Yeah Del boy, it's from a 1936 Bugatti saloon, it's British racing green and has accident damage on the front nearside fender. The only scrote I know owns one of them is the Storekeeper at Nanny Clarke's waterbed factory, Binky 'No Brains' Smithers, he lives at 32 Acacia Mansions, Denton, lives there alone since his mother ran off with a team of unicycling librarians from Willenhall', and still reading from the record card, says, 'Dear oh dear, Del Boy, he's a known associate of Mad Teddy 'Two Barrels' Carew, who's just been released from Broadmoor after doing' a ten spot for blaggin' the Thora Hird Tea Rooms, Newton Le Willows with a loaded water pistol!

The real world of the collator, I think you'll be amazed to learn, is nothing like that. I'm not sure if 'Stocky' himself came to the sunny West Midlands because of disciplinary troubles with his supervisors (Although it wouldn't have surprised me if he had!). 'Stocky' was a Bobbies bobby who had forgotten more than I ever knew! He told me that if a bobby got in bother with his Sergeant or worse, his Inspector, he would again be moved Stations, for the silliest breaches of discipline, to teach the other bobbies a lesson. Which doesn't sound too bad. But if, for example, you worked at Hanley, Stoke on Trent and 'they' wanted to be awkward 'they' could and would be vindictive and cruel enough to transfer you to the most southerly point in the force as a punishment. Smethwick! some sixty odd miles away! Now bear in mind that in those days, most Bobbies lived in Police accommodation and as such would be provided with a police house or flat in the vicinity of their station, it doesn't seem that bad does it? But when you think it meant that your family would have to uproot all ties it had in that locale. . Your close relatives, yours spouses job and your children's schooling where all effected, simply because some nasty bastard of a supervisor took a dislike to you. It's called victimisation and bullying now. Then they called it discipline.

An example of the sort of infraction of the discipline code would be an officer being late for pay parade. You've heard of the phrase, 'Pay Parade', I'm sure. It stems from the armed forces. On police pay days, the whole of the division or sector would have to parade in their stations back yard. Standing in ranks, like in the forces. Marching and Drill would be performed and then the officers would be inspected by the senior officer, usually a Superintendent. If you failed this inspection, you didn't get paid, that was that! During this 'Pay Parade' any misdemeanours would be discussed in front of his peers, the whole section. There were so many minor infractions of rules that these days would tantamount to bullying or harassment. But then, hey..... . They were the good old days, weren't they?

A nice story I like where some gaffers were sometimes just a tad heavy handed on discipline was told to me by a mate of mine PC Bob Lyon, who is due to retire in late 2010, Bob related a tale he witnessed in the early eighties as a young probationer and involves the use of a new invention that in just a few more years was going to revolutionise how we all spent a lot of our leisure time. A senior constable on Bob's shift was a bobby named Kenny Greenhall , a fabulous bobby, who in his spare time was a professional Snooker referee. You know, one of them geezers on the telly that wears a penguin suit with white cotton gloves and keeps saying, "Foul stroke, four away, free ball", that sort of thing! Well, Kenny, who I also remember well, but never worked with, looked a bit like the old horror film actor Lon Cheney Junior and a haircut like Ray Reardon, he had chubby red cheeks, a bostin' black country accent and a fantastic sense of humour. In this tale he'd been off on sick leave, with something trivial, like a bad cold. Upon his return to work at the first briefing he attended in the parade room at West Brom his supervision told him that he had to go upstairs later that morning to report to the Chief Inspector who wished to see him about his weeks sick leave. Nine o'clock arrives and Ken goes to see the Chief Inspector Snoddy who gravely announces that disciplinary procedures are about to be initiated regarding PC Greenhall 's 'behaviour' during the weeks sick leave he'd just taken. A puzzled Ken, started wracking his brains thinking 'Whats he talking about'. Ken had genuinely been ill with whatever he had ailing him or at least thats what everyone thought. Chief Inspector Snoddy said, "Greenhall , at 2100hrs last Tuesday the 29th of Octemder your shift were on late duties. However, you were shown as being off sick with a cold is that correct?" Ken replied "Yes Sir that's correct." "Well Greenhall , what would you say if I told you that you were <u>seen</u> to be fit and well and what's more, rather dapper in your 'other' working suit refereeing a Snooker match between Albie the Hurricane Higginson and Big Bill Tumeric on a television knock out Snooker competition." "Gaffer I was in bed last Tuesday night cuffin' an 'hayvin (Black Country for Coughing and Heaving. In other words. I have a cold) my missis'll back us on that." Ken interjected. "So why is it that I saw you in full colour on my twenty-six inch Ferguson on Tuesday night refereeing a snooker match, no Greenhall , I've got you bang to rights, with the little grey cells as Poirot would put it and unless you have a decent excuse I'm going to sheet you. You were fit and well weren't you Greenhall ?" Chief Inspector Snoddy sat there grinning at him as Ken paused for a second and then as if inspired replied. "Boss, you are quite right, I was the referee on the snooker the other night for the Higginson/Tumeric frame you are quite right, but it didn't take place last Tuesday night. You were watching what the telly people call VT or videotape sir!"

After a short lecture on the pre recording and Video Taping of television programmes from PC Greenhall, Chief Inspector 'Poirot' was very embarrassed and decided to lock himself away in a darkened room for the rest of the day with an ice bag on his noggin to cool the little grey cells, he'd been well and truly snookered.

Ken got back to the shift and elucidated. Bob was out on patrol with Ken later that morning and said to him, "I thought that particular snooker competition was televised live from Pebble Mill?" "It is", replied a smiling Ken, frame to Greenhall I think!

But I digress, yet again. My little Old Hill story. In 1980, Old Hill nick was still all olde worlde, none of this sort of modern finery, like computers, air conditioning, mobile phones, health and safety regulations and the like! The front office at the hill was similar to an old off licence department of a public house. You walked through a big thick oak door into a very dimly lit, cubby hole, a tiny sort of vestibule which I can only describe as a small square patch of hallway, probably 5' x 5', and a dark little box. Straight in front of you was a door which was locked, or at least closed to the public using it as an entrance to the nick. To your left was another locked door. To the right of you there was a hatch, a serving hatch a bit like the old fashioned type hatches you used to see in dentists surgeries and busy restaurant kitchens. It had a small ledge on it where people could rest their weary elbows as they unloaded their problems to the ever alert front office assistant. This serving hatch led onto the old front office, and the office man, who would be a PC, that's a constable for those uninitiated not a computer. Yes the police force had PC's in their offices when Bill Gates wasn't even old enough to open a real window. The PC in the front office on this particular Sunday was a lad called Dave Rhodes , a great lad, who knew the job backwards. The one thing about working the front office was, you only got front offices duties if you were either in the mire because you'd upset the supervision, you had upset a member of the great British public and as a result they had made a complaint and you'd been served disciplinary forms and was awaiting a decision from the Chief Constable, if you were grounded from driving Police vehicles cause you'd been in a Polac (Police Accident) or you'd been injured in the line of duty and had come back to work on light duties (Where you were well enough to come and hobble round the nick and get in everyone else's way but not well enough to go out on the streets and do the proper operational policing).

To avoid any confrontational duties during this period of waiting for a decision on what to do with you, the powers that be would keep you out the way and more to the point, keep you out of trouble by putting you on front office duties. So for whatever reason, Dave Rhodes is the front office PC on this particular evening at Old Hill. Now, being the front office man at Old Hill had its perks. Because of the serving hatch, the front office man could wear literally anything he liked from the waist down, within reason of course. He could wear jeans and trainers or slippers or anything he liked because obviously being a serving hatch, the public visiting only saw you from the waist up! So, if you wore your police shirt and your epaulets (They are the small folded pieces of cloth that bear your metal collar numbers) and your tie when you answered any calls at the serving hatch. People visiting the nick saw a real police officer in uniform, little did they know that down below he could have had on a basque, suspenders and high heeled shoes, and they wouldn't have known it, and of course there were, I would have thought in those days, some officers who were that way inclined! But that is another story.

But, getting back to Dave Rhodes in the front office, this was one those nights when Dave was wearing his slippers and his jeans. From the waist up he was a serving West Midlands Police officer, resourcing the front office at Old Hill Police Station. On this particular evening, the hatch bell went, summoning Dave away from his copy of Titbits. He put down his brew and walked over to the hatch. Where even before he opened the sliding glass door, he could see a middle aged couple through the frosted glass having what we call in the police, a domestic, a temporary breakdown in an otherwise loving relationship. Basically, the lady looked and carried on a bit like Peggy Mount. For those who don't know who she was. She was a gifted actress, who was famous for playing the stereotypical foreboding battle-axe wife, she used to appear in comedy programmes in the 1960's, was enormous, built like a Wakefield Trinity Rugby League front row forward with a face to match. Unlike Ms Mount, she was shouting, bawling, effing and blinding (It was Old Hill remember) at her comparatively tiny breadwinner. The stereotypical, proverbial, quiet, shy, hen-pecked, retiring, four foot nothing of a husband that, in not so many words was becoming a bit of a failure in his marital tasks! They had decided to leave the privacy of their own home, putting on their coats to face inclement weather, all in an effort to save their marriage! Dave Rhodes said, "What's the problem, then", as the little guy goes to speak, the battle axe butts in and says, "It's him aye it, he keeps having a goo at me, tellin me, me cookin's shite. "

She then breaks into a flood tears and so, without further ado, Dave says, "Okay madam, calm down, come through and we'll have a chat about it see if we can sort it all out". Now basically what Dave meant was, I'll unlock the public entrance door, let you into the station, you can come through to the little room off the corridor that we have for witness statement taking, where we can all sit down and discuss the matter in a reasonable, commonsensical way, over a pot of tea. Dave would listen to their woes and give advice where we could. I used to ask such a couple how long they had been together. If they said any figure higher than 3 years. I would tell them that I had only been married for two years and they expect me to advise them about marriage! But of course this being Old Hill, the minute Dave said, 'come through' to the couple, the husband actually mounts the counter and climbs through the hatch into the front office! He stands next to Dave and as he is dusting himself down after his mad scramble and says to his wife, "Come on then, we haven't got all night!" holding his arms out to assist her . His portly wife points and wags a stubby forefinger stuck on the end of a flabby upper right limb directly at the surprised young PC Rhodes and exclaims in a shrieking high pitched drone, 'Listen here cock, if yow think I'm coming through that theer hatch, the same that short streak o' nuthin just did, wearing no corsets to support we, yow can bloody well think again my lad!' and out through the front door she storms in a huff, or was it a Volkswagen? No, it was a huff! Followed closely by her, currently not too significant, other half, hurriedly climbing back through the hatch, he shouted after her "Juliet, my darling, wait for me!" This is a true story, Romeo had climbed through the serving hatch, Juliet, obviously assumed that she was meant to emulate her spouse and thus decided that she'd better go on a crash diet first. So left the scene without the earnestly sought police advice. I wonder if she promised to love, honour and obey during her wedding vows?

That story sums up Old Hill Police Station. The irony of this story is that Old Hill Police Station still has a front office, but unlike the early eighties, due to cutbacks and current police strategies, it has been closed for about the last five years, probably more. The Home Office have the nerve to call their policing policy, 'Neighbourhood Policing'. If you go to Old Hill nick out of office hours now, you have to use an intercom on the wall outside that puts you in touch with a police help desk officer at Smethwick, six miles away. He or she takes your details while you stand getting soaked to the skin and you thought serving the public through a small service hatch was archaic!

THE HUMAN SARDINE

The recognition and understanding of mental disorders have changed over time and across cultures. This job gleans many stories involving people with mental illnesses. This one particular night, I was double crewed in Kilo Mike Two-Zero with a colleague, PC George Ashurst. George was a Police Constable then, but last I heard of him in the job he was working at our headquarters, Lloyd House, as a Sergeant in the Anti Terrorist office. Ironically I recently had a commission to paint a local VIP and when I went to a 'sitting' with the dignitary in question, who did I meet as his Personal Assistant and Chauffeur? None other than the retired George!

I was only young in service then, still in my Probationary period. Which was my first two years in the police. We got a call to go to a mid-terraced three storey town house in Cape Hill, to a job that had come in as a family domestic. A domestic is where a family member, partner or ex-partner attempts to physically or psychologically dominate another person in that household. Usually referring to violence between spouses. But it can include cohabitants, non-married intimate partners or family members. Domestics occur in all cultures; among people of all races, ethnicities, religions, sexes and classes. Domestic violence is perpetrated by both men and women.

On this occasion an elderly black male caller was stating, "Me daughter's going mad, come quick, she's breaking the place up", or at least something very similar to that anyway. I can't remember the actual address but it was in a street in Smethwick that is now called New Hope Road. Why they call it New Hope Road, God knows, the estate is a dump designed to look like a giant rabbit warren. One of those massive patches of grey concrete that modern designers threw up in the nineteen-sixties. The whole estate was the same, little boxes, a bit like the estates we saw during the Tottenham riots, a vast sprawl of synthetic concrete boxes, that are made out of ticky tacky and all look just the same, like the song written by Malvina Reynolds and then immortalised by Pete Seeger, that parodies the development of modern suburbia.

The addresses on the New Hope Road were mainly three storey buildings with the living room on the middle storey on these council maisonettes. Squalid estates, that when you drive around them were a bewildering grey monochrome puzzle where every road, walkway and alleyway look just the same as the one around the corner in the next road. There were cul-de-sacs at every turn, it was like driving in a maze! As we drove around it, I can't remember the number we're looking for, but for arguments sake, lets say we were looking for number three hundred and fifty seven.

George as senior man, is driving the marked police panda, he stops when we see a pedestrian walking a dog. I roll the front passenger side window down, and ask the bloke, " Excuse me mate, can you tell me where number three hundred and fifty seven is please?" He has a think and scratching his forehead is just about to tell us, when and this is no word of a lie. we all see a dining table, a full solid teak dining table, come crashing through the main living room window of the house opposite us, with the almighty crash of cascading, shimmering, fragments of glass. George looked at me, I looked at George, and then we both looked at the bloke walking the dog and said to him in unison, "Its all right mate, I think we've found it". We drove over to the front door of the address where stood a little black fellow, in his late fifties,he was very slim, only about five feet six inches tall. He was in his pyjamas and slippers but still wore a pork pie hat. He was trembling with fright. He still had his phone in his shaking hands. With a really worried and shocked expression on his face, he said in a patois accent, "Officer, she's gone mad, just like her sister, who in All Saints", then he broke down sobbing into George's arms. The poor bugger. All Saints was Birmingham's psychiatric hospital. It specialised in the treatment of serious mental illness, usually for relatively long-term inpatients. Those patients who were an immediate threat of harm to themselves, or could harm other people. If there was uncertainty as to the extent of a patient's danger to themselves or others, they are typically placed in a place like All Saints for safety reasons. This guys one daughter was already there and now her twin was upstairs going the same way.

We could here the sound of braking glass and furniture coming from upstairs, as her dad cried from behind us,"She's going completely doolally tap". He confirmed that the daughter now seeming going off her trolley had got a twin sister who was already a patient at All Saints. It now looked like her doppelganger was going to be joining her quite soon. Oddly, she'd never shown any signs of mental illness and abruptly and unexpectedly she'd gone off the rails.

I went up the stairs first at George's behest, as I say, the house was on three levels, and at the top of the last flight of stairs is this woman. She isn't wearing a stitch of clothing and is covered in oil, baby oil I presumed, at least I hope it was baby oil, from head to foot, and as I say totally naked. She was sitting on the top step of the last flight of stairs with her legs wide open and to make things worse it was that time of the month! She was very pretty, a woman in her mid to late twenties, who was very slim. She had long black straight hair that was dishevelled and tousled, she had clumps of it in her tightly clenched fists as if she'd been pulling it out by the roots. She had wild staring eyes, pupils dilated, like vacant icy cold black pools, gone-out eyes, the kind of eyes that you can't look at for too long without looking away.

The kind of eyes that look totally through you at something else, they're not seeing you but they can see someone or something else. She looked down at me and suddenly acknowledging that I was there said, "Come and ride me Babylon I am the whore of Babylon!", 'Babylon', was a phrase that was used predominately by black people in the eighties Rastafarian movement. It referred to any oppressive power structure. In this case the West Midlands Police. The Whore of Babylon was a symbolic figure of evil in both Christian and Rastafarian ideology. The first time I heard of Rastafarian's and the term Babylon I was as a young probationer on foot patrol with a lad called PC Les Sculthorpe. Who one night shone his little torchlight onto the tax disc of a parked car in Price Street Smethwick and as he did so, two young black girls walking passed him defiantly started singing under their breath, 'Babylon put on di pressure!' in a reggae type beat. But I digress.

As this lady said," Ride me Babylon". I remember gulping! I looked back down the stairs at a grinning George who whispered, "She seems attracted to you Bry, Go and get her son". I went upwards, about three steps away from her. I tried to grab her arm, to arrest her and stop her playing up.

But of course, like a giant sardine, she's covered from head to foot in oil, so I'm slipping and sliding all over the place, my hands are slithering and skidding all over her, and being a young discreet officer, I'm trying to grab arms, hands, legs, feet. Not the other bits, if you know what I mean. As I tried to grab her upper arm and grab her my hands kept sliding down her forearms. It was like trying to grab a slippery oily eel. Her forearm just kept slipping out of my grasp! I was getting nowhere, very quickly. She was slapping me around the face and digging her finger nails into my tunic. She clawed them towards my face and I kept my head back away from their grasp. At the same time her eyes flashed with madness as she continuously kicked and lashed out with her sharp boney knees and greasy feet in all directions. It would not be an underestimation to say she was a real handful, if you can excuse the pun. It was reminiscent of a couple of sumo wrestlers slapping each other before going into a proper maul! While this pre-maul engagement was still in its infancy, the laughing policeman, George, had asked the grieving father for a large cotton bed sheet. George ran toward us both and actually shouted at the top of his voice in an ear piercing tone, as if to distract us both, Geronimo! As he threw said blanket over the slippery harpy, who was taken totally unawares. We both jumped over George's 'catch' and hauled our outsized pre-oiled sardine in! Having eventually overpowered her, she calmed down, a bit. She was put in the car with a terrified policewoman to watch over her and taken down to Piddock Road Police Station in Smethwick. She kept ripping off any blankets or clothes that she was supplied with and constantly danced a very seductive corporeal rumba in the middle of the dimly red bulbed lit female detention cell, under the very watchful and zealous gaze of the Custody Block staff. The Police Surgeon Doctor Wang, was called out and obviously, his examination was brief. Doc Wang virtually sectioned* her on the spot. Strangely, I have dealt with many patients from All Saints and other types of Mental Institution during my time with the police. But in thirty years in the police service I have only seen a Police Surgeon section a patient once and this was the occasion.

*The Legal involuntary commitment of a person not previously brought to the attention of the authorities to a Mental Institution against their will and/ or over their protestation.

I remember going to a small mid terraced house in Rood End, Oldbury, yes a place name that could easily be the subject of a double entendre. But The Black Country is heaving of such locations, for example, Bell End, Mincing Lane and Cock Green to name but a few. I was with my oppo, PC Bob Halsall, who was senior man and driving the Zulu fast response car, a white Morris Marina TC with a big blue flashing light, sirens and six inch fluorescent stripes on either side, that made it go faster! I was the observer, radio operator and 'gopher'. The Observer goes for the chips, goes for messages, goes first out of the car at stop checks, goes first for just about everything in fact! On this occasion I was first to go for the front door of the house in Rood End, Oldbury in response to a call from a child that went something like, "My Dad is hitting my Mum and won't stop". Bob, an advanced police driver or 'graded grain' as police officers would say, got us there at light speed through heavy traffic and we were outside the door in minutes. The front door was opened by a small seven or eight year old asian girl whose quite badly beaten Mother stood next to her sobbing and whispering in Punjabi into her daughters ear, the girl, who acted like this was totally normal, translating for her mother. We all went into the dining room at the back of the house and sitting on the obligatory bed settee that all

Sikh households seem to possess was a small, demure, well dressed asian male, very small, thin and clean shaven. This man sat quietly, hands on his knees and listened intently as the lady told us via her daughter that her husband had violently attacked her throwing her around the room in front of her children. It transpired that her Dad was a voluntary patient at All saints, at the time Birmingham's huge Psychiatric Hospital and that he walked out and went home to beat up his other half quite often! This was one of those times when Dad went AWOL (Absent Without Leave). Presuming that the man on the settee was a relative, friend or neighbour, we were both gobsmacked when we asked the little girl where her father had gone now and she pointed a small accusing right index finger at the meek,mild looking, asian male sitting on the settee, who must have been about five foot two inches tall and six stone ringing wet!

Having ascertained via his daughter that he understood English, I looked at him and said, "OK mate, you've heard what your wife said. I'm arresting you on suspicion of assault". As I started to instinctively out loud, 'caution' the man, who obviously hadn't a clue what day it was,I reached out to lawfully and symbolically lay my judicial (long) arm onto his shoulder. As I parrot fashion, said,"You are not obliged to say anything unless you wish to do so, but whatever you do say will be etc etc." The prisoner jumped to his feet and assumed the stance of a mini flyweight boxer standing fully upright, he stood with his legs shoulder-width apart, his rear foot a half-step behind his lead foot. Obviously right-handed, he lead with his left foot and fist, with his right heel off the ground. His lead fist held vertically about six inches in front of his face at eye level. The rear fist, held beside his chin, his elbows tucked against his frail looking ribcage to protecting a small puny torso, chin tucked into his chest. Eyes fixed on mine as he bobbed and weaved about. I ended the caution with his curious reply of, "Nineteen sixty seven". The strangest reply I have ever heard to the caution. Raising my open palms toward him, I told him to calm down and take things easy, to which he again replied, "Nineteen sixty seven". In fact, to each question put to him, he replied, "Nineteen sixty seven".

Then in a 'light bulb switching on in the mind of an hairy arsed copper moment.' I discovered how to use reverse psychology! I smiled at him and pointed to the door as if I were a waiter directing him to a table and said to him in a inquiring way, "Nineteen sixty seven?" He smiled, a broad, friendly smile, his serious eyes turned into kind, affectionate little globes of joy as he replied in a rapturous way,"Nineteen sixty seven!" We got to the pavement.   I opened the back door of the car like a doorman at the Ritz pointed at the back seat and inquired, "Nineteen sixty seven?", the reply as he sat in the back like, his excellency the Duke of Sandwell on a night out to the Greyhounds, was a regally ostentatious, "Nineteen sixty seven". We drove directly to All saints Hospital and I went through the same rigmarole as before to get him out of the car. Every question and each response was Nineteen sixty seven.

I never knew what the significance of the year Nineteen sixty seven (or MCMLXVII as the Romans would have said) was to him. How would I know? I was only ten years old then. But it was I think you'll agree, a very eventful year which saw: Elvis Presley and Priscilla Beaulieu married in Las Vegas.   The supertanker Torrey Canyon run aground in between Land's End and the Scilly Isles. Celtic become the first British team to reach and win a European Cup final beating Inter Milan 2–1. The Beatles released my favourite album Sgt. Pepper's Lonely Hearts Club Band, The first UK colour TV broadcasts began on BBC 2. Radio's 1,2,3 & 4 all launched in '67. Christian Barnard carried out the world's first heart transplant in Cape Town. Concorde was first unveiled and at Wembley Stadium, Queens Park Rangers became the first third division football side to win the Football League Cup, defeating my beloved West Bromwich Albion 3–2. That'll be it. The poor sod had been to Wembley and seen the Baggies lose!

Another reverse psychology ploy I used was one noisy Saturday morning in the cell block following a busy Friday night of pub scraps. A psychotic prisoner named Barry Bostock, known fittingly locally as 'Barmy Barry', was as Nissed as a Pewt (Thankfully) as the Reverend Spooner would say and was violently but metrically, head butting his cell door from the inside. Working custody block duties and unable to concentrate on my cryptic crossword, everytime I asked Barry, who strangely, had no cuts or bruises at all in spite of the savage head-butting, to discontinue this performance as it may well have been quite damaging, even to someone with a skull as thick as his and it wasn't doing the one and a half inch solid steel door much good either!

By now the Custody Officer, Sergeant Pete Ellaby, was fully contemplating a scenario where about four bobbies would have to enter the cell, wrestle him to the ground and sit on Barry, simply to restrain him till the Police surgeon came out to section him, which could be hours. All this so that Barry wouldn't do himself any damage which sounds a little paradoxical! Of course, we did ask him to stop. But when anyone asked him nicely to stop head-butting the door he told them (In native Anglo Saxon) to go away in short jerky movements, taking no notice whatsoever, quite naturally of course, Barry being a total genetic troglodyte.

How to distract him from this potentially dangerous pastime and keep him amused with a safer task I thought... mmmm The custody block had run out of colouring books, crayons and comics. There were no dirty (Mildly

Pornographic) books in the Sergeants drawer and the toy box kept in the front office for lost or found children to amuse themselves with whilst waiting to be claimed or hauled off by a Social Worker had been locked away in the cupboard for the night.

There was the custody block 'library' of course. It consisted of a new Gideons Bible, a pristine copy of the Police and Criminal Evidence Act 1984 (The legislation governing police custodial operations in England and Wales) and a grubby, well thumbed paperback copy of the The Great Escape, an autobiographical account by Paul Brickhill about life in a German prisoner of war camp Stalag Luft III for captured British and Commonwealth airmen during World War 2. Ironically, Brickhill himself never escaped from the camp, he just wrote about the ones that did! But of course 'Barmy Barry' couldn't read, so that was a negative. I could have offered him a Naxpax coffee or Tea. But,the serenity would only be fleeting and I didn't want to exacerbate matters by asking him to drink freeze dried camel droppings!

In the meantime Barry, worryingly, carried on smacking his cranium into the cell door. All of a sudden, in another 'light bulb switching on in the mind of an hairy arsed copper moment' I once again employed reverse psychology. 'It had worked once before it can work again,'I thought! I winked at Pete, who was on the blower to the Police Surgeon, as strolled down the corridor of the cell block towards the pandemonium. I grinned at Barmy Barry and speaking very softly (and slowly of course) I put my right index finger upright across my pouting lips before saying,"Sshhhhhhh, Listen Barry", I whispered, The Gaffers gone out on patrol, there's nobody in the nick, so I'm gonna go upstairs to the television lounge to watch the big match on the telly, have a nice cup of tea and soak my tired feet in a bowl of hot water and Radox. Do us a favour my mate, carry on nutting the door as hard and as loud as you can. That way, I'll hear you banging and know that you are ok so, I won't have to come checking up on you all night long. You'll do that for me won't you Barry? Ta mate" Barry immediately ceased his head banging session, scrunched up his face in such a way that I could tell that he was properly computing my question slowly, as he mulled it over in his troubled mind he frowned, quite soberly, for a inebriated neanderthal and incoherently mumbled several swear words under his breath before staggering to the bed at the back of the cell, wrapping himself in his home office blankets and going into deep comatose slumber, a rest and peaceful quiet that lasted the rest of my shift!

VARSITY LIGHT BLUES

When I was a PBO, thats a Permanent Beat Officer. Although each beat on the Division was, naturally covered by all the response officers on the four units, imaginatively titled A,B,C & D Units. But, each beat was also allocated a PBO, who, only worked that one beat. I was a PBO on Beat 31, Cape Hill, for eleven years (Said like that it really does sound like a prison sentence). This particular day, I went to an address on ,Cape Hill, Windmill Lane Estate, which was (and still is to some extent) a rough estate and certainly the area with the most crime on K3 sub division, the sub division covering the South of Sandwell, which was K3 then, its now K2 OCU(Operational Command Unit) named after the second highest mountain in the world and by far the best ocu I have ever worked on! The Cape, as its known locally,is a much nicer place nowadays than it ever was (I wonder if my modern counterparts would agree?). Quite a lot of tax payers money was pumped into the area to regenerate it! In fairness to the politicians involved, a couple of million quid later, it is a bit better than it was. Early eighties Windmill Estate was a very rough, dreary, grey, concrete covered, shitty estate. Full of 1950's multi storey blocks of flats that had seen better days and not lasted anywhere near as long as the so called architects had promised they would, they were damp, dim, dreary and by my early days on the beat in the early 1980's, mostly derelict. Inhabited by rent arrear tenants who had insulted most if not every member of staff at the local housing office & and druggies injecting their lives away, totally oblivious to the squalor they existed in. Such a block was located in a part of the Windmill Estate called Baldwin Street, a block of one bedroomed flats, built with God knows who in mind? It had about eight floors,thus, sixteen flights of dimly lit stairs, but no lifts! They were gloomy, Dickensian, flights of stairs, covered in graffito and litter with the overriding scent of natural waste products! The permanently faintly illuminated landings led out onto communal balconies and onward to the postbox red painted front doors of each flat. You see similar flats on The Bill sometimes, there's a lot of 'em in the Smoke. But they have at least been decorated at regular intervals. The flats at Baldwin Street had little walkways outside the whole of the house, with the kitchen window of the flat positioned next to the front doors. They were grotty by most standards, it was like visiting a battleground in Basra or down town Beirut, the kind of area where there would always be burnt out shells of vehicles, half naked toddlers playing with sticks or throwing bricks at each other. The older ones, throwing car tyres over lamp posts, or tossing bricks at passing taxis. The only vehicles that drove regularly threw the estate were in fact Police Cars, Ambulances, Fire Engines and some (brave) Taxis! Nobody in their right mind would drive their car through that estate. One of the things I have just recalled about it, was the feral pack of dogs, about a dozen or more, none wearing a collar, that would would pack together and roam around the area. They would feed at the rear of fast food shops and waste paper bins. I tell people now and they think I'm joking and making it up. I swear by almighty God (Although I'm a fee paying agnostic) that I'm telling you the truth. There really was a pack of 'street' hounds that used to roam around the estate. At the time the council had one, yes one, dog warden for the whole of the borough and I think he or she sensibly strayed purposely over the other side of Sandwell. I remember, I always used to take my tit hat (Police Helmet) off when stray dogs were around, any dogs for that matter. People in Smethwick owned Dangerous Dogs before a Dangerous Dogs Act had even been thought of! I'm not sure why but dogs don't like tit hats, I think its cause bobbies being tall, look even taller in a tit hat. Thats what I read somewhere anyway! That reminds me of a joke. Why do policemen wear hats? So they know which end to wipe!

Anyhow, this particular day, a guy who had recently moved into the flats had telephoned the police station and asked for crime prevention advice in the dingiest part of Britain you could imagine. If the world had needed a suppository God would have stuck it into the Baldwin Street flats! So being just a little curious, I went to see him. He was in a flat on the fourth level. Having left Cambridge University he'd just moved in,with his pretty wife, they must have been in their mid twenties. Very well spoken, too well dressed, too well spoken and frankly, too clean cut for Baldwin Street. Well, for living in Smethwick actually. This prig, and I really do mean prig, had been a complete grade one doom brain from the minute he set foot in the Midlands. What he'd done,he'd badgered the local council to abide by the law of the land and supply him with accommodation on demand. I don't know about now but at the time, UK employment legislation rules had not long been introduced, whereby, on the grounds of seeking employment, one could go to virtually any council area in Britain, and say, "Excuse me, but I've just moved into this area, I've obtained a job and I require somewhere permanent to live". The local council, by law, had to house you! I didn't know this at the time, but it transpired, this guy had done exactly that, with some poor soul at the local Sandwell Council Housing Office getting the verbal wrath of this cultured graduate. This clever get from Cambridge, armed with a still warm degree in origami, was obviously a very erudite man, I can't tell you what his degree was in, but it was probably something like politics, philosophy, airfix model kits or the law, but without doubt, to want to settle in Baldwin Street, Smethwick, proves that because someone has a degree it don't necessarily mean that they are clever! This bloke must have been a sandwich short of a picnic to want to live in this place, a complete grade one pillock.

Accordingly, on this nice sunny morning, I was feeling tippy top, rollin along, singin' a song as I knocked his front door. Next to it, as I said earlier, was his kitchen window, which, being at chest level, would have been a piece of cake to get into, for any novice burglar. Those one bedroomed flats were squalid & down at heel. Upon entering, I followed him into a diminutive, postage stamp sized hallway, with the kitchen door to the left, the hall led onto a small bedroom and finally a reasonably enough sized living room, for a single person, containing an outer facing window, some 50 feet from the ground. Allowing a fine view of the next Council block! On the other side of the vestibule was a scantily furnished but adequate bathroom,finished in whitish, tobacco smoke yellowed, faded and cracked wall tiles, that was it...Shangri-la! A bit like the living space allocated to the entrants of I'm a celebrity get me out of here but without the multi talented presence of Ant and Dec.

Coming the great 'I am', banging desks, indicating to council housing staff that he knew the law, quoting act and section at 'em resulted in him being allocated one of, if not, the worst dwellings the area had to offer! Now believe it or believe it not, this chap wanted a Crime Prevention survey. For the flats in question thats like Jack (of Beanstalk fame) asking Burger King to look after his Cow for a bit! I went in there and said, "Good morning (lets call him) Mr Scholar", "Come in", he said, sharply. He didn't look happy! Far from it in fact. His opening gambit to me was, "You took your time officer (A term that all police officers find truly delightful), I rang your station last night, I expected a police officer here last night!". "Good morning Sir,I said, I wasn't working last night, I got your message this morning when I got to the office". I pointed out that due to limited resources, Smethwick Station have to prioritise any calls that come in and that at weekends we have slightly, ever so slightly, more important jobs in the pipeline than crime prevention surveys on flats in Cape Hill. I got the whole story on how Mr Scholar and his concerned looking, significant other, had come to live in such a place. I then said, " Mate you're not in Cambridge any more, no dreaming spires(Or is that Oxford?) here, this is Smethwick. " He still had an attitude about him, but, police officers are paid by members of the public, even rissoles like him, so, as he was a member of the public, I had to exhibit integrity and be professional. I like to think that I have always treated everyone equally as a beat officer. Hence, I say to him, "Okay you want some advice, what can I do for you". He said, "Officer what is the best crime prevention advice you can give me for living here?". In the job we would call this an S.F.Q. (Stupid Fucking Question)! I thought for, oh easily about four tenths of a second and said "I think you should move to a safer area mate!" There was a curious silence, then, Mr Scholar essentially went a bit red in the face, then crimson as his upper lip began to quiver. His eyes bulged out, and he said in a raised voice, "I beg your pardon?", in that sort of learned disparaging arrogant, bullying teacher sort of 'I'm better than you, tone of voice. He continued, "Did I hear you correctly?" Graduates can be acerbic so and so's can't they? Learned people eh? Always believing that sarcasm was the lowest form of wit. I replied in a lofty but quiet tone under my breath,"There's nothing up with your hearing is there mate?", I said,raising my voice again, "Move house!" He rejoindered, "I want your name and number, I'm going to complain about you and your advice". Within a nano-second, I blurted out my collar number and said, "I am Police Constable Bryan David Connor of the West Midlands Police, currently serving at Piddock Road Police Station, Smethwick. The Superintendent is Mr Karalius, my gaffer is Inspector Cook, my first line supervisor is Sergeant Mantle". I told him my contact phone number, I told him everything, except my inside leg measurement!

Nonetheless, I think he got the message, that I was a tad upset at his attitude, and he said to my surprise, "Look PC Connor,Bryan was it? We've got off on the wrong foot here", and I said "I'd agree with that sir" He went on, "Perhaps we can begin again and please, call me Giles?" I replied "Yes, you're right, of course we can start again,Sir." "Officer", he said, still in a quite condescending voice, "What is the best advice you can give me for living in this flat in Baldwin Street?'. There was a longer pause this time, and he must have been thinking I'm gonna come out with a reasonable reply,like, 'Lets have a look at your mortice locks, lets have a look at your door locks, your door frame, the glass in the door and your kitchen window that faces the balcony outside etc. etc. to be honest a six year old infant could have broken into those flats, that's how easy they were to break into. The door panel alone, you could break through with any size ten universal key (Thats a boot - Mine's a size

Ten, but sizes do vary!) A size Ten boot would make a big enough hole for you you to climb through the door frame and into the dwelling.   But as I say, there was a longer pause this time, and I really did, seriously think of telling him exactly what *he* wanted to hear, along with a leaflet about crime prevention. But of course, what I did say is, "Mr Scholar, I think you and your other half should move from here to a safer area". I thought then that it was the best advice I could have give him and it would still be the best advice today! He went off like a rocket, like a Saturn Five on Guy Fawkes night, I've never seen a bloke lose his rag so much, with his posh accent and all, he really did go into a tirade of, very eloquent words.   But y'know, if he was trying to impress someone, there was only me and his missis there and I wasn't impressed. Quite the opposite! He started to talk to me as if I was something he'd carried into the flat on the sole of his shoe! Before I went, I wrote down my name, my collar number and the phone number for the police station on the back of a police 'pink' calling card and thrust it into his soft sweaty mitt. Needless to say when I got back to the cop shop, I pass on the tale to my mates back at the office. Roy Mantle (My Sergeant) just laughed at me and said, "That didn't go very well then," and I said, "Not very well sarge, no", and he said," Mr Scholar's already phoned me, he asked me the same question and I told him to move somewhere else!" Funnily enough he's spoke to Harry". Harry was our Inspector, Harry Cook, he was a good gaffer, a bobbies bobby, he was one of those Inspectors who looked after his PC's. If you thought you were right and you stood by your guns and you did so with integrity, Harry would support you one hundred percent. Easily six foot two or three inch tall, with muscles in his spit, Harry Cook was a big man, very smart in uniform, very dignified, but he had a face like a blind cobblers thumb, he was ugly!

Harry had a wondering eye,not for the ladies, no literally he had an eye that rolled around in its socket. I can't remember which eye it was, it was what they would call in the Black Country, a bonk eye, I'd never tell him to his face that he had a bonk eye 'cause he'd have brained yer, but Harry had a bonk eye. When he looked at you his eye rolled a little bit, he looked a touch mental. But he had a heart as big as a bucket and he was the kind of gaffer that you'd run through brick walls for! He would smile reassuringly, then, old school like, would always begin his conversations by speaking slowly, thus being able to build up to Vesuvius crescendo if later required. Harry spoke to Mr Scholar in the front office, when he came in to complain about me and eventually after listening to quite a mild verbal assault compared to the tirade he'd given me at the flat. That was enough for Harry, who roared at him, "How dare you talk about one of my officers like that. Given the circumstances you are in, my officer came to your flat as requested and gave you sound, honest, crime prevention advice. Now, unless you've anything else to say, kindly leave the station!" We never saw or heard from Mr Scholar again, so he must have taken our advice! What a pompous man he was. I'm sure that if he had come that attitude with his newly found neighbours in Baldwin Street they'd have probably strung him up and ate him. So, who knows, he might have ended up being part of the foundations for the M6 Toll Road. It is said that a little knowledge is a dangerous thing. In this case it would appear that a great deal of knowledge tends to cloud ones judgement! The Baldwin Street flats were pulled down about twelve months after Giles' departure. We were all relieved about that, especially Stanley Baldwin who I think has just about stopped turning in his grave. Mind you, the former Tory Prime Minister who gave his name to this dump may well have liked it, because, he,after all, like Giles, was a Cambridge scholar!

THE CAPE HILL
BREWERY STORY

Master Brewers, Mitchell's & Butlers (M&B's) had a Brewery in Cape Hill, as far back as 1898. People always associate Cape Hill with the City of Birmingham; wrong, it is located in the, Staffordshire and Black Country township of Smethwick, on it's border of Warwickshire fair enough, you could even see the boundary post of the vast metropolis of Birmingham from its front Car Park, but nonetheless, Cape Hill Brewery was in the Black Country area of Staffs county.

M & B's merged with rival brewers Bass, in the early nineteen sixties. Their most famous beer was Brew XI, "for the men of the Midlands". Their famous logo depicting a leaping deer. An interesting fact about how that logo came about was that at the time the founders bought the land at Cape Hill, it was the ideal place for brewing beer because the site included a natural spring, which in itself gave one of their products, 'Springfield Bitter' its name. But on the original blueprints for the purchase of the site, the distance across the stream that ran from the spring was described on the blueprints as being, 'A deer's leap in width' and that phrase became the inspiration for the company logo! That's the story I was told on one of my 'official' visits to that particular establishment as its local beat officer of course!

Having a Brewery on the patch does of course have its obvious advantages! Every new probationary constable would eventually be introduced to the Brewery and share in their appreciation when would be thieves were locked up or frightened away by the boys in blue! I remember my initiation to this particular establishment. I was on A Unit, on nights with my tutor constable Mick Benyon, checking the perimeter fence of the brewery. There you would see hundreds of crates stacked five or six high filled with fresh bottles or cans of M&B's finest.   You soon knew if there where thieves breaking into the compound because the little tinkers are greedy and not satisfied with stealing one crate they stack them up, near the hole in the fence,before they go back for more, stacking them ready to just pick up at the last minute. They always get too greedy and nearly always end up getting caught. It's a bit like the story of the Lion and the mouse. The Lion protects it's larder full of food and every day the little mouse tiptoes by the sleeping Lion and steals a small piece of cheese from right under the sleeping Lions nose. However, one day the mouse tries to take the whole massive round of cheese and the Lion, who knew all the time about the Lions nocturnal trips, grabs the mouse by his tail and swallows him whole! Moral of the story, don't get too greedy, biting off more than you can chew. It's a good anecdote when warning greedy people about the investigators at HM Inland Revenue. Whose crest ironically is a Lion!

Now, bear in mind Cape Hill Brewery was vast, with loads and loads of barrels, kegs, crates, bottles & cans of the amber stuff, you name it, it was there,a veritable Aladdin's cave, all in this considerable compound. To a thief it must have been a bit like the mouse with the cheese, you don't miss a little bit when it's gone. So, the brewery was a popular place for crims. Anyhow, this particular night Mick Benyon and I are on Kilo Mike One Nine. A marked panda car. I was sent to check the perimeter fencing of the Brewery to theoretically make sure no one had stacked any ill-gotten gains around any weak points of the fence before returning to the Security Hut to meet up with my tutor Alf, who would be having a cuppa with the night security crew at the front of the premises. Sounds easy?

I'm checking everything, there are no crates or bottles near any gaps to indicate a breach, but I do find a hole in the fence and start enthusiastically looking around everywhere, inspecting the compound, walking round the site, now bear in mind, this is in the time before Closed Circuit Television Cameras and it's a very substantial site. All of a sudden an urgent radio message crackles across the airwaves from Yankee Mike, YM, the Force Control Room. To announce that the intruder alarm had been activated at M&B's Brewery Cape Hill! Of course then through the voices on my radio I hear the cavalry starting their charge from all points around the division, Zulu Seven, Zulu Eight, Kilo Mike One Nine, Kilo Mike Two One, Kilo Mike Two Zero, Kilo Mike Two Two. They're all making for Cape Hill Brewery, from all different areas of the borough. I'm already in the Brewery compound, hearing all this radio traffic. Bear in mind I'm supposed to be sitting in Kilo Mike One Nine with Alf. So when the controller says 'PC Connor, what is your location', I'm panicking, thinking, 'What should I say? . Staring at the blue box I keep intermittently tapping the transmit button on my Burndept Radio with my right forefinger whilst blabbering incoherently into the radio mike. My controller Stan Roby says 'PC Connor you are breaking up

, I cannot understand you when this incident at the Brewery is over, come in and change your radio'. Of course, I'm panicking then 'cause I'm already there! So I think, well, if there are intruder's on the premises, I'll go back to the hole in the fence and cut off their escape route (bit of brains there y'know). So, I go back to the hole in the fence, and because its pitch black, I can see all the blue lights of the arriving police cars, at all points around the perimeter fence. Security men who were already on site are there with Alf, my tutor and the head security man, an ex-Birmingham City police inspector called Barry Mees, a really great bloke, I got on well with him 'cause I later became the beat bobby at Cape Hill.

Of course it's a false alarm, there are no intruders, and of course what's happened is, when I was walking round the compound, I broke through an infra red beam, setting off the alarm and of course, my 'in the know' tutor, had sent him round deliberately knowing it would go off, strange that! Then, of course traditionally Cape Hill Brewery and the local constabulary having a good working relationship, Mr Mees delighted and impressed with the response, especially the one shown by the young Connor who had arrived on foot within seconds would say, "Lads here's a couple of crates of beer, for the shift, put 'em in the boot and enjoy 'em with our compliments. Thanks very much for all your help". Off went these couple of crates along with a newly educated probationer. Who, after all, would always from that set of nights on, thoroughly check the perimeter of the Cape Hill Brewery. The brewery was closed in 2002 and production switched to Burton upon Trent It doesn't exist anymore, there's a housing estate there now!

Talking about the Cape Brewery reminds me of a guy name Dennis Toper who lived in an old Caravan on waste ground at the back of the Brewery Yard. I was going to say that Dennis was a likeable Rogue, but he wasn't. He was a detestable, loud, foul mouthed thief. He was in his late 50's when I first knew him. Now what made him memorable was that he was a uni-dexter. Anyone who has heard the hilarious Peter Cook and Dudley Moore sketch about a one legged man applying for a film role as Tarzan the Ape-Man will know that he only had one leg! Dennis' left leg was fine. It was a good leg. I had nothing against his left leg. Problem was, neither did poor old Dennis! Dennis was deficient in the right leg division by one and so, wore a prosthetic limb. It was an odd prosthetic, not like the modern ones that look very lifelike. It was more like an unvarnished pine dining table leg that tapered from six by four inch at the knee to a three by two inch stump on the business end, covered in a thick bulbous black rubber sheath making his prosthetic table leg look a little like a spent match!Very odd, a bit Long John Silver-ish. Why are one legged men called Dennis so cantankerous? Because they ARRRRRR Jim lad (Couldn't resist)! Dennis liked his beer (a lot) and was more of a nuisance when he'd either been smelling the barmaid's apron or when he needed a new shoe! You see, most shoe retailers have rows and rows of left shoes displayed on metal stands both in and outside the store. Why they display only the left shoe, I do not know. But this situation was excellent for a one (left) legged shoplifter. His Modus Operandi (Method used) for obtaining a new, pair, err sorry new single left shoe was firstly, view the shoes displayed, then choose a modish shoe appealing to sense of taste, then pick up said shoe from the display and finally hop it (Couldn't Resist) with the new shoe! This one day, Dennis had gone shoe shop lifting along Cape Hill, a busy shopping area. He'd stolen a shoe from a shop display and was being pursued along the Cape towards the Seven Stars (Public House) traffic lights. At this location stood young WPC Christine Lowe (She would be PC Lowe now, in our Politically Correct world) on foot patrol, who also gave chase.

Dennis, upon seeing a diminutive female officer, suddenly got quite courageous and turned on the lone officer, discharging a complete tirade of swear words that no lady, let alone a police one, should hear. Dennis grabbed the young officer and a struggle ensued. Chris, managing to press her Burndept Radio 'transmit' button sufficiently long enough to request assistance. When police officers hear the word 'assistance', boom from their blue boxes the cavalry come a-running! On that particular morning I was riding shotgun in Kilo Zulu Seven, a fast response marked police vehicle with bright flashing blue lights and deafening woo woos. The driver was PC Martyn Flannery, Christine's fiancée! I think we were tootling around the Brandhall Council Housing estate at the time we heard the assistance call, about three miles from the Cape, contemplating finding a tea spot. We were suddenly launched into light speed! I flicked the switches that turned on the woo woo's and the beacon and made sure my seatbelt was secure. Junctions flew by at a fast rate of knots. We swerved at warp speed around bends and the adrenalin was flowing like vino. I'd never seen Martyn drive like this; it was fantastic and admirable to witness a man and a machine working together in unison to rush us to an Emergency Scene. Flanners was a police trained advanced driver, a graded grain, we used to call 'em. Because we all held Grades 1 to 4 for standard levels of driving ability in the job. One: Being the crème de la crème advanced level. Four being a bog standard panda grade (Which everyone starts off with). I was a Grade Three. I could drive Panda Cars, Police Carriers (Vans) and the odd petrol driven lawn mower. If really stretched to the limit of my driving skills, I could take a whole van load of hairy arsed bobbies from the back yard of any nick in England and Wales straight to the mortuary in no time at all! Zulu Seven TA'd first on the scene. Martyn, like the cowboy in the films, jumping out of the car to save his gal! Which reminds me of a joke. What time is it when the Cowboy races to the girl tied to the rail tracks and saves her? Ten to Ten! Do you get it? You will. Anyway, by the time we got to Cape lights. Chris is safely trapped inside the public telephone box outside the bingo hall in Windmill Lane and Dennis is hopping up and down on his newly shoed good leg, whilst hammering the outside of the phone box with his artificial appendage! In those days the phone boxes had about 24 panes of glass on the two solid sides and door. Dennis had smashed about a dozen of them. Luckily Chris was managing to keep the door pulled firmly shut but she'd acquired a few bloody abrasions from flying glass. Of course, Cape Hill being a busy shopping area, there were an abundance of people witnessing this incident and not a living soul assisted that young policewoman, not one.

Of course, upon the arrival of two male officers our brave unidexter ceased his attack. Continued with the 'gobbin off' but suddenly lost his bottle (Must have gone to the same place as his right leg) and didn't want to be aggressive anymore when male officers arrived. What a surprise! The only other thing I would add about Dennis was that every time he was put on the sheet in the Custody Block. The Custody sergeant would say, "Name?" He would comply. Next question would be, "Address?" to which Dennis would always answer,"I live by the cut (Black Country word for canal), drop in anytime!" How droll Dennis. Funny the first few times.

That was about twenty seven years ago now. Martyn and Chris are still together, they were married not long after the incident with Toper. They have a grown up son who once had a three legged Hamster called Dennis. In Todays

Bryan Connor

Metro newspaper (Feb 10th 2010) I read an item in the 'send us your txt' section from a chap named James Lavelle in Essex who wrote, 'So a one armed 'bandit' in Bexhill stole a single cufflink from a jewellers in Leigh-On-Sea.' He added, 'Am I the only person wondering how he is planning to attach it to his shirt sleeve?' Well, Jim, if he can't get it onto his shirt sleeve he could always sell it to Dennis.....via a second hand shop!

SANTA' s LAST SUPPER

It was the week before Christmas in the Black Country town of West Bromwich and it is one of the stories retold to me, I didn't go to this, it was one that a good friend of mine, Steve Long, witnessed, Longy is a bobby that I partnered up with when I worked out of West Bromwich, which is in the North of the Borough of Sandwell in the West Midlands. Its a job Steve went to around 1990, West Bromwich Police Station was the divisional headquarters of the then K Division. With four response units, imaginatively titled A,B,C and D Unit! The Units were made up of One Inspector, Three Sergeants,One Patrol Sergeant,One Custody Sergeant and a Station Sergeant. The Shift had in the region of Twenty Constables. There were two Zulu Crews to staff two 'Zulu' cars. Yes, they were still calling them Z-Cars in those days. These vehicles in my early police days, were marked Morris Marina's,with blue lights and Air Horns that went NER-Ner NER-Ner when you switched on the large plastic the NER-Ner button on the middle of the dash. These vehicles were meant to be used for fast response to 'Immediate' 999 calls such as serious Road Traffic Accidents (RTA's) or Suspicious Persons still on the Premises calls. Thus,

they were also fitted with both Burndept (Local) Radios &
VHF radios that received Yankee Mike (YM was the Force
Control Room at Bournville). So they received even more
voices in their magic boxes. Then there would be four single
crewed,panda cars, in my early days, Austin Allegro's, again
light blue, marked police vehicles with a blue light on the
roof but unfortunately no Ner Ners and the ordinary local
Burndept radios! Steve, an advanced police driver and his
Zulu partner on this particular night, get a message via
Yankee Mike at the Force Control Room at Bournville Lane
that the West Midlands Fire Service have turned out to a
gas explosion at a block of flats on the Lyng state in West
Bromwich. Bobbies of a certain age, like me, instantly think
of the incident at Ronan Point in Newham East London.
Where in May 1968, a whole corner of a twenty three storey
council tower block collapsed, following a gas explosion,
killing five people. So, when Steve arrived and the damage
was just to one flat it was with some relief that the officers
TA'd (Time of Arrival on the log). They trudged through
freshly fallen snow that was deep and crisp and even. The
brave officers of the West Midlands Fire Service were already
at the scene and had brought out a burns victim, a forty-two
year old white male, from his devastated flat. Our service
colleagues from the West Midlands Ambulance Service had
already hurried chummy off to the Burns Unit at the Queen
Elizabeth Hospital in Edgbaston, Birmingham.

As he'd already been rushed off, understandably quickly,
Tat and his mate had to liaise with the Fire Fighters to get
details of who the victim was. Once they knew who the
victim was they got the low down on what had gone on. It
transpired that just like every good Anglo Saxon male that
goes out on the razzle he had returned to his two bed roomed
council high rise flat after attending his local Social Club
where this particular year it had been his turn to be Father

Christmas at their annual party for members' children. Post party and mainly due to thankful parents of the kids, Santa returned to his grotto twelve parts cut to the wind and as tight as the belt that went around his appropriate festive girth. Now in half reds and boots exchanged with carpet slippers our St Nick was tootling around his flat from room to room, getting his bearings, opening and acknowledging the Christmas cards he'd amassed the previous night and displaying them around his living room, as you do. Chris Cringle turns living room light on. Switches on TV and still full of the Christmas spirits stumbles into the hallway through to the bathroom to water the reindeer as it were, singing, *'Its beginning to look a lot like Christmas'*. He strolls into the bedroom turning on his bedside lamp and his electric blanket, to keep him snug on this bleak mid winter night. It's about half past twelve, quarter to one in the morning, and in this semi comatose state Santa is routinely ferreting round his flat and decides that before he visits the land of Nod and start dreaming of a white Christmas, he is rather peckish. Realises that he has eaten all six of his Netto economy mince pies so makes his mind up to have a couple of rounds of hot, freshly buttered toast. Still unsure on his pegs, he bimbles into the kitchen, twists on the cooker knob for the grill, puts two slices of bread onto the wire tray of the cooker and pushes it under the grill, then, whilst that's doing, off he shuffles to the bathroom for more ablutions singing *'Jingle Bells'* as he goes. He does the kind of things that slightly inebriated Santa's do when they are about to go to bed do. Takes off the beard, throws off the boots, removes the red uniform hanging it over a chair ready for Christmas Eve. Then the mundane getting undressed, ready for bed, looking and smiling into the mirror as he wiped away the lipstick marks of admiring mothers from his rosy cheeks like you do. Still shuffling around his flat doing

239

walkabout flat type things, tired and yawning decides he's now its time for bed, having turned off the TV and walked back into the bedroom, he sits on the edge of the bed, sheets now lovely and warm. Taking his slippers off and kicking them under the bed he makes a life changing decision. He thinks just before I go to bed I'll have a cigarette. Still very tipsy, he fumbles a fag out of the box from the drawer of his bedside cabinet, puts it in his mouth, gets his box of Swan Vesta matches, dextrously manages to separate one match then holding it loosely between the end of his index finger and thumb clumsily strikes it against the sandpapered side of the matchbox.

Now our Santa, all alone and bereft of little helpers, had forgotten to do one important thing before retiring. The doughy white un-toasted slices of bread were still lying on the metal tray under the grill on the cooker in the kitchen. What Santa had failed to do was to ignite the gas supply to the grill! Unfortunately, as soon as he struck the match & started to suck on the end of the Rothmans King Size that hung from his bottom lip, he also ignited the invisible cloud of domestic gas that had by now filled most of his flat. Result...BOOM!

Literally, the whole place blew up. Now, the crazy thing about this story is that, like every British Anglo Saxon male who has been out on the pop, our Santa was a creature of habit in more ways than one. More than just being a bit peckish after a night on the ale and being too boracic to buy a takeaway and too drunk to know he'd left the gas on in the kitchen. The Fire Officers at the scene first pointed it out. "We know that he was in the bedroom when the flat blew up". The senior fire officer stated. "We know exactly what happened, what he'd done and what he was preparing to do," It become apparent that they also knew that, from the side of the bed that he was sitting on at the time of the blast, he had got up suffering horrendous burns. Had, post-BOOM, raised himself painfully up off the bed, walked down around the bottom of the bed and up the other side of it. Once there, in abject pain and fighting for every breath he'd opened one of the drawers in his bedside cabinet, took out a pair of clean underpants from the drawer and in what must have been excruciating pain, put on the clean underwear. He'd gone through this agonising ordeal because of course, like every Anglo Saxon son is instructed by, nay had it drummed into him by his Mother, for years and years,'If you ever have to go to hospital be sure to wear clean underpants.' Yes, yes, it's true! This is what we all grew up being told and exactly what Santa had done on this occasion. The fire service officers even knew that this is what he'd done. How did they know that his story was true? Because, not only had they found his discarded soiled pair of grundies by the bedside cabinet and lets face it, I think I'd evacuate my bowels if I had suddenly supplied the source of heat responsible for a gas explosion in a multi storey block of flats! He was so badly burned that when he had walked around the the foot of and up the other side of his divan, he left a trail of melting skin along the route that had dripped and trickled off him onto his bedside carpeting. That's how the Fire crew knew that he'd gone around the sides of the bed and changed his underwear. Amazing eh? The pain that poor man must have been in when he remembered to take his mothers advice and change his undies. Yes, it is amazing isn't it, but that's not the end of the story.

Steve and whoever he was partnered with that night, go down to the Burns Unit at the Queen Elizabeth Hospital Burns Unit. They had state of the art equipment there, still do, I think. When they walked into the admissions ward of the burns unit, festooned with Christmas decorations, they were astonished to find a grinning red faced Father

Christmas, not long brought in from a gas explosion accident, lying on one of those special beds that blow warm gusts of air underneath badly scorched bodies, so, in effect; he was floating on a cushion of air! An air bed if you will. It sounds funny saying an air bed, he wasn't in a tent in the middle of a cow field and he wasn't camping, he was on a special bed that blows a layer of lukewarm air. He was actually compos mentis, wide awake, laughing, smiling and joking with the fantastic nursing staff.

When Tat speaks to him he sounds great and confirms everything that the Fire Officers had already stated about the circumstances of the explosion. Even down to the tale about the underpants, all parties laughed and joked about it! Now, because it was the early hours of the morning and medical staff are prepping him for treatment to come and stuff like that, doing what they do extremely well, easing his pain, calming him down and helping him relax in the best way they can. Steve says to him, "Look mate, you've got to be treated by the nursing staff, you just get well, let the hospital staff do what they've got to do, we're on nights again tonight, we'll come straight over from Bromwich at ten o'clock and get a statement off you then, OK mate?". He said, "Righto lads, fine by me." Off trot the bobbies to liaise with the ward sister, to let her in on the plan, "There's nothing more we can do tonight", Steve explains," We've enough details for now, he's not really in a fit state to get a statement from tonight, we'll come and see him tomorrow night he looks like he could do with the rest". The very experienced sister, used to dealing with these sorts of cases, answered something along the lines of, "Officer, with the huge percentage of burns that that lads got, I don't think he'll see the rest day out". Sister was right of course. Santa died some time during the following afternoon and didn't see the day out. I don't know what percentage of burns he had, but they were obviously fatal. It just goes to show you, it is very tempting to say something facetious like 'smoking is bad for you', but it really does bring home the fact that it is so easy to have an accident in the home, especially when you are under the influence of mind altering substances like booze and we've nearly all been there!.

Steve and his mate managed to speak to the guy again, quickly and compassionately gleaning enough information for what would be a coroner's inquest into the fatal explosion. Off they went sombrely, in their police vehicle back to Bromwich where snow was still falling, snow on snow, in that sad bleak mid winter morning, long ago. Later that day, the badly scared patient, who had no living relatives, passed away alone in that Burns Unit.

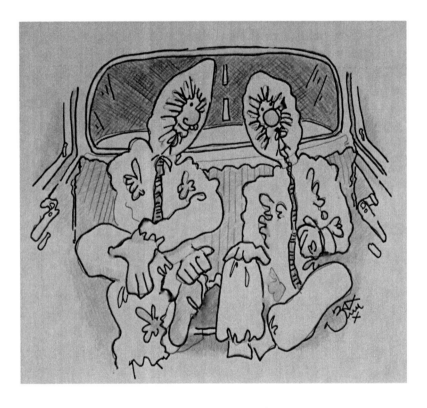

'Low Sperm Count'

THE MEN IN WHITE

In the very early hours of one Sunday morning a mate of mine, who I mentioned earlier, PC Dave Bullman was sent to a Public House in Cradley Heath to a report from the landlord which read, 'Two youths who were thrown out of the pub earlier this evening and are barred from my pub have returned and are throwing stones and breaking the pub windows'.

Upon arrival both of the local grubby, unkempt, troglodytes, lets call them Kay and Jay, were somewhat the worst for drink, apprehended and housed at the local lock-up for the usual procedures to be carried out.

It transpired that Kay and Jay had been customers in the pub the previous evening and had been kicked out and barred for rowdy behaviour by the licensee. By the time they had sobered up enough to be interviewed the two 'suspects' understandably I suppose, given the dire circumstances, were having an attack of chronic amnesia and were going 'no comment' on their tape recorded interviews.

Dave asked the night detective, lets call him DC Zed, if he could proffer any of his vast criminal experience and knowledge to this dilemma and Zed wisely suggested that he take Kay and Jay's clothes off them for forensic examination, as, if they had broken the windows, they would have microscopic particles of powdered glass caught in the fibres on their clothing that, if present, the findings could then be match up with the glass broken at the scene. Brilliant! Thought Dave and the suspects were released on bail to return at the lock up in a few weeks time, on this occasion a month, to give the police time to send off the items for forensic examination at the Home office Labs in Birmingham.

Kay and Jay were told to strip by the custody officer, Sgt Sid Stratton; who oversaw the strict bagging procedure. Coming from the notorious Briers Lee Estate in nearby Dudley, where a bath is something you store coal in, the two temporary guests of Her Majesty had a certain odour if you get my drift. It certainly drifted into the nostrils of the officers. To cover their humiliation the 'suspects' were each given a new one piece white paper hooded disposable suit to wear for their remaining time in the block, thus, Kay and Jay became 'The Men in White'. After being bailed to return in a months time Bully gave the men in white a lift towards home in the police vehicle. Guests of Her Majesty don't normally like being dropped off outside their homes. Funny that, especially when they are wearing retina scorching one piece paper suits. Unless its snowing of course, then they'd be camouflaged.

As he drove along the quiet early morning streets he could see both miscreants, via the rear view mirror, in the back seat with his 'oppo' a probationary Constable sitting between them for the ride. It was then that Kay, turned to Jay, his soap retardant, grubby little features peeking through the little drawstring paper hood, grinning a brown tobacco stained, toothy smirk toward his partner in crime and said, "We look just like a couple of sperms".

Which really does say a lot for our modern comprehensive education system. Kay couldn't read or write but did know what a sperm cell was and even what one looked like! With the hoods on their one piece paper suits up over their heads obscuring most of their faces. Dave couldn't help chuckling as they did very much resemble sperm cells, especially when they slid off into the early morning mist along the High Street

That reminds me of one of my favourite police jokes. "What's the difference between a Hedgehog and a Panda Car? A Hedgehog's got the pricks on the outside! But I digress. The following weekend, Bully, now on a late shift was sent to Warrens Hall Nature Reserve, an area of quiet greenery straddling the border between the West Midland Districts of Sandwell and Dudley, once covered by heavy industry encompassing coal mines, boat yards, blast furnaces, iron works and timber yards. Now, Warrens Hall Country Park & Nature Reserve is a place for walkers, courting couples and other wildlife. It's the sort of place that the local kids take their bikes for a scramble, both push and motor. When it's the latter the park rangers usually call the police.

Dave received a radio message that some youths were riding around the Reserve on a quad bike. An all-terrain vehicle, informally referred to as a quad bike or quad, that travels on low pressure tyres, with a seat that is straddled by the rider, along with handlebars for steering. As the name implies, it is designed to handle a wider variety of terrain than most other vehicles. The rider sits on and operates these vehicles like a motorcycle, but the extra wheels give more stability at slower speeds. Now, although not a rare sight nowadays, when youths from the Council Estate close-by have a quad bike you have to suspect foul play! So Dave drove up there expecting to find a stolen quad and few more guests for Her Majesty.

Upon arrival, he saw a group of about six youths standing around a very unroadworthy looking quad parked but ticking over on the car park of the nature reserve. The plume of thick toxic white smoke coming out of the exhaust didn't mean there was a new Pope it meant this quad bike was a knacker. As he got closer, the group saw the liveried nerr nerr (Marked Police Car to you) approaching and they all starburst off in all directions legging it down the small adjoining 'warrens' that help give the area its name. The quad was driven straight up a very steep grassy bank, quite adroitly, by a youth who couldn't have been much older than 12 years old. An older youth standing astride the quad, straddling behind the rider with both feet balanced on its rear axles and both hands on the riders shoulders, let go one secure left donnie (hand to our none Black Country readers) and turning toward the police vehicle with the obligatory crafty smirk on his face, stuck up two fingers, a la Harvey Smith, toward the officers in bold insolence. It was then that this 'hanger on' lost his foothold, fell backwards off the quad bike and came rolling down the hill like a ball of Double Gloucester cheese at Coopers Hill towards the salivating and attentive officers, who stood waiting in the slips to catch the ball before it cleared the boundary. There is a police phrase, used quite often when a villain slips off the hook and gets away from his lawful captors, for whatever reason, the phrase, "He'll come again" would be the idiom uttered by one or more of experienced bobbies on such an occasion. Chummy had come again!

The Bobbies grabbed the rolling malefactor and were surprised to discover that they had caught young agent Kay One of the men in white that Dave had dealt with some seven whole days before! Walking him to the car Dave couldn't help but notice that there was something awfully familiar about Kays lower apparel. He was still wearing the paper suit that he'd been issued with at the police station the week before. Kay had cut off the arms, shoulders and hood of the garment, well it was a disposable suit, then rolled down the torso tightly around his waist finishing off the overall ensemble with green and yellow plastic coated electrical wire. So you could say he was well earthed.

Kay, without any awkwardness, explained to the amused officers that he only possessed one pair of trousers in the world and the police had sent them off for forensic examination! But not only had Kay modified the suit, he'd personalised it. He was the only possessor of a disposable paper suit bottom with a crude self drawn Nike type logo daubed on the right hip with a blue indelible pen, which it was later discovered had soaked through the paper and onto the top of his right thigh. Other liquids had also soaked through the paper trousers in the ensuing days but I will not digress.

According to my encyclopaedia, most sperm cells cannot divide and have a very limited life span, but this sperm born in a cell was ejaculated back into its natural surroundings, lasted at least seven days before going back into yet another cell!

Did he get another paper suit? Of course! We're not total fashion philistines in the police dearie. We allowed Kay the right to once more express himself, we even gave him a grey felt pen and suggested pinstripes were this seasons 'must have' in the Sandwell and Dudley 'club scene'. We disposed of the first fashion statement in the station incinerator, mind you; The Tate Modern did show a keen interest and unfortunately Sandwell Council hadn't wasted millions of pounds on an art gallery at that time or Kay might have made a fortune by exhibiting his trousers at 'The Public' Art

Gallery in West Bromwich. His trousers could have been hanging there now. In a well aired room of course.

Did Kay get his own trousers back? Yes. Were there fragments of glass on them from the broken pub windows? Of course! This isn't Hollywood this is the real world. Kay, I don't know if you are carrying on a life of crime but, if you have, might I suggest you invest in at least one spare pair of trousers as a contingency in future!

I was tempted to call this story "The wrong trousers" but settled on the men in white for obvious reasons. I wonder if Tommy Lee Jones will be interested in being deneuralyzed for his role of Kay in the Black Country Films production of 'Men In White'?

'Andy's Viking Impression'

A TRIBUTE TO ANDY

This chapter is a tribute to a dear colleague and friend, Andrew Armstrong. The stories were retold to me by Andy shortly before he passed away in May 2009 at the age of only fifty six. I was honoured to be asked by his wife, Carol, to read the following account at his funeral service. I have left it as I first read it to Andy who I last saw when I left the office to go to some mundane work related committee meeting. As I walked through the office I shouted over to Andy who had just finished reading the stories you are about to read and asked "Are they alright?" Andy still holding the A4 copies of my draught print grinned broadly and stuck up his thumb. That was to be Andy's last day at work, he began a holiday tour of Eastern Europe and Scandinavia the following day with Carol. I wished him a good holiday and said goodbye for what was to be the last time.

Andy told me the about the night the shift Inspector, let's call him Eric, asked him for a 'meet'. A regular check made by the shift supervisors on the foot patrol beat officers during a tour of duty. Supervisors would ensure that officers were on their designated beat, update them on current intelligence, sign their pocket books, then have five minutes of chat with them before driving off in their warm, cosy supervision car in search of the next half frozen beat officer.

It was around midnight and Andy had just purchased a sizzling hot portion of fish and chips liberally dosed in showers of Salt and Vinegar & lovingly swathed in half a dozen sheets of last weeks Express and Star from a reliably good chippy in the Old Hill area of the old K1 Sub Division. Andy left the chippy with the firm intention of secreting himself in a nearby shop doorway for the hasty consumption of the said cuisine. But, as he left the chippy his Burndept Radio crackled to life, the voice in the box asking for a 'meet'. "Kilo One - PC Armstrong - What's your location – Over?" It was Sergeant John Platt, the shift controller calling from his centrally heated office at West Bromwich PS. "Elbow Street Sarge - Over," Was Andy's hastily thought-out reply. "Andy, Inspector Sloane is in Halesowen Road, stay there, he'll be with you in a minute or so for a meet - Over". 'Oh dear', thought Andy, or something similar to that anyway! The gaffer was literally only a few streets away. So, with not much time to spare, Andy improvised by shoving the blistering hot, convenience food inside his police helmet and balancing it perilously onto his head just as the supervision car rounded the corner of King Street!

The Inspector pulled up in the unmarked white Austin Allegro supervision car and young Andy threw up a respectful and balanced salute. The Gaffer routinely chatted police business to the hot headed young beat officer. Andy concurred and nodded in all the right places as the Inspector imparted his update for what seemed like an age! A very uncomfortable Andy was becoming quite anxious. The red hot chips were starting to burn his scalp! And unbeknown to him, the steam from his recent purchase was discharging through the air holes situated on either side of his custodian police helmet. Making the fair haired, bearded Andy, resemble a wild eyed marauding Viking warrior with huge steamy horns protruding from both sides of his hat at once! Andy had a lobster pink complexion, as long beads of sweat mingled with chip fat trickled down his distressed face. Having cottoned on to this the Inspector said, "Andy lad, you look a bit warm. Do you want to take your hat off son?" "Yes please Sir!" said the despondent beat man. Who of course learned yet another lesson in policing street craft? That was; to always make sure that when you buy hot food out on the patch. Give the controller a location that's impossible for the supervision to drive to!

Andy did get his own back on the sardonic Insp Sloane, in more ways than one. One morning tea break at Old Hill nick, Andy had nipped out to his car for something and on the way back into the station spotted Insp Sloane in his shirtsleeves, doing what could only be described as 'lurking' in the high growing bushes situated underneath the small slightly opened, frosted glass, vented window above the squad room where half the shift were now drinking their morning brew at break time and discussing among all the usual internal politics of the day their usual moans and groans regarding Eric and the awful way he ran the shift. Yes, Eric was eavesdropping on his own shifts gossip outside the open window from the safety of the clump of bushes below! Andy came back into the room and deliberately turned the conversation to Eric and whatever was Eric's current ridiculous idea for improving productivity on the shift. During this debate he stealthily started to write in ballpoint pen across one of his fellow officers newspaper crossword puzzles what he'd seen on his way in and after a knowing wink, continued to praise Eric loudly whilst at the same time gathering everyone's slops from the bottom of their teacups adding them to the three-quarters of a pint of lukewarm stewed tea already stagnantly ignored along with the seven stodgy catering tea bags lying at the bottom of the five gallon brown enamel shift tea pot. Andy, a former swimming champion, took off the lid and in one movement adroitly jumped onto the wooden chair situated under the small slightly opened frosted glass vented window and threw the liquid contents, the strong slightly milky dark brown dregs from the teapot very accurately through the open window and over the bushes outside. "I believe cold tea is very good for getting rid of irritable little pests from plants" Andy shouted as the tepid & stewed concoction sprayed the bushes beneath, including its irritable inhabitant, who let out an understandably stifled groan. After another quite satisfying fresh brew, half of the shift ended their morning break and made their way out of the building back onto the streets. As they passed the supervision office, Andy asked the shift Sergeant if the Inspector was about as he needed some advice about a file he was working on, only to be told that the Gaffer had been called away suddenly to cover a change of duty up at Divisional Headquarters. To be strictly accurate, Eric had nipped home to change his soiled white police uniform shirt!

To make things worse for Eric, Andy struck again, when, one afternoon, not long after the Viking episode, whilst out on foot patrol, a helpful member of the public handed Andrew a stray dog. It was a Tipton Flock Hound, aka, a Heinz 57. When he got the mutt back to Old Hill Andy found that the dog pound was already full and that there were no RSPCA officers on duty until the following morning. Andy was faced with a predicament. Where could he put the growler? He made sure the dog was fully fed and watered before booking off duty and decided that the best place for the dog would be to 'house' him in Inspector Sloanes office. Where, using the much copied Barbara Woodhouse method, he told the dog to sssiiitttttit! I think the dog must have misheard the word sit!

It was everywhere. The grateful hound left many 'gifts' all over Eric's office. The following day, upon discovering the waif and the mess, the Inspector went ballistic, but, surprisingly; didn't sheet Andy. Mind you, as Andy later told me that there'd been enough sheeting done for one day! The Inspector (whose office now incidentally reeked strongly of Jeyes Fluid) decided to castigate young Andrew by placing him on a football duty at the Hawthorns Stadium, the home of West Bromwich Albion Football Club. Now, unlike most of his police colleagues, Andy couldn't stand football and tried his best to avoid being placed on match day duties at all costs.

On this particular match day, Andy, was stationed at a fixed point in Halfords Lane, outside the player's entrance of the ground. Andy was far from impressed with being placed on football duties by the Inspector and as the opposition team coach arrived late for the fixture & pulled up outside the players entrance, he belligerently informed the driver authoritatively, "You can't park there on double yellow lines!" pointing at the said restriction markings in the gutter. The driver explained the importance of his passengers, rationalising with the officer that they were the away team due to play West Bromwich Albion at the Hawthorns that very day and were already late for the fixture. This of course failed to impress the indifferent Andrew who said to the driver, "I don't care if it's Mother Theresa on a world fund raising tour, you are not parking that coach there." Andy pointed down the road in the direction of Smethwick and says, "The football coach park is down there." With a loud Pssssttt the embarrassed coach driver reluctantly closed the automatic door of the coach and drove away in the direction of the coach park. Resulting in the Albion's match day opponents performing a brisk pre-match warm up – a ten minute yomp back to the Hawthorns and a further delayed kick off! Which got Andy's supervising Inspector. 'Eric' *noticed*. Andy never worked so near a sporting venue again. He unfortunately couldn't remember who the opposition were that fateful day. But it's be odd to imagine the Manchester United first Team legging it briskly up Halfords Lane to the ground with their kit bags in tow!

"Why did you all call the Inspector Eric, when his actual name was Roy?" I asked Andy, when we chatted and chortled over these tales. "Well, we as a shift decided that the gaffer was so dim, we all reckoned we could include him in on the joke and he wouldn't clock that the joke was on him and so we started referring to stories about a fictitious 'Eric' whilst in the gaffers presence and he would start to join in the laughter. Never at all knowing that *he* was indeed *Eric*!" said a grinning Andy. Adding, "He never twigged it, never and towards the end of his time on the shift with us at 'The Hill' he even started blaming the fictitious 'Eric' for things that went wrong at work, for example, he'd announce that someone had cocked up the shift overtime rota's and in the next breath he would exclaim, it must have been Eric! How astute was that!"

I had the privilege to serve with Andy at varying times during my own thirty year career. Following his retirement, he was working part time as a Police Staff Member (posh phrase for civilian support officer) of the West Midlands Police at the K2 ocu glidewell unit based at Hawthorns House and thoroughly enjoying his life. Ironically, Hawthorns House is approximately one hundred and fifty yards up the road from West Bromwich Albion Football Club. Only a few weeks before he sadly passed away Andy related these stories to me admitting to me that sometimes even he himself was mystified that he had managed to remain in the police service for the full term of his thirty year contract, considering how many senior officers he had crossed swords with and the amount of times he had been counselled by them, being told not to cut his nose off to spite his face. Well, Andy had the last laugh and could wear any type of spectacles he wished. When I last saw him he still possessed a moderately sized proboscis! Andy took ill and was hospitalised in Copenhagen, Denmark on the penultimate day of his holiday. He sadly passed away there after being diagnosed with cancer.

Andy served the people of the West Midlands and Sandwell in particular, admirably, with impartiality, integrity and without fear or favour. He was the proud possessor of a framed certificate awarded upon his retirement which certifies that he indeed was a Member of Her Majesty's Constabulary for thirty exemplary years and not many British citizens can affirm to that!

I once heard someone say that time is a sort of hunter that stalks us all our lives, but I would rather believe that time is a companion. That goes with us on the journey through life. Time itself reminding us all to cherish every moment. Because they'll never come again. What we leave behind is nowhere near as important as how we live our lives and what we do for our fellow men and women. Thanks Andy, it was a privilege to have known and served with you. I will never forget you.

TOILET HUMOUR

My introduction to 'toilet humour' started at a very early age. My Uncle Clarrie, my mam's brother, who passed away quite a few years ago now, but genetically I still see, every time the barber shows me the newly cut back of my head in the barbers mirror, because I inherited his bald patch, used to work at the local council sewage treatment plant in St Helens. A shitty job, yes, but somebody had to do it. A bit like policing really!

When we, my cousins and I, as kids, asked him what he did at the 'farm' he told us he worked at, he'd say, "I'm a sorter". Winking at the assembled adults, an enormous grin covering his face. When one of us would inevitably ask, "What do you sort?" "I sort the mens from ladies with a big stick," he'd reply and with an extremely dead pan face he'd add, "The mens are perfectly straight and the ladies are slightly bent". Mind you, on each visit to our house with my Aunty Edie he always brought my Mam a big fresh bag of Tomatoes that grew wild on top of the filtration beds, they always tasted lovely too. Uncle Clarrie, grinning broadly would say, "Them's organic they are. Cost yer a fortune in the shops, they would". This was years before organic gardening was as popular as it is now!

My professional police life gave me a whole new outlook to toilets. Naively, I used to think they were places where the public just relieved themselves. Public washrooms and restroom facilities provided for Joe Public to 'release the chocolate coloured hostages' In Britain and around the globe for that matter public bogs are, due to heavy usage and the lack of available staff to keep up with the cleaning, most of the time, dirty, squalid, smelly, dimly lit places and very much the last place you'd want to 'go' into, to euphemistically spend a penny or more of your hard earned brass. There used to be at least five public washrooms in our policing area alone and most had an attendant to keep them clean, tidy and fit to use. But over recent years politicians (Bless 'em) have decided to save money by making cutbacks. Cutting off this important service to the public.

I remember one attendant complaining to me one day, "Officer, I've seen young business folk snorting coke, drug addicts mainlining in the cubicles, couples occupied in various positions of the Karma Sutra, others engaged in diverse, nefarious sexual exploits, pimps & prostitutes of both sexes candidly plying their trades, with crooks & vagabonds engaged explicitly in the trading of illicit merchandise, its truly awful and enough to make the most hardened police officer blush. You know, a fella came in here about ten minutes ago, had a shit and left and it was like a breath of fresh air!" It's a fact that there are more germs growing under your fingernails than on a toilet seat. So, where theres muck there's success and to prove it, I have only ever received one Chief's commendation in the job and that was centred around public toilets!

During the mid-nineties a bobby named Dick Anderson and myself worked together in the neighbourhood police office, then called the Permanent Beat officers or PBO's. I think it was our Sergeant Roy Mantle who first decided to put us together working the bogs but we became good at fishing for sexual deviants in them. Most people would call this activity, 'cottaging' and although the term is often associated with gay men, it really can apply to anybody. The term cottaging is rarely used outside gay communities and as attitudes towards the gay community becomes more tolerant, fewer individuals find themselves limited to covert and illicit ways of meeting others. I know that a lot of the modern age diversity ridden, politically correct, liberal cops would probably cringe at the thought that police officers once went undercover into public toilets to try to catch sexual deviants! For example, some people in modern society would try to condone the fact that George Michael went looking in public toilets to find other men interested in having sex with him there. But in my book that is out of hand, especially when there is the possibility that children might go into those same toilets to use them for what they were originally purpose built for!

I remember one of the new wave, politically correct Inspectors coming into the parade room one morning and seeing an intelligence 'Wanted' type briefing poster, bearing a photograph of a local well-known villain, under whose fizzog I'd just written '**PERVERT**'. The Inspector catching me in the act as it were, in front of numerous witnesses, began to tear me off a strip in front of a group of young officers for writing such, "Typical old school, insensitive, comments' over a photo of someone, who after all is only a suspect and therefore innocent until proven guilty." I couldn't agree more", I told the Inspector, "but the man on the poster is wanted for perverting the course of justice, hence my abbreviated appendage Ma'am!" I left a bemused and silent slightly reddening Inspector to face a group of confused officers.

One Friday night on late shift, at about nine o'clock on a very cold wintery evening I was driving a Public Order carrier van full of bobbies when I felt a bit 'took short' as it were and in need of a pee. Sergeant Roy Mantle was in the front passenger seat and suggested as we weren't far from the Albion football ground we could go to the public bogs on the Brummie Road, just down the road from Bradford's bakery. I parked up the van in the adjoining lay-by and walked up the long dark path to the unlit toilet entrance at the side of the building. As I got in there, it was pitch black. You literally could not see your hand in front of your face. Not surprising for such public buildings to have vandalised lighting I thought as I instinctively found the urinals (By smell,possibly?) and started to unzip & rattle my change, as it were. I had the unerring impression that I wasn't alone. You know, when you can't see anyone, but you can feel a presence around you. My Burndept police radio cracked into life and the radio voices echoed loudly in the eerie silence of the gents loos. I then heard a very slight shuffling sound, but thought nothing of it as I continued 'watering' as it were. A few moments later I returned to the van and was greeted by a grinning Roy who said, "What did you say to upset that lot then?" Explaining that not long after I'd entered to bogs, a stream of men, approximately thirty or so, some still adjusting their dress, came rushing down the path and upon seeing the Carrier, rapidly starburst from the scene in all directions, at a rate of knots. So fast in fact, that by the time I came out of the bogs, the area was completely clear of any members of her majesty's subjects.

Dick Anderson and I were good at doing plain clothes obs(ervations) in public toilets. I don't really know why, but young Dick (An unfortunate name given the subject matter. Try and not think of Sid James and his saucy laugh as you read this. I bet you can't) was a clean-shaven young officer, who, if you'd put a blazer on him would have passed for a fifth former at the local comprehensive school. We would mainly go into the Gents by Vicky (Victoria) Park, Smethwick on early evenings or Saturday and Sunday afternoons.

There are two main types of deviance we used to look for. Firstly there would be the men looking to pick up other men for sex and/or actually committing the act in the cubicles or there were also some males who would just enjoy exposing themselves to other men in the toilets because they were big in the southern region as it where. When performing these observations we would both stand at the urinals and 'pretend' to pee, leaving some sections of urinal free for any would be 'tiddlers', if you'll excuse the fishing phrase, to walk into our trap. The main thing to beware of was, to not speak to any would-be suspects, for fear of being accused of acting as agent provocateurs. You would simply wait, quietly and let them make the first move. Mmm, does sound like a few dates I've been on!

On one of our early soirées into this genre, I remember one guy that propositioned PC Anderson and myself who, when I had identified ourselves as police officers, must have thought we were joking, either that or he had an extremely low retention span and it had slipped his mind that he'd been arrested. As cheekily, whilst sat handcuffed in the back of the plain police vehicle he said, "Are the cuffs part of the act are we going to go to your place or mine?" Slightly taken aback, I said, "Well, I have already cautioned you, so we'd better go to our place". Just to make sure, I cautioned him again after which he just laughed again as if we were pulling his leg (Only his leg, mind). Only minutes away from the police station we turned left off the main drag, and stopped on the ramp, controlled by automatic barrier at the rear yard of the police station. The prisoner, finally realising that we were genuine police officers and that he had been arrested exclaimed in a shocked shrieking high pitched voice, "I thought we were going to your place?" to which I replied, "This is our place, we've a room ready for you you may have to stay the night. " He said, "What's the charge officer?" to which I replied, "There's no charge. It's all part of our friendly service" (Sorry couldn't resist).

The public toilets by Victoria Park were well frequented by men propositioning and it gleaned quite a few prisoners. It would be busier in the spring and summer months. Word would get around the access magazines and things would be quiet for a while, so we wouldn't work obs on one place for too long. Just prior to the commendation collar, we received complaints from parents of young boys who were playing football in junior Sunday league fixtures at Victoria Park and that Men had begun congregating around the gents loos in the park again.

On the following Sunday afternoon, in late July, at around four in the afternoon PC Anderson and me were joined in the darkness of the gents loos when we were joined by a middle aged white male wearing motor cycling gear. Full Leathers, full face crash hat, the lot. The kind of bloke who you would think would use this sort of facility if they were on a long cycle ride, so when he started to hang around for more time than the average toilet visitor would hang around (If you'll excuse the phrase, 'hang') I began to think this man was here for something, other than spending the proverbial. Dick and myself, both aware of his presence, just stared forward at the wall, silently, rocking slightly forward and back on our heels, pretending to piddle, but not of course, not speaking for fear of being thought of as acting as an agent provocateur. It sounds funny, it is. It sounds embarrassing, it is. It sounds like a strange thing to do, it is. Very un-natural. It seems to last an age, those few moments, but eventually the 'ice' was broken, by the suspect

cyclist of course, who asked Dick if he was interested in what
he was holding and waving about and did he fancy going
somewhere where they could be alone to discuss the matter
further. I, of course heard every word, and therefore could
corroborate that this man was attempting to importune
another male for an immoral purpose. I introduced myself
and showed the motorcyclist my warrant card to confirm
that I was a police officer. PC Anderson got his out and
waved it in the bikers face. His warrant card I mean!

We take chummy out into the cruel sunlight of day
and there saw his expensive machine, locked, still making
those clinketty clink cooling sounds as it leaned next to the
concealed brick walled entrance of the bogs. The bike did
look the part and when we saw our prisoner in the light,
bedecked in full motorcycling gear.

He was ashen white, obviously shocked at being
'caught'. But he appeared to be more nervous than the
usual punters we'd catch, cottaging. Making me suspect
that we'd caught a big fish. There are many historic cases
involving celebrities and politicians who have succumbed
to this particular activity and I started to wonder if he was
someone of note. He certainly didn't look very familiar.
He was a bespectacled middle aged white guy, not very
tall, about five foot seven inches tall and very slim. He
was well but abruptly spoken. Limiting all responses to
"Yes","No", "Don't Know" answers. We searched him, what
little there was to search and found a small but sharp knife
in a zip up fabric pouch he had fastened around his waist.
As we conveyed him to the station he was very nervously,
asking how long he would be detained as he was a waiter
in a restaurant and was due at work later that evening. He
kept asking, "What will happen, to me, will I be charged?
Which is of course quite normal for people who have been
arrested but this was strangely different, he was asking the

question as if the rest of his life depended on it. I explained that as per PACE, the Police and Criminal Evidence Act, it was not my decision to make. Strangely, he didn't even want a solicitor. He asked the custody officer if the process would be quickened up if he fully co-operated. Again, very strange behaviour.

Dick and I interviewed him on tape and he readily admitted the offence and was full of remorse. When the interview finished he reiterated his concerns about being late for his job and asked what the next stage was. I told him that we would be checking him on the the computer for any previous activity, then the Inspector would decide how to deal with the matter. He seemed to know about judicial proceedings and asked that if he'd not been dealt with for a like offence, then it was possible he could be cautioned. I agreed, but restated that it would be my Inspectors decision. Dick and I knew that because of the presence of the small six inch bladed knife on his person, chummy was going nowhere, but we weren't going to tell him that at this stage.

When checking the Police National Computer with the mans details, it transpired that the man we had in custody had only six months earlier been released from a high security prison in the North of England and was still out on licence for murder. If someone is out of prison on licence, it is known as a temporary licence, formally called release on temporary licence (ROTL) and also informally known as temporary release. The Home Office use it as a form of temporary parole for prisoners who have 'behaved' themselves whilst serving their sentence. Now because it was a Sunday, it had been very difficult to find someone 'in' at the Home Office, as they have to decide how to deal with anyone who breaches this privilege. But,after a hell of a game to find the right section, I was told by the Home Office representative (He sounded like posh TV presenter/ex

Member of Parliament Gyles Brandreth) that I spoke to that he'd have a look at the papers and get back to me shortly. and I thought, oh well, we'll never hear from him again.

So, having already discussed the case with the gaffer, who'd decided that he could be cautioned, pending the Home Office decision. I started to prepare the papers for chummy to be cautioned. Now bear in mind I said chummy had been inside for murder. There are all sorts of Murder, as defined in common law. The unlawful killing of another human being with intent (or malice aforethought), and generally this state of mind distinguishes murder from other forms of unlawful homicide (such as manslaughter), There are some murders that are crimes of passion. Where some people were pushed over the edge by a domineering spouse and killed them in a fit of rage. Murders committed where people are genuinely mentally ill. Then there are the sort of murderers where people are killed by accident, for example, a fight outside a pub that goes a bit Pete Tong when one of the participants hits their head on the edge of a kerbstone and fracture their skull. It's still murder! Then of course there are the pathological individuals like Fred West, Harold Shipman or Ian Huntley. I didn't know the circumstances of our prisoners 'murder' until within only a quarter of an hour or so, the Gyles Brandreth sound alike rang me back.

Our man was sentenced for the murder of two men in the city of Nottingham. They were both gay and it was discovered that our man had killed both men in separate incidents that took place in public toilets. After ascertaining that they were gay men this homophobic individual had attacked them with a knife, killing both. Gyles confirmed to us that the Home Office were going to revoke his licence. This meant that he would go back to prison to serve the rest of his life sentence. He would not pass go and would not collect two hundred pounds.

After letting my supervision know, I went down to the cell block to collect our man and take him into the custody block to be spoken to by the Inspector. Who read out the details of his earlier Victoria Park incident offence and informed him that due to the fact that he had admitted the offence he would be cautioned. He asked the little leather clad motorcyclist to sign and date the caution card and the colour returned visibly to is relieved face. Then the gaffer said, "Just one more thing. Upon making the routine checks my officers spoke to the Home Office who confirmed that you are currently out on licence from Her Majesty's Prison Service is that correct? He replied in the affirmative in a subdued meek little squeak, "Yer, yer, yes, why is there a problem?" The Inspector said, "No there isn't a problem, take notice that this licence has been revoked." The blood visibly drained from his face and he whispered to me, "Can they do that?" Having quietly walked the short distance along the corridor I placed him back in his cell, I loudly slammed the steel door and looking at this pathetic creature through the small hatch in the cell door I said, "They can and they have".

I remember going to an incident at a public toilets with a young PC called John Ledger. I hadn't been back on the shift long and John was at the end of his two year probation. The caller from Sandwell council was reporting that one of their toilet janitors had locked a member of the public in the bogs for his own and the protection of the public. Apparently, the cleaner was trying to mop the urinals and had asked the chap to finish his 'James Riddle' and exit the toilets, so that he could clean them. Whatever the man was doing, was taking quite some time doing it and the impatient janitor, who wanted to get on, asked him to hurry and that was when the man became even more aggressive and told the janitor to go forth and multiply. The bellicose male made all kinds of verbal threats and so the janitor decided the best plan of action, wisely, was to lock him in the bogs!

When we arrived, the huge steel outer door to the gents was still tightly closed and a total maniac could be clearly heard going ape shit on the other side of it, his booming, echoing voice muffled by twelve inch thick pebble dashed council toilet walls. The janitor explained that he had given the hulk, every opportunity to leave, without having to get on the bat phone, but alas, felt impelled to incarcerate the troglodyte within and wait for the protectors of justice to arrive.

John went up to the closed bog door and asked the man to stop banging and kicking the same, so discourse could begin. From behind the door came a booming voice that announced, "Officer, when I get out of here I am going to kill the janitor". Throw in a handful of F-words and you would have the exact account. It seemed the longer the man remained in the blacked-out stinking public urinal the more vocally threatening he got.

It was a siege situation but I had a plan. I told the janitor to open the door and in trepidation the young Johnny Ledger started to chat to the monster in an effort to keep him occupied, while I lay in wait, by the side of the door ready to jump on him. You can't beat old fashioned policing can you! As the massive steel door creaked open and light burst into the watering hole the huge moron could be clearly seen, shouting loud obscenities and making a bee line for the janitor with a probationary police officer hanging around his neck, trying to persuade him to calm down.

Remembering all my human awareness training I dove straight down on all fours between the stalking beast and his his prey. Now, nut-cases who are going off on one and about to strangle an innocent member of the public going about their normal business, do not tend to listen to the voice of reason no matter how loud, neither do they tend to look clearly where they are going. With this in mind, the thug didn't see me going down on all fours and fell over me, head first at a quick rate of knots into the granite hard pavement beneath me. Before John could say, "I can't find my handcuffs", I'd cuffed Goliath and was dragging him to the car. He was a big bloke, well over six foot, he was a stocky white guy, was casually but well dressed. He continued to bellow obscenities at the top of his voice in a Australasian accent. There was no evidence of alcohol and so clearly the man was in need of a doctor, preferably a psychiatrist.

John cautioned the man as he rattled off a string of repugnant one liners, mainly questioning both our parentage and insulting our dear mothers. When we got him to the station he stubbornly wouldn't get out of the car and swore blind that there was nothing we could do that would make him budge I used an old time honoured and tested ploy to remove him from the motor. I tickled him under his arms and eventually an embarrassed troglodyte removed himself from the car and walked up the ramp in the rear yard to the cell block. I remember in the old cell block at Smethwick, we didn't have an official height measuring apparatus for checking how tall prisoners were. But, I do remember that we had the measurements marked on the door jambe of the Doctors Room in felt tip and when it got to over seven feet, some wag had written **INNOCENT**! in large red felt tip block capital letters at about the seven foot three mark. Hey, no word of a lie, the top of this little chaps head reached the innocent mark.

The man mountain was charged with public order offences and strangely pleaded not guilty. So we all went to court for a not guilty trial, at the tax payers expense. The stupid thing was, had he put his hands up and admitted the offence, he'd have received a caution and that would have been that. But to receive a caution, the offender must admit the offence and show some remorse. This oaf was far too proud and much too stupid to admit that he was in the wrong. More proof of his doltishness was that he decided that he fancied himself as a bit of a Perry Mason and defended himself at court.

At an eventful but witty court case at Birmingham Magistrates Court he responded to every point made by each of the witnesses like an Antipodean version of the Churchill Bulldog, "Oh,No,no,no,no,no,no," with no logical mitigating arguments coming from his lips. I remember the Magistrates Clerk during his cross examination of myself, eventually and infuriatingly weighing up the mental condition of the accused by asking him if he had ever received psychiatric treatment. After a long pregnant pause came the considered reply, "Not in this country,no". After much consideration, perhaps it was a very wise decision to permanently close most of the public toilets in Sandwell.

TAKE HIM DOWN THE STEPS OFFICER

On my first visit to a Crown Court, the highest court of first instance for English and Welsh criminal cases. I visited the one at Wolverhampton. It was a fine Monday morning in June 1981. God was in his heaven,the birds were singing in the trees, everything was right with the world. Having ascertained that the case I was involved in was listed for court two and was second on the listing. So I was sat on a bench in the main entrance hall by the entrance to court two worrying about having to give evidence in that theatrical circus for my first solo case when I was tapped on the shoulder by an usher who said, "His Lordship in court one wants a word with you, follow me".

I pursued the elderly usher, who was wearing a cape like teachers wear at prize giving day. We went through the two pairs of enormous double sound proofing swing doors into Court number one. I'd never been in a court room before. It was just as you would imagine. The strong smell of pledge on all the ornate wooden panelling which adorned all the walls. The huge, opaque windows flooding in bright natural light. The atmosphere was electric, an expectant hush, the sort you get seconds before the first line in a play, filled the room. A sea of inquisitive faces, that all seem to know the reason for your being summoned when you don't, looked around in my direction, like a wedding congregation watching the shy sacrificial bridegroom walking up the aisle. I could see the prosecution and defence barristers, their wigged bonces buried in thick case papers, paying no attention to me at all.

I stood in the shadow of the precipitous witness box, a large wooden dais, towering over me like an unholy church pulpit, a timber polygraph apparatus awaiting the next martyr to justice in the Yes/No interlude game. Then I saw the Judge. His Honour Judge Craven Moorhead, who was glowering down over his horn rimmed spectacles at me from high on the top of his lofty bookcases. This was an official representative of the crown, demonstrated by the huge Queen's Coat of Arms which sat behind him on the wall bearing the words Dieu et mon droit. that appears on a scroll beneath the shield & refers to the divine right of the Queen to govern Britain. Serious stuff eh! His Honour Judge Craven Moorhead beckoned me to stand within 'pay attention' distance and began in a very posh voice that I'd only ever heard on Radio 4, it sounded like he had a mouth full of marbles, "Officer, can you hear the noise of the roadworks outside my court?" he said, It was only then that I became conscious of a dull droned chorus of pneumatic drills breaking up asphalt outside. Not loud enough to halt proceedings but maybe an irritant. "Yer, Yer, Yes Mi Lord", I nervously squeaked. "You had better go out there and tell them to discontinue this insufferable commotion officer" said His Lordship, obviously rattled. "Yes Mi Lord," I replied. Out I toddled in my best dress tunic and instantly saw the 'offending' group of road construction operatives.

Picking out the most important looking hard hatted workman and ascertaining that he was the Foreman, had a name badge with 'Mr Murphy' clearly printed on it, I politely asked him to stop the work, explaining what the Judge had said. "Ok, that's not a problem sor" Came the reply in a soft Irish droll from the supervisor who instructed his crew of about four jackhammer men to down tools and switch off the droning, rattling, diesel compressors. Result!

Minutes later I was sitting back in the main entrance hall of the courts, quite pleased with myself, I resumed my personal anxiety, that of trying to remember what to say when you have to swear in, along with trying to rehearse the evidence of the case in my mind. Whispering to myself over and over again, 'I swear by Almighty God that the evidence I shall give will be the truth the whole truth and nothing but the truth, so help me'. No, wrong! Start again. So embroiled was I, that I hadn't realised about twenty minutes had elapsed and the work men outside that I had spoken to had re-commenced their excavations! An ashen faced usher approached me yet again and mouthed the words, "He wants you back in court one now" I knew who he meant and who *he* was!

The Judge, wearing a pained expression on his face, leaned over the bench and said to me in an irritated, pretentious tone, "Officer, did you speak to those workmen?" I answered in the positive and told him what had happened earlier. To my surprise, he then instructed me to bring Mr Murphy into the courtroom. An incredulous Mr Murphy, who at first thought I was pulling his leg, was eventually persuaded that I was in deadly earnest (You thought I was in Wolverhampton didn't you?) and he accompanied me into court to confront wig wearer supreme. Murphy, a middle aged road worker, walked through the court toward His Honour in his one piece bib and brace denim overall, a yellow fluorescent sleeved jacket, thick blue denim work gloves and black wellingtons bearing his companies famous logo. As he stood before the beak he nervously removed his hard hat, which he timidly clutched in his arms like a newborn baby. "You are the person responsible for the noise that interrupted my proceedings?" said His Lordship. 'He's sharp as a button', I thought, 'Obviously the product of an Oxbridge education. "Err, Yes Sor, Yer Lordship, Mi Honour Sor" said Murphy anxiously. "This officer (the judge pointing an official boney forefinger in my general direction) instructed you to stop making an excessive hubbub, in the interests of judicial process, what ?" "Err, Yes Sor, Yer Lordship, Mi Honour Sor, that he did Sor" his retort. I thought a hubbub was a chewing gum! "I suppose in the interests of fiscal revenue you continued your excavations?" I whispered the rough translation of the question in Murphy's ear, "You decided that it was going to cost a fortune if your lads downed tools for much longer ?" "Thats roight officer," he said, "Don't tell me, tell the Judge," I continued out of the corner of my mouth. "Err, Yes Sor, Yer Lordship, Mi Honour Sor" Murphy told the moderator, whilst squeezing more life out of his hard hat. "Then, I hold you in contempt of court and I will review this matter at the end of todays proceedings, take him down officer." Said the sober arbitrator. "Yes, Mi Lord" I replied, taking Mr Murphy by the arm and guiding the bemused site foreman down the proverbial wood panelled steps situated at the back of court one, that led down to the holding 'day' cells under the court buildings.

"Whats going on?" said Murphy, as I explained to the full circumstances to the Custody Sergeant of what His Honour Judge Craven Moorehead had ordered me to do. "Better house him in cell no.6 then", the Sergeant said, in a matter of fact way, as if it happened all the time. A terrified Mr Murphy was, at first, bravely threatening to take all concerned regarding his 'false' incarceration to court. That would be interesting I thought, who would a Crown Court Judge be judged by? The Lord Chief Justice I suppose. Mmm, I wouldn't fancy giving evidence in that court!

After five hours, several cups of freeze dried tea and a congealed dish of lukewarm Irish Stew at lunchtime, that the incarcerated celt referred to as 'slop'. Mr Murphy made sure that he followed it all swiftly with massive helpings of humble pie! When hauled up in front of His Honour Judge Craven Moorhead Mr Murphy was sufficiently remorseful. I mean, how dare he carry on his livelihood like that! A compliant and contrite Murphy assured His honour that the Road works would be completed out of court hours. He was dismissed and His Honour went off doing whatever High Court Judges do when they aren't maltreating court officials and the general public.

I always retell this story to police officers to emphasise the sheer power that these High Court officials have. Some bobbies, new to the courts and inexperienced in the ways of the judicial system, show their ignorance and naivety by refusing to respond to a court summons by saying,"Well I'm on rest day that day, so I ain't going to court to give evidence!" And I tell them, "If a High Court Judge says, 'Jump' I would advise you to say, How high would you like me to Jump Your Honour?" I don't think the judges are as powerful as they were when I was first in the job. But, I wouldn't advise any road crews to start digging up the road way anywhere near court one at Wolverhampton when His Honour Judge Craven Moorehead is sitting.

THE CON-ORDINATOR

These are a few stories about the Neighbourhood Watch scheme. This is a Crime Prevention initiative that began in the United states (Of Course) whereby, individuals and the police, work together in an effort to reduce crime and make their communities safer places to live and work in.

The schemes are administered by the police, but residents have designated co-ordinators, whose task is to organise meetings, distribute information received from the local police and pass on to the police any useful information about possible criminal activity in their areas. The scheme has been very popular in the States and has its supporters in this country. Schemes actually do reduce the chances of members becoming victims of crime. I have visited many schemes that really possessed a great sense of community spirit. I remember one scheme in particular in Warley that used to have an annual outing to Weston Super Mare! There are now many facets of the scheme including Business Watch, Pub Watch and even Dog Watch. I think its good that schemes exist. Lets face it, in a Neighbourhood Watch area, Billy Burglar is walking around the street looking for opportunistic dwellings where Joe Public makes it easy for him to take rich pickings. He (or she, lets not discriminate against lady tea leaves even if the courts do) looks for open windows and doors. But, in a Neighbourhood Watch area, they don't know who is watching from behind those twitching net curtains or venetian blinds!

Billy Burglar hates inquisitive people & thats the main advantage of the scheme. The members are its eyes and ears, they make the area a safer place to live in. Plus, Neighbourhood Watch groups get discounts from Security Companies for alarms and locks. Being a scheme member also reduces the premium you pay on your household insurance policies, which makes the little nodding Bulldog happy, Oh Yes! One Christmas I helped set up a scheme for all the Meat retailers in South Sandwell. We called it, appropriately, 'Butchers Watch'. Now that was a memorable set up evening, or rather the buffet was at the end of the night! I even suggested we have a Toy Watch at Christmastime but the gaffer, Inspector Cook thought I was taking the Michael. I remember Mr Cook once sending out a questionnaire to all the Neighbourhood Watch membership in the borough asking them, among other things to list what they thought was the most important crimes that they thought should be tackled in their area. He didn't include a tick in the box type questionnaire to assist them, as modern spin doctor politicians might, he just gave them a blank canvas. Resulting in an honest (and eye opening) list of 'issues' that the watch members felt were not being tackled by their local plod. Oh yes they were worried about Assaults,Burglaries,Street Robberies and Criminal Damage but the top offence they thought should be tackled on their list. Drivers parking cars outside their houses! What is this obsession with parking? Is it just a British thing? People ring the police, sometimes using the 9's emergency system to report that someone has parked a car in front of their house.

How dare they! The fact that the car is taxed is irrelevant. The fact that we point out to these sad individuals that the highway outside their house doesn't belong to them is also irrelevant. You know, there are some sad people in this world. I remember one irate lady, who lived by Sandwell District Hospital complained that she couldn't park outside her own home at Hospital visiting times. When I spoke to her and ascertained that she had not long moved there and that the Hospital had been there for some thirty years. I think she still expected me to ticket a car that bore a valid tax disc! At the time of writing this, I have just seen an item on the local TV news where a man in Warwickshire is that miffed that he gets approximately 90 service buses driving passed his home every day, he has created a full scale model of the back of a bus and attached it to the front of his house to highlight the problem of noise, thus provoking the local 'stirrers' of swill in the bucket to swarm around his house to sympathise with him. This, at a time when thousands of our brave service men and women are fighting and dying for their country in Afghanistan. These idiots, whose biggest worry in life is cars parking outside their drums or buses driving past their little castles, should be utterly ashamed of themselves.

But I digress, Neighbourhood Watch schemes that are run well, can be very good and can glean criminal intelligence. You see, Billy Burglar walks down a street and as I said, he doesn't know who is watching from behind those quivering nets. When I worked in Community Services Department at Smethwick following a serious injury following a road accident. I assisted the police Neighbourhood Watch officer Martyn Flannery, who I had known from my first day at Smethwick nick. One day he took me to meet a Neighbourhood Watch co-ordinator in the Black Patch area of the division. Black Patch, Smethwick borders Winson

Green in Birmingham, home of HM Prison Birmingham. It was a rough area, where one day a colleague of mine, PC Fred Myler was visiting the block of flats there and foolishly (?) left his panda car on its front car par just that bit too near the front door of the block. When he returned from this mundane address check visit he returned to find a rusty old enormous fridge-freezer on the roof of the car that had been accurately discharged from one of the blocks loftier balconies. Just as well, he was on his own that morning and hadn't left a colleague in the front passenger seat to fill in their pocket book or they might have been filled in for good! Black Patch was that sort of place, where the majority of the population had a healthy disregard for the defenders of law and order! Funnily enough Salters Spring factory was the largest employer in the area, making weighing scales. Not much justice in this neck of the woods! This Neighbourhood Watch co-ordinator from Black Patch was a bloke with a speech impediment and used to say, con - ordinator instead of co – ordinator. He was the conordinator for a small block of maisonettes in a small cul de sac on the edge of this very troublesome inner city estate that 'progress' had turned into a dirty, grey, cold, uninhabitable, forgotten wilderness. I remember being sent to the Community centre in Black Patch Park for a European election once. From about eight thirty that morning until Ten O Clock on the night they registered six voters and one of them spoiled his voting slip making it null and void! But it gives you an idea what the area was like. By day it was a hive of activity with all kinds of light engineering company's based in the area. It had once been the home of the famous Raleigh Cycles factory. The weighing scale company Salters were still there. There are numerous small manufacturing works in the area. As I say, it is a hive of activity. In fact also in the area is the site of James Watt's first steam engine, James Brindley's first major canal runs through it and the highest spanning metal bridge in the world was built in the area.

This conordinator was a retired military man, thin and wiry, he always dressed immaculately wearing an oversized beige three-quarter length, double breasted macintosh, like Inspector Clouseau's, he also wore a burgundy beret. You would have thought that his speech impediment was the most memorable thing about him , but no. This gentleman had a pencil line moustache and above it hung the largest nose I have ever set eyes on. It was huge. Now, a colleague of mine, PC Paul Nicholls, a very great friend of mine, over the years, had a fantastic phrase that described this mans nasal appendage perfectly. A little cruel, bur none the less, very accurate. Paul described his curvaceous conk as resembling that of an 'arabs dagger',which paints a picture in the minds eye and it did resemble a very large Arabian Jambiya, or jambia a specific type of dagger with a short curved blade. If you could imagine drawing a Jambiya for a caricature cartoon, that would be about the right proportions! Thinking about it I think the football manager Neil Warnock has a similar but slightly smaller konk on his mush. I would have thought this conordinator would be long gone now, 'cause that was in the 1980s and I think he was a pensioner in his seventies then, so I would guess he's long gone, I can't remember his name, he was a military type guy, not very tall but always very immaculately dressed, y'know how these ex-military guys are, where they wear blazers with military badges on 'em, like their regiment badge and they wear a regiment tie, and when he was in public he wore his beret proudly, his grey slacks and black well polished shoes,hidden behind the macintosh. He always walked erect, upright, with great pride in his appearance, and I think he had a little moustache, like David Niven. And he was, very rare for his age, very physically fit. He was the Neighbourhood Watch conordinator for the Black Patch Neighbourhood Watch scheme. For the sake of the tale lets call him Colonel Blimp.

In the early days of Neighbourhood Watch the coordinators got very very zealously keen on scheme reporting all kinds of things, anything, the least thing that went on would be reported with the utmost gusto. Its no wonder that traditionally the general public think of Neighbourhood Watch coordinators as curtain twitchers, but basically they're not really like that. Well, not the majority of them! 'Neighbourhood Watch coordinators are just general normal average ordinary people who are just concerned about crime in their area, but unfortunately Colonel Blimp was a curtain twitcher, a bit of a 'Billy No-Mates' and the type of guy who would sit on just about any public committee going, overzealous is the word that would describe him. When he'd see you on the beat, he'd literally be like the nudge nudge, wink wink, say no more type character from Monty Python, he'd say, "Listen officer, there's been a bit dodgy deeds going on at such and such a place", he'd then pull out a small notebook where he'd jotted down car registration numbers and notes on any incidents that he regarded as out-of the ordinary. "I'd keep an eye on if I were you, those young 'uns look as if they're up to no good, he'd say, relating to a group of six or seven acne ridden youths trembling in the doorway of the local chip shop. I'll keep an eye on 'em and I'll let you know if I see anything suspicious. " We would smile politely and thank him for his help whilst looking to make a swift escape or as the gaffers would say an 'exit strategy'. One eventful morning I was on foot patrol walking passed the flats in the Black Patch area of Smethwick when along strolled Blimp. He beckoned me toward him, Eric Idle like, knocking the side of a bluish, runny, 'Arabs Dagger' with his right forefinger, winking at me and nodding knowingly,in my direction, irritatingly tapping my arm with his elbow as he whispered from the side of his mouth, "If I see anything suspicious going on or if I've got any criminal intelligence to report to you, obviously I don't want my cover blown as the Neighbourhood Watch conordinator". He pauses to look around furtively before continuing, "I don't want the ruffians and the criminals to see you coming to my front door see, cause then they'll know that I'm the conordinator, right. So,"He pauses, looks around again, as if the KGB have put a tail on him, then grabs my arm drawing me closer to say, "What I'll do, right, when I see a bobby in the street, right, I'll stop in front of them and then fasten one of my shoe laces, this will mean I have crime information for them and you can either give me a ring or come to my house after dark when they can't see you visiting me". Following a crafty wink he said, "If I don't tie my shoe laces and just walk past, that means there are no messages for you. Do you understand officer?". He looked around again Jason Bourne-like waiting for my response. "Yes I think I follow you", I warily informed him. "Fine," he said in a business like way as he stole away into the drabness of the Black Patch flats.

So, a few days later I'm walking through Black Patch park, gods in her heaven and the birds are singing in the proverbial trees, when I see a large 'Arabs Dagger' walking toward me at a rate of knots. Its wearing a three quarter length beige mac, a burgundy beret and is underlined by a David Niven tash, yes, it was the Colonel. He makes a bee-line towards me and in his zealous scuttle to deliver his message to me, wink, wink, nudge nudge, crouches down to fasten his shoe lace, directly in the path of a park keeper carrying a huge cardboard box full of dead leaves. The unsighted Parkie, falls over the crouching MI5 man and goes rolling down the path like an Arsenal striker tripping in a Penalty box. Legs akimbo, grazes on his chin, his box of leaves proving Sir Isaac Newton absolutely right, Parkie tumbled indiscriminately along the path he'd just cleared. It caused a head turning incident, to say the least. Attention that 'Arabs Dagger' said he'd try to avoid. But I think on this rare occasion he actually had genuine criminal intelligence for me and I think the parkie had a message for him too! It wouldn't have been so bad but, Blimp was wearing shiny black slip on leather jodhpur boots with no laces at the time of the incident!

Tying laces, reminds me of a young albino boy I once came across named Arthur Street. I first knew Arthur when he was a pupil at a local Infants School in Smethwick. He obviously stood out, with his pale skin. He didn't have pink eyes and that, but was an albino Afro-Caribbean lad, with white curly locks, can't be missed. One day, whilst giving a Stranger Danger talk to the Infants assembly at his school. Arthur raised his hand during any questions at the end and said, "My Mum says that Police Officers are supposed to help people". I clearly nodded in agreement, saying, "Yes, Your Mum is right". With that, Arthur raised an unfastened trainer on his right foot towards me and said, "Fasten my shoelace for me then will you". That was an eventful morning. I had started the assembly dressed in a large Brown shop keepers overalls, a tartan flat cap and a West Bromwich Albion scarf which was covering my uniform underneath. I had the headmistress introduce me to the kids as Mr.Connor. I then started to undress, steady now, with the intention of slowly dressing into my police uniform and asking the children to keep shouting out, trying to guess what I did for a living. It sounded like a decent idea at the time!

As I had removed the overalls, following decent suggestions from the kids as, shopkeeper and caretaker. I had got to half blues, which was, my black shoes, black police trousers and white long sleeved shirt minus my police epaulettes (The ornamental shoulder piece containing my collar numbers). Because the shirt has two large chest pockets and straps on the shoulders for my epaulettes the kids had cleverly started to guess 'like' occupations such as Fireman, Ambulance Driver, Airline Pilot and Nurse as well as the obvious. But the vast majority where still struggling. My ultimate aim was of course to help them identify me in full police uniform and then I was to instruct them that if they were ever lost they should not be afraid to approach anyone in a uniform and ask them for assistance. It really annoys me when I hear parents tell their kids in the presence of a police officer, "If you don't behave, I'll take you to the police and they'll take you away and put you in prison!" Nice one Mum and Dad. So, when your kids are in genuine trouble and need help they will run a mile when they see a police officer! Rant over.

As I got down to half blues I still kept saying to the children, "What do yo think my job is?" It was then that I saw a tiny blonde girl sitting cross legged on the front row, the reception classes, you know, the classes that sit in tiny pools of.... er I digress, this little angels hair was tied back with little curly ringlets and she had a broad smile on her little face as she held up her tiny hand catching my undivided attention. The assembly hall went quiet as I leaned forward and smiling, I looked at her and said, "Whats your name?" "Poppy" she said in a squeaky cute little toddler voice. "Thats a lovely name", I said. "Well Poppy, what do you think I am?" She then said in a very distinct and clear announcement to the whole assembly, "A Fart Arse!"

The place erupted into bawls of infant laughter and somewhat flabbergasted I was slightly taken aback as the visibly apologetic looking headmistress walked over to me. She was about to make her apologies when I whispered in her ear, "What very astute pupils you have here Mrs Norton!"

DECEIT, SCROUNGING
& CAJOLING

'When you believe in things you don't understand, then
you suffer'
Stevie Wonder

You'll be surprised to learn that this chapter isn't
about politicians! It's about superstitions. I myself am not
superstitious but lots of coppers are. A prime example of
Police Officers being suspicious would be the utterance of
the 'Q' word. If you find that a particular tour of duty is
dragging along slowly with little or no jobs are coming in, one
officer will invariably be tempted to say "It's quiet innitt?".
But of course, most officers believe that if the Q word is
mentioned, then all hell will break lose and that mention of
the Q word causes the phones to melt it gets that busy and
invariably does! So like the Scottish Play with Actors, the
'Q' word is never uttered by operational bobbies. Bobbies
are very serious when it comes to police procedure but they
are also very fond of playing pranks on each other. We call
them blags. A dictionary would describe the word blag as:

To obtain something by deceit, scrounging, or cajoling, i.e. He blagged his way in. Blagging is very acceptable in a job that see's so much sorrow and despair. As I'm sure you would understand. Some of the funny stories I have shared with you in this publication were 'blags'.

The first blag I remember being played on me was on Tuesday 1st April 1980. I was on nights on foot patrol in Bearwood Road, Smethwick. My tutor Constable PC Chris Murphy (Who was in on the blag) said he'd been forced to stay in the station to write a statement and so, I was told to 'leg it' for an hour or so. Of on foot patrol I went. My first solo patrol. I hadn't received a call on my radio until at one minute past midnight I received a message from the controller, Sergeant Colin Huddart to go immediately to the front steps of Smethwick Council House as we had had an anonymous call to say that they had seen a baby abandoned on the front steps of the Council Building. I ran as fast as I could towards the Council House and on my way I could hear the Sergeant sending virtually all the shift to the location. As I ran through the entrance gates I could feel a stitch in my stomach I'd been running that hard. Panting and breathless I scanned the steps and couldn't see a cradle or cardboard box or any bull rushes for that matter, but I couldn't see any other officers arriving either, which was strange given the serious nature of the message.

As I got level with the steps I saw the head, quite motionless, just the head mind, which had been bitten off! It was a red jelly baby by the door of the council house, it had been placed on a piece of A4 copier paper bearing the distinct message 'I ain't got no body!' With that most of the shift appeared from behind trees, bushes, walls and street furniture in front of the Council House and began to cheer clap and and laugh!

I immediately radioed the message that I had found the deceased and mentioned that the baby appeared illegitimate. Sgt Huddart asked me to explain how I could tell it was illegitimate and I said, "Well sarge,you can decide the legitimacy of jelly babies by opening the packet and turning it upside down because you see when you turn it upside down all the little bastards fall out!" The members of the shift at the 'scene' laughed but Sgt Huddart's voice went very serious and he said to me, 'PC Connor that is unprofessional misuse of the radio system. Get back to the station the Inspector wants a word with you, now!' PS Huddart said this on what was known as 'talk through' where the rest of the shift were also privy to the message. My chuckling audience tutted and several voices piped up stuff like, "You're for it now" and "The Gaffer don't take too kindly to radio abuse of his supervisors. "

Worrying all the way back as I trudged the short distance to the nick, I went through the back door of the station, walked up the corridor to the gaffers office and knocked the door. Inspector Johnny McRae immediately shouted, "Come". I entered sheepishly and stood to attention, my helmet tucked under my arm in regulation fashion. He looked really miffed as he said, "We can't allow this can we eh?" I stood silently, not having a clue what he meant. "I said, we can't allow this can we?" he bellowed. "Allow what Sir", I said. "Some bastards had all my red jelly babies, you'll have to have a green one!" With that he thrust the open bag of Jelly Babies under my nose & burst out laughing, as did the rest of the shift who were now congregated in the corridor outside.

The same night I was dropped off by a Police Car at the motor part stores at the Bevan Police Garage at Brierley Hill, some seven miles away from Smethwick, to get a 'long stand' for one of the Panda cars. I'd been there about forty minutes before one of the mechanics there asked me if my stand there had been long enough or did I want to give it another ten minutes! Yes, It was still the 1st April. Very Funny I thought.

But it didn't stop there upon my return to Smethwick nick, one of the lads Huggy Bear (aka Paul Hopkins) told me, straight faced, that I had a message to ring a DC Lyon at Dudley Police Station accompanied by a contact number for him. I rang the given number which did start with the Dudley dialling code of 01384.from the front office at Smethwick, a sleepy sounding male voice eventually answered and I told him that I'd like to speak to DC Lyon please. The man answering laughed and said, "Are you are a Probationary Copper then?" After confirming this he said, "The Sea Lions are all still asleep but you can have a word with Mr Eagle Owl from the Flying Squad if you like, he was awake!" I'd been given the number of the nightwatchman at Dudley Zoo!

Some years later when I had moved to West Bromwich Police Station when working on the dreaded 1st of April. I got a written message left on my desk to speak to a Mr Judge on a given number! I was a lot older and wiser now. I wasn't gonna fall for that old nutmeg. Presuming the number was one for a Court building somewhere I wrote on the note in huge letters,for the leavers of the note to read,'I'LL RING MISTER JUDGE NEXT WEEK SOME TIME!'.

A few days later there was a young man in the front office asking for me stating that he had some urgent business to discuss that couldn't wait any longer. His name? Gary Judge!

A MATURE STUDENT, LATE FOR HIS LECTURE

If you have read some of my stories I think you'll agree that as a Beat patrol officer, discretion must be exercised when carrying out day to day events. For example, if we locked up every driver exceeding the speed limit as set by statute, the cells would be overflowing! Some discretion is always required when it comes to the law, if officers dealt with everything they went to without using common sense we'd all be robotic automatons, regurgitating what we'd been told to do during our training and arresting people for all kinds of minor incursions. A lot of people in our society now treat everything as black and white, where in reality the world is a quite a grey place. There has long been a conflict in law enforcement between enforcing the exact letter of the law and understanding the spirit of the law. Should an officer enforce every little violation of the law he or she sees, or should his time be spent dealing with the crimes that society truly want punished? This grey area is where the concept of police discretion comes in. Police discretion is the judgment officers use on the streets, whether it be letting someone go after a stern lecture, or taking someone to jail for a minor offence because they may be a danger to themselves or others.

One night I was the observer in the Zulu car (A marked police fast response vehicle, fitted with two tones & go faster red stripes!) with PC Del Prescott, a very old friend and an extremely good advanced driver who hailed originally from the town of Rowley Regis, one of the six towns of Sandwell Borough. At about quarter to one on the Tuesday morning of the as yet fairly uneventful first night of seven nightshifts, that always started on a Monday night. We saw an old but very well maintained Vauxhall Viva saloon car being driven a little erratically, and suspiciously slowly along Windmill Lane, Smethwick. Del decided to follow the Viva, just to see how the driver responded to our 'presence'. After the Viva jumped the traffic lights at the Seven Stars junction of Cape Hill on amber, it was obvious the driver had no idea of our presence, following him at a safe distance.

Del flicked the unique large plastic switch located in the centre of the dashboard of this Morris Marina saloon that flashed the bright but unmistakable blue flash of light across the the facades of wet shop frontages that most drivers who'd been sniffing the barmaids apron on that previous evening would immediately recognise as their cue to instinctively pop a polo mint or two into their beer breathed gobs, but on this occasion the oblivious Viva pilot carried on driving along for another fifty yards or so before pulling over, quite aptly by a twenty four hour taxi office in Waterloo Road. The smartly dressed Viva driver, a gentleman in his late sixties seemed a little unsteady on his feet, as he got out of the car I could see he was very smartly kitted out wearing a slightly skew-wiff green beret, white shirt collar, regimental tie and blazer, light brown corduroy slacks and very shiny oxblood coloured Doctor Marten shoes. On his jacket was emblazoned the unmistakable 'Star of Burma' insignia, a six–pointed gold star, which indicated that this man had served in the Far East during World War 2 and been awarded the Burma Star medal. Awarded to all allied military service staff serving in the jungle battlefields recognizing in particular the rigorous nature of climate, topography and the extremely debilitating conditions in which the holders of the award waged a savage but successful campaign against a determined and fanatical Japanese foe, thus making this particular association unique among post war ex-service associations. The war hero precariously approached us both, stopped about six feet away from us, stood bolt upright, and looking me in the eye, immaculately saluted and said, "Good morning officers is there a problem with the old Viva then?" At which he let off a thunderously rasping fart, so loud, in fact that I think it could have rattled nearby shop roller shutter doors. He grinned a wide toothy grin and said, "It's alright lads, I haven't followed through, er, yet" I informed him, eventually, when we had stopped laughing that he had a break light out on his Viva and upon suspecting that he may have had a drink or two, 'persuaded' him to leave his pride and joy locked, secured and parked up for the night and take a taxi from the nearby taxi office, home. The man appeared to sober up quite quickly at this suggestion and readily (& somewhat wisely) agreed to the suggestion stating that he'd get a taxi home and replace the offending faulty light bulb as soon as possible. He frowned sincerely and apologetically in our general direction, his dark silvery grey bushy eyebrows meeting in a defiant, and almost Churchillian 'V' sign, saluting again as he span around and marched off the imaginary drill square in the direction of the dimly yellow ochre lit steamy taxi office. We resumed our normal patrol, still amused at the old soldiers explosive chords.

About fifteen minutes later, the veteran of jungle warfare had decided to by-pass the taxi office and had walked off along Bearwood Road, in the direction of the Barleycorn Public house. As he passed the Hadley Sports Stadium he was stopped by a foot patrol officer from our unit, PC Tom Tyrer, who the shift had christened 'Two Dot'. Why? Well, it appears that when a member of Mensa International or the like, perform an intelligence test on someone and that someone is that dull-witted that an intelligence quotient or IQ score cannot be derived following several different standardised tests designed to that assess their intelligence, then an IQ number cannot be allocated for that person and instead are awarded two small dots. Now, need I explain why Tom was nicknamed 'Two Dot?' "What are you doing out here at two thirty in the morning?" Two Dot asked the dapper pedestrian. "I'm going to a important lecture. " chuckled the old warhorse. "A lecture? Who is going to give you a lecture at this time of night?" said young officer. "My Mrs." said the man in a tremulous tone.

Luckily, Del and I were driving along the Bearwood Road in time to witness Two Dots encounter with the orderly but intemperate war hero and before the freezing cold beat officer could even think about returning to the warm cosy police station and a hot cuppa with a drunk in tow. We'd pulled up alongside the couple and I declared to Two Dot, "Its OK Tom, we'll take care of this one". Bundling the bemused and fortunate holder of the Burma Star into the back of the fast response vehicle which immediately sped off down Bearwood Road in completely the opposite direction to the police station, much to the surprise of Two Dot, who was still thinking about his next response to the man he'd just been talking to and had now mysteriously vanished!

Del tilted and raised his head slightly to the left and looking at the passenger in the rear view mirror said with a view to running him home, "Where do you live then old mate?" I live in Harborne offisher", he retorted. "F****** Harborne!" exclaimed Del. We began to tootle the three miles or so off our police area into Lardy Land (aka Birmingham) and the mans address. As he chatted about how he'd been honoured the previous night becoming a lifelong member of the Handsworth branch of the Burma Star association I was just about to say something like, "You must be very proud" when the man leaned over on one buttock shut his eyes and rasped a loud two noted fart, which sounded exactly like the first two bars of Ricketts' famous military tune Colonel Bogey!

Always being quick witted when it comes to van humour, I immediately sang out loud the the remaining first line of the famous alternative stanza, "Has only got one ball!" Del then sang the next line, "Goerring has two but rather small" I continued, "Himmler, is, very similar". Culminating in us all singing, "But poor old Goebbels has got none at all!" Which ended in resounding laughter from all present!

Having ascertained that our fare had eaten quite a large roast meal at the previous evenings festivities we were now unfortunately suffering the consequences of such a lavish and sumptuous blowout, if you'll excuse the phrase, but it does tend to describe the after effects well. We were outside the mans address in a matter minutes at that time in a morning and unceremoniously we hastily ejected him from our safekeeping. As we sped back to our patrol area, God knows what would have happened if. our unit Inspector had caught us, I glanced into the observers' rear view mirror and could see the appreciative veteran, still standing to attention, saluting toward us below the sulphur glow of the street light on the corner of his road. "Least we could do" said Del, breaking the silence. "Yeah" I said, being of the same mind. We drove back to the patch and our normal duties safe in the knowledge that we had done the right thing, discretion, literally being the better part of valour and all that, to quote the Bard.

We thought nothing of it until the following night we were sitting on parade at about 9:55 pm. Parades for duty were always held fifteen minutes before the shift was due to start. On nights quarter nine (2145hrs), on earlies quarter to six in the middle of the night (0545hrs)and quarter to two (1345hrs) in the afternoon for late shift. I remember on one occasion being late for parade (Not a rare event for this individual) Inspector Robinson and the shift already beginning parade without me! Still fastening the silver buttons on my tunic, I clumsily rattled the old handle opening the large oak victorian door and barged my way into the quiet parade room full of attentive eager bobbies, who, having been inspected where now being briefed by the shift supervision prior to plodding the mean streets. As I half ran, half tripped into the room, I seemed to have aroused the attention of the Inspector. Who sarcastically challenged my entrance with," Ah, Good Evening PC Connor, you should have been here ten minutes ago!" To which I, in my broadest, slightly Les Dawson-esque Lancastrian accent, retorted, "Why, what happened?" to which the quietly attentive congregation, worshipping at the temple of Sir Robert Peel's policing tradition, 'A' Unit Smethwick, suddenly burst into laughter.

I could even see smirks on the faces of the sergeants, who would normally try to stay straight faced on such occasions or disciplinary reasons & to support the Boss, standing behind Inspector Robinson, whose smug and slightly arrogant grin during his original question had now turned into a red faced, unoriginal, embarrassed bully who couldn't think of an original put down reply for the young tardy and i'll admit a little disrespectful Constable Connor. Mr.Robinson came back with the rather predictable response, "PC Connor, Get out of this parade room and wait in the corridor outside my office, I'll deal with you after parade." As I skulked out of the parade room with my tail, or was it my truncheon, between my legs, I looked up to see the admiring looks on the faces of my shift companions and that really meant the world to me at the time.

I have really always believed in life that respect is earned. There are so many gaffers in the police now that 'hide' behind their pips and in a nutshell, they can't manage people. They couldn't run a whelk stall, let alone a squad of professional police officers. Officers have to and MUST respect the rank, its true, but it doesn't mean that they have to respect the idiot wearing the badges of rank. That respect as I say is earned.

But I digress, the following night we were sitting on parade at about 9:55 pm. When we were disturbed by the humdrum, monotoned ring of one of the two parade room telephones (Very Hi-Tech eh?. Well it was the eighties). This normally meant a three 9's emergency scramble for the Zulu crew to a serious RTA (Road Traffic Accident) or an attack alarm at a commercial premises where for example burglars had set off the security contraptions. But no, one of the crew answered the call and after a short wait, with at least two Zulu crews preparing for a 'shout' the young officer answering the blower said to Robinson, "Sir, There's an old military looking gentleman in the front office asking to see the shift Inspector. " Inspector Robinson finished parade and went to see the old chap. You of course can guess who this man was…. but for the police officers amongst you, he was wearing a blazer with the Star of Burma Insignia.

It transpired that our Viva owner had been an Army Sergeant Major and he'd explained to Robinson exactly what had happened the previous evening and he'd brought a box of biscuits as a donation to the shift, which Mr.Robinson accepted with a sincere thank-you. As soon as the old soldier had gone, he summoned Del and I to his office and asked us why the man hadn't been breathalysed. We explained that in our professional opinion the man was just barely over the legal limit for intoxication and rather than taking him into custody we decided that to advise him to secure his car and take a taxi home would be the best course of action in the circumstances. A red faced Mr.Robinson later ascertained (we presumed from Two Dot) that we'd taken him home. He reminded us that we were not a taxi service and that had we been involved in an accident we wouldn't have been insured! I was very tempted to tell Mr Robinson to wind his neck in, but he'd have flipped and I would have experienced some of that anarchic discipline that I touched on earlier.

Ironically, I saw Mr Robinson only a few months ago on the automatic escalator in Asda. As he approached I could see that he was screwing up his little ferrety eyes and starting to recognise me. As we passed he exclaimed, "Hello Bry, great to see you!". I blanked him completely. Which gave me immense satisfaction. I thought of every probationary constable that Robinson bullied in his time with the West Mids and there were quite a few, and thought of them, as a bewildered little browbeater clutching his shopping bag went back to the humdrum little world he habituates and which no doubt still rules like a Black Country Ceaușescu.

'Voices from a Blue Box'

'Death Rattle'

GOATS AND GHOULIES

As I stated in a previous chapter lots of coppers get superstitious at some incidents but to quote Hannibal the Cannibal, "I myself cannot." I am a positive, glass half full type of person, with little or no issues. I am claustrophobic though, I found that out after being trapped in a broken down, tiny, stainless steel, coffin-like, urine soaked, council lift, with half a dozen hairy arsed Bobbies one Sunday morning. I actually forced the doors open just to get a breath of fresh-ish air!

But, when it comes to the supernatural, well, I am a died in the wool sceptic. I am a paid up member of the British Humanist Association and I think mediums like Derek Akorah (Or should we say Derek Johnson the real name of the medium) are just con artists taking gullible peoples hard earned cash by making up stories about the 'afterlife'. If there was anything existing after this life, I think we'd know about it. We don't and there isn't. The only credible medium is the one in between small and large!

Derek Akorah's credibility has been questioned many times but following his work on the TV programme *Most Haunted* with that woman who used to make dolls houses out of sticky back plastic on Blue Peter, who, quite frankly for a Ghostbuster, gets worryingly 'spooked,' every time a light bulb blows on set, so its God help her if she ever see's a *REAL* Ghost which of course she won't, because they don't exist. On numerous investigations for the programme, Akorah appears to become possessed by spirits or an evil entity & would appear lost and confused (Not difficult for Liverpool football supporters). On one such occasion, when not talking to a deceased Yorkshire Terrier who loved to bark at postmen, Akorah claimed to be possessed by the spirit of a man called Kreed Kafer. In a later interview, the programme's parapsychologist, Ciaran O' Keeffe claimed that he'd made up the Kreed Kafer character (an anagram of "Derek faker") and miss-fed the information to Akorah who subsequently presented Kafer on the telly as fact!

But I digress, I am a skeptic, but very open to any real proof. It reminds me of my first ghostly episode at a sudden death at a pensioners ground floor flat where I as a probationer was sent, when neighbours had rung the police to report that they were worried about this chap, as he hadn't been seen for a few days. I was on nights and was sent to the man's flat at about eleven o'clock that evening. Having ascertained the gentleman's name, I called it through the letterbox, "Mr. Smith?" I tentatively shouted, with no response. I then tried the outside windows of the ground floor dwelling, all tightly fastened with closed curtains obscuring outside observance. I had to put the door in. I put my shoulder hard to the locked front door and as I have shared in previous chapters, was very surprised at how easy the locked door flew open. I discovered the deceased in the small living room of the flat. He'd passed away watching TV, a small 17" black and white set that flickered snow or white noise across the dimly lit room. I turned on the light and saw the dead man still fully dressed, lying in a recumbent, TV watching position, on an old two seater fifties style, sit up and beg, settee, eyes still openly fixed on the hissing idiot box in the corner. I radioed in my findings and asked the controller for the undertakers to turn out, as a matter of routine. There were no suspicious circumstances evident, but also, as a matter of course, I began to search the flat for some details of the dead man's next of kin.

During this time I struck up a very nervous one sided conversation with the deceased, telling him who I was and explaining the normal police procedure for this type of incident. As I opened a very old fashioned looking 'built in' cupboard next to the fireplace I was startled, as a large amount of banknotes, in various denominations, cascaded over me like a tickertape parade! There must have been thousands of pounds there. I radioed the downpour into control and asked for the shift supervisors to attend. In the meantime, I counted the cash, still nervously chatting away to my new 'friend'.

As I sat cross legged on the rug in front of the gas fire I counted out the money in small piles of £5, £10 and £20 pound notes. Still chatting nervously to the deceased who lay about two feet away, behind me. Asking him basically, why he had hoarded so much cash, instead of spending it!

As I chided him for this self neglect, the remaining air in his lungs, made its natural way up past his vocal chords and with a very loud heart wrenching AHHHHRRRRGGGGGG!!!!!! It escaped across the room in the general direction of my eardrums. Out through dead lips came the death rattle of the dead man. When he started to emit this unearthly sound I had been sat cross-legged on his hearth rug counting his money. By the time it died down (No pun intended) I was somewhere between his front door and the front gate of the premises which I cleared like Colin Jackson the Olympic hurdler! I ran and ran and ran. I was convinced that his ghost, not happy with my lawful burgling of his flat, was after me for rifling through his privates. I must have been a good two hundred yards away from his flat when the supervision car pulled up, the sergeant stopping to ask what was wrong, I grabbed his arms and dementedly ranted to him that the dead man was alive and had shouted at me because I was counting his cash! The Sarge calmed me down and together we went back to the 'haunted' flat. Where of course, the poor old deceased was still exactly that, quite dead and no harm to the living.

I have heard the death rattle a few times since. You never get used to it, but, you do learn to accept it, as part of a not too pleasant part of the job. I have been to quite a few 'haunted' houses. I remember one in particular was an old lady called Mrs.Warley, who lived in a small two up two down mid terraced house in Oldbury. She rang to complain that she could hear children in her upstairs bedroom. I was on foot patrol not far from her address and volunteered to go to her house. Upon arrival, she met me at the front door and was much shaken up stating that these children 'visited' her bedrooms most evenings and that on this evening The Devil had told her not to go up the stairs.

I have to admit that It was a little spooky and like the modern films that centre around the occult, the house was freezing cold, in spite of the fact that it was a summers evening. I was followed to the bottom of the stairs by the old lady who was convinced that there were laughing children in the upstairs rooms. I went up there, armed with my trusty truncheon 'Simon' and started to loudly chastise these 'invisible' intruders. I went back downstairs and a very relieved and reassured old lady made me a cup of tea as I sat in a now, warm, living room.

The following day, I spoke to her doctor at the local surgery. Discovering that the drugs she was on for mild depression, following the death of her husband, can cause mild hallucinations. The doctor reduced her dosage and she never heard her tormentors again.

I remember using a ghost story on community camping trips, were a group of police officers and members of staff from the local authorities community services would take under privileged children on trips to adventure holiday centre's around the country. We would normally have about two dozen locals miscreants to look after. On this particular trip we visited an old converted Victorian school house in an unpronounceable mid-welsh village. On the first night, the kids, all between thirteen and sixteen years, were very excited, some had never been away from their West Midland homes until then. I told them the story about the ghost of the tailless dog that roamed around that village on nights when the moon was full. I told the quietened throng of avid listeners that many years ago, a witch had been burned at the stake in the village and that her dog, a huge hound, had tried, unsuccessfully, to save its mistress from the rampaging villagers and that during the proceedings they also killed the dog, but cut off his tail and placed its preserved remains in a large glass case behind the bar of the local pub, to remind them and future villagers of the dastardly goings-on. I pointed out that the tail was still kept in the bar to this day and that on nights when the moon was full, co-incidentally just like that very evening, that the ghost of the witches dog roamed the streets of the village howling and searching for its tail. Why, because he couldn't enter doggy hell without being whole. I went on that on one particular night the dog had scratched and clawed at the front door of the local tavern and that right on the stroke of midnight the licensee had seen the hound scratching the door. The hound looked at the landlord and said, "I am the tailless hound of the village and I cannot enter eternal rest in Hades without my tail. I demand you give it to me now!" With that, the landlord, clutching a cross in one hand and a copy of his Magistrates License to carry on his noble trade in the other, said to the dog, "I am sorry, I cannot give you what you wish, as being a licensed vitular I cannot retail spirits after half past ten at night!"

I have the late and very great comedian Les Dawson, to thank for that joke. Which was of course was received with stifled mirth by the assembled adults, but with misunderstood cynicism by the youngsters who, were by now convinced that they could hear the hound howling but were ready to form a search party to hunt down the hound from hell in the village as young would be forerunners of the Most Haunted team format!

I remember an Inspector at Old Hill nick who was convinced that the Inspectors office was haunted. It is a very old station as I have mentioned in the chapter about Peggy Mount, the Hill was around in the 1880's and it would be easy for the weak minded to believe that the building was haunted by maybe prisoners that had died in custody there! The weak minded one, in this case, the Inspector. Who, when he arrived to open his locked office would enter to find hot drinks and half eaten, warm, bacon or sausage sandwiches on his desk! This happened on many occasions and the Inspector decided that his office was haunted. These were in the days before CCTV cameras were readily available. The Inspector not only locked the door, he sealed it with tape to make sure no one had entered using a duplicate key. I think he even bought and fitted a shrewd padlock on the door, thinking that naughty constables were trying to pull his leg, heaven forbid!

The following morning the inspector checked the tape. It hadn't budged. He unlocked the padlock, with the only key that was in his possession at all times and finally unlocked the mortise lock on the office door which he tentatively pushed open followed closely by a small group of inquisitive officers.

On his desk were a half eaten breakfast and a half drunk cup of tea. The meal was still hot and the tea still had steam whipping upwards into the atmosphere. On that day, the story became even more sinister, as the Inspectors Marked Police Mini Van which he'd left parked in the back yard was missing! Only to be found parked outside the front of the station locked of course. These strange goings on only happened when this particular Inspector was on duty and these suspicious happenings continued for months. The Inspector becoming convinced that Old Hill nick had a ghostly visitor.

It was a few months after the Inspector had been moved onto pastures new that some of the lads at the nick took me into their confidence and I discovered that a cupboard in the corner of the Inspectors office that later became the stations TV/Rest Room had a small opening in the ceiling that opened up into the roof space of the building and that all along the lads had been setting up the Marie Celeste type greeting for the Inspector to test his, obviously crap, investigative skills!

One night, one of our number decided to have a kip in the rest room during his stint of night shift and decided to 'lock' himself into the room to remain, undisturbed. It was then that I showed the rest of the shift the alternative entrance, via the attic and terrified the life out of our poor sleeping and unsuspecting guardian of justice. Didn't it Bob?

It was at Old Hill that a very good mate of mine, PC Tom Killeen, was working one set of nights when he was sent in a single crewed panda car to an automatic alarm at the artificial ski slope in Haden Hill Park. Yes, in the seventies, some one thought they could make lots of cash by building a man-made synthetic ski slope in Old Hill, three hundred and twenty five miles from the only legitimate UK 'snow' covered ski slopes in the Scottish Cairngorms, which resembled a huge criss-crossed upside down sweeping brush, carpeted over a huge slope that some people actually paid good money to ski down in the heights of mild weathered Sandwell winters and summers for that matter! The ski slope had an office for its operators to stay out of the rain and snow that resembled a blue portacabin. In fact; it was a blue portacabin, the intruder alarm of which went off, usually falsely, at regular times.

This particular night was a very dark night with no moon. Police patrol car, 'Kilo Mike 4' driven by Tom had parked up the car at the base camp at the end of the slope and trudged up to the dizzy heights of the office armed only with a very weak torch light and a thin piece of wood in his truncheon pocket. It was a mild night as Tom made his way towards the portacabin, but it was pitch dark and a very lonely and deserted location. He trudged toward the hut that stood in the grounds of the abandoned and derelict Haden Hill House (Now renovated and used as Council Offices once more). The usual sounds made by scurrying nocturnal animals and the cracking noises of twigs breaking under foot disturbed the silent approach of the diligent officer. Who upon arrival at the portacabin could see that it appeared to be 'in order' and that it was to be yet another 'fault on system' report to the controller. As he rattled the handle of the secured front door the intense audible alarm leaped into ear piercing life causing the startled officer to recoil back on his haunches and think about evacuating his bladder! Upon regaining full control of his endocrine system, the officer let the controller know that the building was in order and that it appeared that there was a fault, asking if the key holder could attend to reset the alarm.

It was whilst waiting for the key holder to arrive that Tom noticed a light in the West Tower of the old Haden Hill House. It shone brightly from inside and appeared to be a dull candle lit sort of light which emanated from within that room only. He immediately ran toward the building thinking that intruders had entered the old ruins but as he got closer the light became fainter and fainter and by the time he got to the remains the light had expired altogether. Tom checked the building, to find no visible means of entry. The building seemingly totally sealed. It was when the key holder came for the portacabin that he was told that Haden Hill House was supposedly haunted by the ghosts of Monks and Nuns that used to be on the sight of an old Monastery.

Tom still isn't sure to this day, whether he saw ghostly goings on that night but I do know that Tom was a reasonable rugby player in his younger days and like lots of men who play with odd shaped balls, like me in fact, he has been punched in the head on countless occasions and therefore cannot be held fully accountable for some of the strange tales he has witnessed since receiving these blows!

Another such tale, was remembered by 'old' Tom, who when sat in the control room at West Bromwich one dark lonely evening, received more than a few strange telephone reports from a council block on the Riddings Mound area of Old Hill, where local, 'sober' residents were reporting strange goings on at the flats. Windows were supposedly opening and closing by themselves; doors were being slammed and rattled. Ordinary household pets were suddenly acting very strangely howling or chattering uncontrollably. Residents could hear people screaming and howling. Windows were shattering outwards and a loud rushing wind could be seen and heard gusting but only inside the vicinity of the flats. Car alarms were sounding and people were reporting seeing sunroofs opening by themselves and car headlights turning on and off. Tom asked PC Dave Hunte to take a ride up in his little panda car and when he got there he reported that although it was about two thirty in the morning about three quarters of the inhabitants of the flats where in the street outside dressed in varying states of undress and completely terrified, refusing to re enter the block until the flats had been exorcised! They explained that this sort of behaviour had been going on for several months and that the local Catholic priest had already visited a number of his flock from the Riddings!

Father Kelly, the chain smoking, slightly sozzled middle aged man of the cloth was sent for and with the assistance of PC Hunte and his panda car he drove around the perimeter of the flats with tea cups full of holy water dousing the walls and exorcising whoever or whatever was causing the unrest at the block. It seemed to do the trick and the disturbed residents returned, happy in the knowledge that Father Kelly had defeated the powers of darkness! There have never been any further developments of that nature there and the local papal representative was along with most of the residents, convinced that something devilish had been going on in the flats. Well, anyone who knows the Riddings wouldn't argue with that remark! I don't know if there was an ancient Red Indian burial ground on the site but perhaps some readers of the Black Country Bugle might know the reasons for the unexplained phenomena that appeared over that short period of weeks? Derek Akorah would no doubt say in his broad scouse accent that there had been a visitation from members of the spirit whairled.

By the nineties the block had become a haven for rent arrear merchants and crack heads and was a neglected desolate hell hole where the dogs walked around in threes for their own protection. At sometime during this decade PC Dave Barrow was sent to a report that residents could hear animals being maltreated in some way in the block. It was a warm balmy summers night in those ignorant pre-mad cow disease and foot & mouth days. Dave and his oppo searched the stairwells, the best way to traverse the Riddings blocks, the urine soaked, vomit covered lifts being a distinct health risk! The two officers could hear the usual screams, cries for "Help" and the distant drone of several domestic arguments permeating the windswept stairwells which blew a weird icy blast, even on this very warm summers evening. As they reached the eighth floor our two pillars of justice thought they could hear the bleating of livestock, either sheep or goats, coming from one of the flats! In the dimly lit corridor that reeked of rancid dead meat, amid the usual miss-spelt graffito such as 'Eyeleen Grimm-Shore Hiss a Porstitue' or 'All Koppahs arr Bastherds' and the fantastically complimentary 'Pee Cee Konner is a t**t (Believe me, when you have graffiti written about you, you know you're doing something right!). The almost obligatory MacDonald's or KFC fast food wrappings strewn about and of course the occasional human Richard the Third was evidence of sheep or goat droppings. Little shiny black beads of baa baa doo doo blazing a trail from the door of the flat to the lift doors. Obviously, these clever livestock were au fait in the use of modern mechanical devices, such as elevators, as of course, they wouldn't have encountered stairs in their normal agricultural/pastoral habitat.

Dave rang the doorbell of the now suspected illicit abattoir and a small, grubby, weasel faced middle aged man opened the door of the flat, the door ajar by about five inches held closed by a door chain. He was somewhat taken aback by the sight of two uniformed police officers and asked them, bravely, "What do you want, I'm busy?" It was ascertained that this gentleman was indeed keeping sheep and goats (about a dozen at a time) and butchering them in the bathroom of the premises in the jewish/halal method of food preparation. With little or no evidence of animal welfare. Both the Jewish and Muslim religions state that such slaughter should be carried out with a single cut to the throat, rather than the more widespread method of stunning with a bolt into the head before slaughter,even in a council block of flats. It was obvious to both officers that this man was causing severe suffering to these poor animals. The tenant had been preparing meat in this unhygienic way and selling it in local pubs along with illicit tobacco for some months and genuinely couldn't see that he was doing anything wrong! Stating that his method of killing was humane and not cruel to the animals which he'd legitimately bought at a livestock auction in Kidderminster.

It really is worrying that in modern Britain, when a sizeable percentage of our populace ask no questions about where their food comes from and have no worries about buying their next meal from unlicensed disreputable 'traders' who prepare the food literally in stinking squalor and are genuinely not bothered where it came from and how it was produced.

Seemingly, if the price is right, it's alright! Mind you, that more or less sums up every person that ever put unprescribed drugs into their body. Which I'm sure you'd agree is totally stupid and would be just like playing Russian Roulette with your health? Wouldn't It?

WATCH WITH MOTHER

This particular tale is set in the depths of winter and a full set of nights where the then K3 Sub Division, Smethwick was having a bending from a very professional 'foxy' burglar.

This burglar chose to attack prosperous premises with slat louvre type windows which unfortunately for Smethwick police were extremely popular with the public (not to mention burglars). They were a window, with narrow, usually six inch wide, horizontal slats, that were angled to admit light and air, but kept out rain, direct sunshine, and noise. The angle of the slats being adjustable, usual in blinds and windows, or fixed in a thin aluminium frame.

The vast majority of the huge old edwardian terraced houses that populated about eighty percent of the Bearwood area of the patch were fitted with louvered windows mainly at the rear of the premises.

To a professional burglar specialising in louvred windows it was like shelling peas! To call the spate of burglaries that we were having in the area an 'epidemic' would have been an understatement! We were having two and three houses done per night. The burglar attacking addresses in the affluent area of Bearwood during the early hours of the morning used a simple Modus Operandi, always attacking rear ground floor louvered windows, forcing the poor locking mechanisms with a screwdriver or jemmy type tool, opening the slats and quietly removing the strips of glazing before entering the premises and mainly stealing the sort of property that would easily go into a pocket before leaving either voluntarily or when disturbed by awakened victims. The felon, leaving no footwear prints at the scenes and obviously wearing gloves during his visits was doing terrifically well.

So high was the Burglary dwelling crime figures on just one are area. That the then Detective Chief Inspector for the Division decided enough was enough. All the Detectives and Neighbourhood Constables on the Sub-Division was ordered to work a full set of nights and some forty officers were paired up and given 'fixed' points on the Bearwood area to perform static observations for the 'louvre burglar'.

Working on the theory that even great burglars get greedy and don't know when to quit when they are ahead. Plans were put in lace that would lead to our foxes downfall.

That set of nights in February was cold. I was paired up with PC Glyn Wellens a good mate whose own Permanent Beat, bordered mine. So we had worked together on operations together before.

The first few days had been uneventful. Our fixed point was half way down an entry or gulley at the ear of a row of commercial shops. This gulley backed onto and gave a great view of the rear of a row of numerous terraced dwellings. The very type our quarry was selecting for his night time dalliances. Other couples were placed at strategic points all over the patch and everyone was connected by the Burndept Radio System. We were given a separate channel from the normal night shift response officers and so therefore only relevant information was being passed via the voices from the blue boxes.

Glyn and I had been parked up sitting in a plain unmarked police vehicle. However, we couldn't start the engine and turn on the heater as this would of course alert any would be burglar to our presence.

For a couple of nights we froze to death, silently, only making the occasional noise when we ate or left the car for a call of nature.

On the third night I went for an early call of nature and when standing in the frosty gulley I could see the rear of a famous Pharmacy chain in the moonlight. I then clocked some very large cardboard boxes in the rear of the store. These boxes that measured a good four feet cubed and were filled with hundreds of small blue moulded polystyrene 'S' shaped chips. I had the wonderful idea of sitting in these boxes and surrounding ourselves in polystyrene chips to keep warm. We would still see the rear of the domestic premises vulnerable to attack from the burglar but would also keep toasty warm because of the polystyrene super quilt. I went back to the cold car and explained my idea to Glyn who readily agreed that we should at least give the idea a try!

We giggled quietly as we both climbed into a box each. We were next to each other and it became apparent in a very short time that thanks to our body heat and the polystyrene chips the boxes were indeed toasty warm. Being a camper I was fully aware that most of a persons body heat is lost from the head and we were both wearing hats to retain our body heat. I think we originally had a giggle because we resembled Bill and Ben the Flowerpot Men....Two four foot cardboard cubes with tiny human heads pooping out of the folded tops. and not a weed in sight!

It was going so swimmingly....by about four o clock in the morning we were as snug as two bugs in a rug and the next I know I can hear the alarmed voices emanating from my Blue Box. I opened one eye and the blackness of the chilly February night I last remembered had gone only to be replaced by a thick blanket of snow, around six inches deep! I glanced over at Glyn's Box, if you'll excuse the phrase, and saw a dark brown four foot cube surrounded by white with a human 'dozing' head wearing a flat cap...on top of the flat cap was six inches of snow. Glyn looked like he had a small thick cheesecake resting on his noggin!

I whispered Pssst Glyn, finally getting his attention, His scrunched up eyes, slowly adjusting to the white-out. 'Kilo Three PC's Wellens or Connor, whats your location.... over', came blasting from our radios. Glyn answered and the friendly voice of Sgt Roy Mantle came over the air. "Did you hear the message for everyone to stand down and come in...over?" Glyn replied 'Yes, Yes...just taking it easy on the roads due to the snow over."

Because of the snowfall the Gaffer had called the 'obbo' off for that night and shouted everyone in...unbeknown to the Flowerpot men! We got back to the nick which was a hive of activity bursting to the seams with all the 'called in' bobbies from the operation who where now gradually thawing out and slurping copious amounts of Tea and Coffee. Even the fox wasn't going to come out in this weather!

I remember one of the lads asking the Gaffer if there would be any proper drinks served...Inferring that he break out the medicinal scotch. "That will come out when we've something to celebrate lad", came his light hearted reply.

We didn't have to wait long though....about three nights later, the Fox decided to come out to play. We all were on our fixed points. You'll be glad to know that Glyn and I had discarded the box idea. Which would be ok if you were a street dweller trying to stay alive on the cold streets of Britain but, not if you are vigilantly waiting for a Burglar to strike. Doing observations in plain clothes sounds very grand and brings to mind all those Hollywood stake out scenarios. The reality is....Its boring.....very Boring. We sat in the cold car waiting for some action. We would hear the odd radio check or someone asking for a PNC check on a suspicious vehicles registration number. In the meantime we would watch the paint drying and count the number of bricks on the frontages of the houses opposite. I even decided to write a short letter to my Mum...anything to keep me awake and watchful!

Suddenly at about three in the morning, the radio coughed into to life and Roy Mantle's reassuring voice came on the air...Like an Angler seeing a float bobble under the surface for the first time he related the details that a member of the public had seen someone in the rear garden of the house opposite and seemed to be suspiciously eyeing it up. He calmly passed the address and numerous members of the plain clothes operation started to stealthily make their way toward the address.

Roy put the radios on 'talk-through' so now Glyn an I had a running commentary to listen to as the adrenalin started to flow. The Bad News was for the Burglar as It became fully apparent that the he was being chased on foot by several officers.The good news was that he was running in our direction!

We then saw PC's John 'JJ' Jenkins and Pete Connolly walking up the street towards us. The street we was in was a typical side street in Bearwood, Edwardian Terraced Housing either side, built up into three storeys. The sort that have small gated entries in between them leading to the rear gulley and the back gardens. JJ and Pete waited in the gateway of one of these entries and Glyn and I alighted from the car and stood opposite them in the shadows of a gated entry.

We were constantly monitoring the radio and the 'runners' were still heading our way! For what seemed like an eternity but was only a matter of minutes we monitored the chase....The fox was heading straight for our our street.

We could hear footsteps running, at that time of night the steps echoed loudly as they approached. Glyn and I ran into the road and crouched between two parked cars as the silhouetted figure of the disturbed Burglar spun around the corner of the street and sped toward us. As he reached our car Glyn sprang out, cat like onto the shoulders of the Olympic sprinter. I ran out behind them and trying to keep up I dove rugby style at the spring heeled crooked quarry. He went down like a ton of bricks, all three of us rolling around on the snow covered paving slabs. Over ran JJ and Pete and before you could say overwhelmed, he was! But just to make sure he didn't go anywhere in a hurry 'JJ' undid and pulled the Burglars trousers down around his ankles so he couldn't run off!

The Burglar was a well known professional from Birmingham called Robin Banks. He only chose houses with louvred windows and always covered his shoes with a pair of socks so as not to leave footmarks at the scenes of his burglaries.

When we got back to the station the Gaffer kept his word. He was a Northern Irishman and had a particular passion for Bushmills Irish Whiskey which he cracked open and liberally distributed to all the members of the successful 'hunt'. Everytime I sip a drop of that little peaty drop of Ireland in a glass, I drink a toast to 'Mr Banks' and thank him, wherever he is, for indirectly introducing me to that wonderful celtic nectar.

Do you know, when people ask me what gives you the greatest satisfaction in the job. It is the thrill of the chase, to seek out and find Billy Burglar and all his other criminal cohorts. There is no feeling in the world like that of stopping, questioning suspicious criminal characters and locking up those guilty offenders that are out and about at all times of the day and night with the express purpose of breaking into houses and factories to steal your loved ones belongings.

It was a privilege to have the opportunity to do just that and to all those lucky men and women still fortunate enough to be in the greatest job in the world I would simply say; Always do the right thing, put the public first in everything you do. Act with fairness, honesty and integrity and you will succeed - Thats how a winning team thrives!

Don't be afraid to improve yourself, we are all, all of us, always learning new things. Strive to be someone that your friends and family can be proud of.

To those individuals still blessed, empowered and contracted to find Billy Burglar I wish you Good Hunting and Tight Lines!

About the Author

Born in 1957 in North West of England Bryan Connor was brought up, the youngest of three children, in a third generation Anglo-Catholic Irish household. Educated at Cowley School, St Helens. After a three year youth and community course in Birmingham. Bryan's life changed completely, when he joined the police having no idea of the strange adventures to come. Bryan has worked on response units before becoming a permanent beat constable on 'Cape Hill' a busy inner city area for eleven years. After working in the Forces' Community Services Department as a School Liaison officer, which culminated in a visit to St James' Palace to receive an award from Her Majesty the Queen. Bryan returned to operational policing. But following a road traffic accident, Bryan faced spinal surgery which left him permanently restricted from operational policing. He then 'piloted a desk', firstly as Case Builder preparing files for court before moving into Ops Planning, arranging resources for mutual aid requests. When he wasn't washing the car, mowing the lawn and helping bring up three daughters, Bryan played rugby representing his force and is a fully paid up member of 'The Hookers Union', in both 'codes'. Now too old and frankly too stiff to play 'the greatest game', he begrudgingly watches his beloved 'Saints', St Helens RLFC, his hometown club, whenever he gets the opportunity. He also follows his local football team West Bromwich Albion FC, 'The Baggies' who where, ironically, the first Football League side he ever saw play when he was thirteen years old whilst on a family holiday in Blackpool, at the 'seasiders' Bloomfield Road ground (Albion lost that day too!). For more information on Bryan's public speaking engagements, his art or indeed if you wish to send him a story for his next book project, please contact him at his e-mail address: bryan@bryanconnor.co.uk